W9-BZG-851

Kwasi Sarkodie-Mensah, PhD
Editor

Helping the Difficult Library Patron: New Approaches to Examining and Resolving a Long-Standing and Ongoing Problem

Helping the Difficult Library Patron: New Approaches to Examining and Resolving a Long-Standing and Ongoing Problem has been co-published simultaneously as *The Reference Librarian*, Numbers 75/76 2002.

*Pre-publication
REVIEWS,
COMMENTARIES,
EVALUATIONS . . .*

"THE ADVICE AND SUGGESTIONS ARE SOUND AND PERTINENT. This book deserves the warmest welcome and the highest praise. At a time when problem patrons abound in some library and information center settings, the purchase of this book will make a good start toward solving the troubles they create."

Dr. A. J. Anderson
Professor
Graduate School of Library and Information Science
Simmons College, Boston

PJC WARRINGTON CAMPUS LRC

More pre-publication
REVIEWS, COMMENTARIES, EVALUATIONS . . .

"**F**INALLY! A book that fills in the information cracks not covered in library school about the ubiquitous problem patron. REQUIRED READING FOR PUBLIC SERVICE LIBRARIANS. . . . This book defines the issues surrounding patron interactions and offers solutions to problems in an upbeat way, addressing central service issues for libraries and librarians everywhere. AN INVALUABLE RESOURCE for those serving diverse, post-Columbine digital generations, individuals marginalized by society, the technologically disenfranchised, and the rest of the library-using world."

Cheryl LaGuardia, MLS
Head of Instructional Services
for the Harvard College Library
Cambridge, Massachusetts

"**U**seful in public, special, and academic library collections and as SUPPLEMENTAL READING IN LIBRARY MANAGEMENT AND SERVICE COURSES IN SCHOOLS OF LIBRARY AND INFORMATION SCIENCE. Of special note are the sections on the 'new' problem patron challenges that arise from the electronic environment (email, chat rooms), insights on recovering from angry confrontations, the components of a workable plan for preventing violence in public buildings, and how to improve organization through complaint management."

Richard Rubin, PhD, MLS
Director
School of Library and Information Science
Kent State University, Ohio

The Haworth Information Press
An Imprint of The Haworth Press, Inc.

Helping the Difficult Library Patron: New Approaches to Examining and Resolving a Long-Standing and Ongoing Problem

Helping the Difficult Library Patron: New Approaches to Examining and Resolving a Long-Standing and Ongoing Problem has been co-published simultaneously as *The Reference Librarian*, Numbers 75/76 2002.

The Reference Librarian Monographic "Separates"

Below is a list of "separates," which in serials librarianship means a special issue simultaneously published as a special journal issue or double-issue *and* as a "separate" hardbound monograph. (This is a format which we also call a "DocuSerial.")

"Separates" are published because specialized libraries or professionals may wish to purchase a specific thematic issue by itself in a format which can be separately cataloged and shelved, as opposed to purchasing the journal on an on-going basis. Faculty members may also more easily consider a "separate" for classroom adoption.

"Separates" are carefully classified separately with the major book jobbers so that the journal tie-in can be noted on new book order slips to avoid duplicate purchasing.

You may wish to visit Haworth's Website at . . .

http://www.HaworthPress.com

. . . to search our online catalog for complete tables of contents of these separates and related publications.

You may also call 1-800-HAWORTH (outside US/Canada: 607-722-5857), or Fax 1-800-895-0582 (outside US/Canada: 607-771-0012), or e-mail at:

getinfo@haworthpressinc.com

Helping the Difficult Library Patron: New Approaches to Examining and Resolving a Long-Standing and Ongoing Problem, edited by Kwasi Sarkodie-Mensah, PhD (No. 75/76, 2002). *"Finally! A book that fills in the information cracks not covered in library school about the ubiquitous problem patron. Required reading for public service librarians."* (Cheryl LaGuardia, MLS, Head of Instructional Services for the Harvard College Library, Cambridge, Massachusetts)

Evolution in Reference and Information Services: The Impact of the Internet, edited by Di Su, MLS (No. 74, 2001). *Helps you make the most of the changes brought to the profession by the Internet.*

Doing the Work of Reference: Practical Tips for Excelling as a Reference Librarian, edited by Celia Hales Mabry, PhD (No. 72 and 73, 2001). *"An excellent handbook for reference librarians who wish to move from novice to expert. Topical coverage is extensive and is presented by the best guides possible: practicing reference librarians."* (Rebecca Watson-Boone, PhD, President, Center for the Study of Information Professionals, Inc.)

New Technologies and Reference Services, edited by Bill Katz, PhD (No. 71, 2000). *This important book explores developing trends in publishing, information literacy in the reference environment, reference provision in adult basic and community education, searching sessions, outreach programs, locating moving image materials for multimedia development, and much more.*

Reference Services for the Adult Learner: Challenging Issues for the Traditional and Technological Era, edited by Kwasi Sarkodie-Mensah, PhD (No. 69/70, 2000). *Containing research from librarians and adult learners from the United States, Canada, and Australia, this comprehensive guide offers you strategies for teaching adult patrons that will enable them to properly use and easily locate all of the materials in your library.*

Library Outreach, Partnerships, and Distance Education: Reference Librarians at the Gateway, edited by Wendi Arant and Pixey Anne Mosley (No. 67/68, 1999). *Focuses on community outreach in libraries toward a broader public by extending services based on recent developments in information technology.*

From Past-Present to Future-Perfect: A Tribute to Charles A. Bunge and the Challenges of Contemporary Reference Service, edited by Chris D. Ferguson, PhD (No. 66, 1999). *Explore reprints of selected articles by Charles Bunge, bibliographies of his published work, and original articles that draw on Bunge's values and ideas in assessing the present and shaping the future of reference service.*

Reference Services and Media, edited by Martha Merrill, PhD (No. 65, 1999). *Gives you valuable information about various aspects of reference services and media, including changes, planning issues, and the use and impact of new technologies.*

Coming of Age in Reference Services: A Case History of the Washington State University Libraries, edited by Christy Zlatos, MSLS (No. 64, 1999). *A celebration of the perseverance, ingenuity, and talent of the librarians who have served, past and present, at the Holland Library reference desk.*

Document Delivery Services: Contrasting Views, edited by Robin Kinder, MLS (No. 63, 1999). *Reviews the planning and process of implementing document delivery in four university libraries–Miami University, University of Colorado at Denver, University of Montana at Missoula, and Purdue University Libraries.*

The Holocaust: Memories, Research, Reference, edited by Robert Hauptman, PhD, and Susan Hubbs Motin (No. 61/62, 1998). *"A wonderful resource for reference librarians, students, and teachers . . . on how to present this painful, historical event." (Ephraim Kaye, PhD, The International School for Holocaust Studies, Yad Vashem, Jerusalem)*

Electronic Resources: Use and User Behavior, edited by Hemalata Iyer, PhD (No. 60, 1998). *Covers electronic resources and their use in libraries, with emphasis on the Internet and the Geographic Information Systems (GIS).*

Philosophies of Reference Service, edited by Celia Hales Mabry (No. 59, 1997). *"Recommended reading for any manager responsible for managing reference services and hiring reference librarians in any type of library." (Charles R. Anderson, MLS, Associate Director for Public Services, King County Library System, Bellevue, Washington)*

Business Reference Services and Sources: How End Users and Librarians Work Together, edited by Katherine M. Shelfer (No. 58, 1997). *"This is an important collection of papers suitable for all business librarians. . . . Highly recommended!" (Lucy Heckman, MLS, MBA, Business and Economics Reference Librarian, St. John's University, Jamaica, New York)*

Reference Sources on the Internet: Off the Shelf and onto the Web, edited by Karen R. Diaz (No. 57, 1997). *Surf off the library shelves and onto the Internet and cut your research time in half!*

Reference Services for Archives and Manuscripts, edited by Laura B. Cohen (No. 56, 1997). *"Features stimulating and interesting essays on security in archives, ethics in the archival profession, and electronic records." ("The Year's Best Professional Reading" (1998), Library Journal)*

Career Planning and Job Searching in the Information Age, edited by Elizabeth A. Lorenzen, MLS (No. 55, 1996). *"Offers stimulating background for dealing with the issues of technology and service. . . . A reference tool to be looked at often." (The One-Person Library)*

The Roles of Reference Librarians: Today and Tomorrow, edited by Kathleen Low, MLS (No. 54, 1996). *"A great asset to all reference collections. . . . Presents important, valuable information for reference librarians as well as other library users." (Library Times International)*

Reference Services for the Unserved, edited by Fay Zipkowitz, MSLS, DA (No. 53, 1996). *"A useful tool in developing strategies to provide services to all patrons." (Science Books & Films)*

Library Instruction Revisited: Bibliographic Instruction Comes of Age, edited by Lyn Elizabeth M. Martin, MLS (No. 51/52, 1995). *"A powerful collection authored by respected practitioners who have stormed the bibliographic instruction (BI) trenches and, luckily for us, have recounted their successes and shortcomings." (The Journal of Academic Librarianship)*

Library Users and Reference Services, edited by Jo Bell Whitlatch, PhD (No. 49/50, 1995). *"Well-planned, balanced, and informative. . . . Both new and seasoned professionals will find material for service attitude formation and practical advice for the front lines of service." (Anna M. Donnelly, MS, MA, Associate Professor and Reference Librarian, St. John's University Library)*

Social Science Reference Services, edited by Pam Baxter, MLS (No. 48, 1995). *"Offers practical guidance to the reference librarian. . . . A valuable source of information about specific literatures within the social sciences and the skills and techniques needed to provide access to those literatures." (Nancy P. O'Brien, MLS, Head, Education and Social Science Library, and Professor of Library Administration, University of Illinois at Urbana-Champaign)*

Reference Services in the Humanities, edited by Judy Reynolds, MLS (No. 47, 1994). *"A well-chosen collection of situations and challenges encountered by reference librarians in the humanities." (College Research Library News)*

Racial and Ethnic Diversity in Academic Libraries: Multicultural Issues, edited by Deborah A. Curry, MLS, MA, Susan Griswold Blandy, MEd, and Lyn Elizabeth M. Martin, MLS (No. 45/46, 1994). *"The useful techniques and attractive strategies presented here will provide the incentive for fellow professionals in academic libraries around the country to go and do likewise in their own institutions." (David Cohen, Adjunct Professor of Library Science, School of Library and Information Science, Queens College; Director, EMIE (Ethnic Materials Information Exchange); Editor, EMIE Bulletin)*

School Library Reference Services in the 90s: Where We Are, Where We're Heading, edited by Carol Truett, PhD (No. 44, 1994). *"Unique and valuable to the the teacher-librarian as well as students of librarianship. . . . The overall work successfully interweaves the concept of the continuously changing role of the teacher-librarian." (Emergency Librarian)*

Reference Services Planning in the 90s, edited by Gail Z. Eckwright, MLS, and Lori M. Keenan, MLS (No. 43, 1994). *"This monograph is well-researched and definitive, encompassing reference service as practices by library and information scientists. . . . It should be required reading for all professional librarian trainees." (Feliciter)*

Librarians on the Internet: Impact on Reference Services, edited by Robin Kinder, MLS (No. 41/42, 1994). *"Succeeds in demonstrating that the Internet is becoming increasingly a challenging but practical and manageable tool in the reference librarian's ever-expanding armory." (Reference Reviews)*

Reference Service Expertise, edited by Bill Katz (No. 40, 1993). *This important volume presents a wealth of practical ideas for improving the art of reference librarianship.*

Modern Library Technology and Reference Services, edited by Samuel T. Huang, MLS, MS (No. 39, 1993). *"This book packs a surprising amount of information into a relatively few number of pages. . . . This book will answer many questions." (Science Books and Films)*

Assessment and Accountability in Reference Work, edited by Susan Griswold Blandy, Lyn M. Martin, and Mary L. Strife (No. 38, 1992). *"An important collection of well-written, real-world chapters addressing the central questions that surround performance and services in all libraries." (Library Times International)*

The Reference Librarian and Implications of Mediation, edited by M. Keith Ewing, MLS, and Robert Hauptman, MLS (No. 37, 1992). *"An excellent and thorough analysis of reference mediation. . . . Well worth reading by anyone involved in the delivery of reference services." (Fred Batt, MLS, Associate University Librarian for Public Services, California State University, Sacramento)*

Library Services for Career Planning, Job Searching and Employment Opportunities, edited by Byron Anderson, MA, MLS (No. 36, 1992). *"An interesting book which tells professional libraries how to set up career information centers. . . . Clearly valuable reading for anyone establishing a career library." (Career Opportunities News)*

In the Spirit of 1992: Access to Western European Libraries and Literature, edited by Mary M. Huston, PhD, and Maureen Pastine, MLS (No. 35, 1992). *"A valuable and practical [collection] which every subject specialist in the field would do well to consult." (Western European Specialists Section Newsletter)*

Access Services: The Convergence of Reference and Technical Services, edited by Gillian M. McCombs, ALA (No. 34, 1992). *"Deserves a wide readership among both technical and public services librarians. . . . Highly recommended for any librarian interested in how reference and technical services roles may be combined." (Library Resources & Technical Services)*

Opportunities for Reference Services: The Bright Side of Reference Services in the 1990s, edited by Bill Katz (No. 33, 1991). *"A well-deserved look at the brighter side of reference services. . . . Should be read by reference librarians and their administrators in all types of libraries." (Library Times International)*

Government Documents and Reference Services, edited by Robin Kinder, MLS (No. 32, 1991). *Discusses access possibilities and policies with regard to government information, covering such important topics as new and impending legislation, information on most frequently used and requested sources, and grant writing.*

The Reference Library User: Problems and Solutions, edited by Bill Katz (No. 31, 1991). *"Valuable information and tangible suggestions that will help us as a profession look critically at our users and decide how they are best served." (Information Technology and Libraries)*

Continuing Education of Reference Librarians, edited by Bill Katz (No. 30/31, 1990). *"Has something for everyone interested in this field. . . . Library trainers and library school teachers may well find stimulus in some of the programs outlined here." (Library Association Record)*

Weeding and Maintenance of Reference Collections, edited by Sydney J. Pierce, PhD, MLS (No. 29, 1990). *"This volume may spur you on to planned activity before lack of space dictates 'ad hoc' solutions." (New Library World)*

Serials and Reference Services, edited by Robin Kinder, MLS, and Bill Katz (No. 27/28, 1990). *"The concerns and problems discussed are those of serials and reference librarians everywhere. . . . The writing is of a high standard and the book is useful and entertaining. . . . This book can be recommended." (Library Association Record)*

Rothstein on Reference: . . . with some help from friends, edited by Bill Katz and Charles Bunge, PhD, MLS (No. 25/26, 1990). *"An important and stimulating collection of essays on reference librarianship. . . . Highly recommended!" (Richard W. Grefrath, MA, MLS, Reference Librarian, University of Nevada Library)* Dedicated to the work of Sam Rothstein, one of the world's most respected teachers of reference librarians, this special volume features his writings as well as articles written about him and his teachings by other professionals in the field.

Integrating Library Use Skills Into the General Education Curriculum, edited by Maureen Pastine, MLS, and Bill Katz (No. 24, 1989). *"All contributions are written and presented to a high standard with excellent references at the end of each. . . . One of the best summaries I have seen on this topic." (Australian Library Review)*

Expert Systems in Reference Services, edited by Christine Roysdon, MLS, and Howard D. White, PhD, MLS (No. 23, 1989). *"The single most comprehensive work on the subject of expert systems in reference service." (Information Processing and Management)*

Information Brokers and Reference Services, edited by Bill Katz and Robin Kinder, MLS (No. 22, 1989). *"An excellent tool for reference librarians and indispensable for anyone seriously considering their own information-brokering service." (Booklist)*

Information and Referral in Reference Services, edited by Marcia Stucklen Middleton, MLS, and Bill Katz (No. 21, 1988). *Investigates a wide variety of situations and models which fall under the umbrella of information and referral.*

Reference Services and Public Policy, edited by Richard Irving, MLS, and Bill Katz (No. 20, 1988). *Looks at the relationship between public policy and information and reports ways in which libraries respond to the need for public policy information.*

Finance, Budget, and Management for Reference Services, edited by Ruth A. Fraley, MLS, MBA, and Bill Katz (No. 19, 1989). *"Interesting and relevant to the current state of financial needs in reference service. . . . A must for anyone new to or already working in the reference service area." (Riverina Library Review)*

Current Trends in Information: Research and Theory, edited by Bill Katz and Robin Kinder, MLS (No. 18, 1987). *"Practical direction to improve reference services and does so in a variety of* *ways ranging from humorous and clever metaphoric comparisons to systematic and practical methodological descriptions." (American Reference Books Annual)*

International Aspects of Reference and Information Services, edited by Bill Katz and Ruth A. Fraley, MLS, MBA (No. 17, 1987). *"An informative collection of essays written by eminent librarians, library school staff, and others concerned with the international aspects of information work." (Library Association Record)*

Reference Services Today: From Interview to Burnout, edited by Bill Katz and Ruth A. Fraley, MLS, MBA (No. 16, 1987). *Authorities present important advice to all reference librarians on the improvement of service and the enhancement of the public image of reference services.*

The Publishing and Review of Reference Sources, edited by Bill Katz and Robin Kinder, MLS (No. 15, 1987). *"A good review of current reference reviewing and publishing trends in the United States . . . will be of interest to intending reviewers, reference librarians, and students." (Australasian College Libraries)*

Personnel Issues in Reference Services, edited by Bill Katz and Ruth Fraley, MLS, MBA (No. 14, 1986). *"Chock-full of information that can be applied to most reference settings. Recommended for libraries with active reference departments." (RQ)*

Reference Services in Archives, edited by Lucille Whalen (No. 13, 1986). *"Valuable for the insights it provides on the reference process in archives and as a source of information on the different ways of carrying out that process." (Library and Information Science Annual)*

Conflicts in Reference Services, edited by Bill Katz and Ruth A. Fraley, MLS, MBA (No. 12, 1985). *This collection examines issues pertinent to the reference department.*

Evaluation of Reference Services, edited by Bill Katz and Ruth A. Fraley, MLS, MBA (No. 11, 1985). *"A much-needed overview of the present state of the art vis-à-vis reference service evaluation. . . . Excellent. . . . Will appeal to reference professionals and aspiring students." (RQ)*

Library Instruction and Reference Services, edited by Bill Katz and Ruth A. Fraley, MLS, MBA (No. 10, 1984). *"Well written, clear, and exciting to read. This is an important work recommended for all librarians, particularly those involved in, interested in, or considering bibliographic instruction. . . . A milestone in library literature." (RQ)*

Reference Services and Technical Services: Interactions in Library Practice, edited by Gordon Stevenson and Sally Stevenson (No. 9, 1984). *"New ideas and longstanding problems are handled with humor and sensitivity as practical suggestions and new perspectives are suggested by the authors." (Information Retrieval & Library Automation)*

Reference Services for Children and Young Adults, edited by Bill Katz and Ruth A. Fraley, MLS, MBA (No. 7/8, 1983). *"Offers a well-balanced approach to reference service for children and young adults." (RQ)*

Video to Online: Reference Services in the New Technology, edited by Bill Katz and Ruth A. Fraley, MLS, MBA (No. 5/6, 1983). *"A good reference manual to have on hand. . . . Well-written, concise, provide[s] a wealth of information." (Online)*

Ethics and Reference Services, edited by Bill Katz and Ruth A. Fraley, MLS, MBA (No. 4, 1982). *Library experts discuss the major ethical and legal implications that reference librarians must take into consideration when handling sensitive inquiries about confidential material.*

Reference Services Administration and Management, edited by Bill Katz and Ruth A. Fraley, MLS, MBA (No. 3, 1982). *Librarianship experts discuss the management of the reference function in libraries and information centers, outlining the responsibilities and qualifications of reference heads.*

Reference Services in the 1980s, edited by Bill Katz (No. 1/2, 1982). *Here is a thought-provoking volume on the future of reference services in libraries, with an emphasis on the challenges and needs that have come about as a result of automation.*

Helping the Difficult Library Patron: New Approaches to Examining and Resolving a Long-Standing and Ongoing Problem

Kwasi Sarkodie-Mensah, PhD
Editor

Helping the Difficult Library Patron: New Approaches to Examining and Resolving a Long-Standing and Ongoing Problem has been co-published simultaneously as *The Reference Librarian*, Numbers 75/76 2002.

The Haworth Information Press
An Imprint of
The Haworth Press, Inc.
New York • London • Oxford

Published by

The Haworth Information Press®, 10 Alice Street, Binghamton, NY 13904-1580 USA

The Haworth Information Press® is an imprint of The Haworth Press, Inc., 10 Alice Street, Binghamton, NY 13904-1580 USA.

Helping the Difficult Library Patron: New Approaches to Examining and Resolving a Long-Standing and Ongoing Problem has been co-published simultaneously as *The Reference Librarian*, Numbers 75/76 2002.

© 2002 by The Haworth Press, Inc. All rights reserved. No part of this work may be reproduced or utilized in any form or by any means, electronic or mechanical, including photocopying, microfilm and recording, or by any information storage and retrieval system, without permission in writing from the publisher. Printed in the United States of America.

The development, preparation, and publication of this work has been undertaken with great care. However, the publisher, employees, editors, and agents of The Haworth Press and all imprints of The Haworth Press, Inc., including The Haworth Medical Press® and Pharmaceutical Products Press®, are not responsible for any errors contained herein or for consequences that may ensue from use of materials or information contained in this work. Opinions expressed by the author(s) are not necessarily those of The Haworth Press, Inc. With regard to case studies, identities and circumstances of individuals discussed herein have been changed to protect confidentiality. Any resemblance to actual persons, living or dead, is entirely coincidental.

Cover design by Thomas J. Mayshock Jr.

Library of Congress Cataloging-in-Publication Data

Helping the difficult library patron : new approaches to examining and resolving a long-standing and ongoing problem / Kwasi Sarkodie-Mensah, editor.
    p. cm.
Co-published simultaneously as The reference librarian, nos. 75/76, 2002.
Includes bibliographical references and index.
ISBN 0-7890-1730-X (alk. paper) – ISBN 0-7890-1731-8 (pbk. : alk. paper)
    1. Libraries and readers. 2. Libraries and community. 3. Libraries–Public relations. 4. Libraries–Security measures. 5. Customer relations. 6. Conflict management. I. Sarkodie-Mensah, Kwasi.
Z711.H437 2002
025.5–dc21
                                        2002001916

Indexing, Abstracting & Website/Internet Coverage

This section provides you with a list of major indexing & abstracting services. That is to say, each service began covering this periodical during the year noted in the right column. Most Websites which are listed below have indicated that they will either post, disseminate, compile, archive, cite or alert their own Website users with research-based content from this work. (This list is as current as the copyright date of this publication.)

Abstracting, Website/Indexing Coverage......... Year When Coverage Began

- *Academic Abstracts/CD-ROM* **1994**
- *Academic Search: data base of 2,000 selected academic serials, updated monthly: EBSCO Publishing* **1996**
- *Academic Search Elite (EBSCO)* **1995**
- *Academic Search Premiere (EBSCO)* **2001**
- *BUBL Information Service: An Internet-Based Information Service for the UK Higher Education Community <URL:http://bubl.ac.uk/>* **1994**
- *CNPIEC Reference Guide: Chinese National Directory of Foreign Periodicals* **1995**
- *Current Awareness Abstracts of Library & Information Management Literature, ASLIB (UK)* **1991**
- *Current Cites [Digital Libraries] [Electronic Publishing] [Multimedia & Hypermedia] [Networks & Networking] [General]* **2000**
- *Current Index to Journals in Education* **1992**
- *Educational Administration Abstracts (EAA)* **1991**
- *FINDEX <www.publist.com>* **1999**
- *FRANCIS. INIST/CNRS <www.inist.fr>* **1983**
- *Handbook of Latin American Studies* **1999**
- *IBZ International Bibliography of Periodical Literature <www.saur.de>* **1994**

(continued)

Special bibliographic notes related to special journal issues (separates) and indexing/abstracting:

- indexing/abstracting services in this list will also cover material in any "separate" that is co-published simultaneously with Haworth's special thematic journal issue or DocuSerial. Indexing/abstracting usually covers material at the article/chapter level.
- monographic co-editions are intended for either non-subscribers or libraries which intend to purchase a second copy for their circulating collections.
- monographic co-editions are reported to all jobbers/wholesalers/approval plans. The source journal is listed as the "series" to assist the prevention of duplicate purchasing in the same manner utilized for books-in-series.
- to facilitate user/access services all indexing/abstracting services are encouraged to utilize the co-indexing entry note indicated at the bottom of the first page of each article/chapter/contribution.
- this is intended to assist a library user of any reference tool (whether print, electronic, online, or CD-ROM) to locate the monographic version if the library has purchased this version but not a subscription to the source journal.
- individual articles/chapters in any Haworth publication are also available through the Haworth Document Delivery Service (HDDS).

Helping the Difficult Library Patron: New Approaches to Examining and Resolving a Long-Standing and Ongoing Problem

CONTENTS

PROVIDING SOLUTIONS TO THE PROBLEM: IDEAS
FROM OTHER PROFESSIONS AND THE WORLD
OF LIBRARY AND INFORMATION SCIENCE

ABOUT THE EDITOR

Kwasi Sarkodie-Mensah, PhD, is Manager of Instructional Services at the O'Neill Library, Boston College. He is also an adjunct professor in the College of Advancing Studies, where he teaches one session of the required research methods and data course to adult students. Dr. Sarkodie-Mensah is the author of over two dozen articles, several book chapters, and some 100 book and video reviews, and has presented several workshops on the difficult library patron issue. He is editor of *Reference Services for the Adult Learner: Challenging Issues for the Traditional and Technological Era* (The Haworth Press, Inc., 2000).

ALL HAWORTH INFORMATION PRESS
BOOKS AND JOURNALS ARE PRINTED
ON CERTIFIED ACID-FREE PAPER

Introduction

Kwasi Sarkodie-Mensah

The issue of the difficult or problem library patron is as old as the library profession. From time immemorial up to the present time, library staff have had to deal with this dilemma. In this publication, library and information professionals take a look at this ostensibly immortal fact of life that affects almost every facet of our work, and provide practical solutions that in the long run will improve reference services to the people we serve, and make the work of library staff less stressful, more productive, and enormously meaningful.

This volume is divided into three sections. In the first, contributors take a look at the nature of the problem: they delve into the nature of the topic, examine it from historical perspectives, take a critical look at the situation as it exists in academic and public libraries, and examine questions dealing with the mentally ill and people of different sexual orientations. A review of current literature dealing with the difficult or problem patron concludes the section.

It is obvious that the development of various technologies that impact our lives and our library work has produced a community of newly bred difficult patrons. The Internet continues to transform and influence our work in countless ways. Cellular phones are also an integral component of our lives and work, but they can also become a strong ingredient in the recipe used in preparing many unpleasant library staff and patron encounters. In the second section, contributors examine the nature, scope and extent of these e-problems and how they can affect our work. The practical solutions the contributors provide will serve to mitigate the various components of the problems.

[Haworth co-indexing entry note]: "Introduction." Sarkodie-Mensah, Kwasi. Co-published simultaneously in *The Reference Librarian* (The Haworth Information Press, an imprint of The Haworth Press, Inc.) No. 75/76, 2002, pp. 1-2; and: *Helping the Difficult Library Patron: New Approaches to Examining and Resolving a Long-Standing and Ongoing Problem* (ed: Kwasi Sarkodie-Mensah) The Haworth Information Press, an imprint of The Haworth Press, Inc., 2002, pp. 1-2. Single or multiple copies of this article are available for a fee from The Haworth Document Delivery Service [1-800-HAWORTH, 9:00 a.m. - 5:00 p.m. (EST). E-mail address: getinfo@haworthpressinc.com].

© 2002 by The Haworth Press, Inc. All rights reserved.

1

Finding solutions to these problems will not only improve the services we provide, but also provide avenues through which we can truly make our services to our users meaningful. In the third section contributors generously and elaborately provide various solutions: what we can learn from other professions, different ways of life, and from our own profession, such as empowering front line library staff, rewriting library policies, and partnering with resource people in our communities.

How unchallenging our daily work lives would be if we did not have such a daunting and practical problem as the difficult library patron to deal with. There is no evidence that this issue will disappear any time soon. By dialoging with our colleagues in the library and information science profession and many others in the communities where we work, we will be able to meet these challenges which are always unwritten but a crucial component of our job description.

THE NATURE OF THE PROBLEM: DEFINITIONS, SCOPE AND EXTENT, HISTORICAL PERSPECTIVES, AND DIVERSE CLIENTELE

Problem Patrons: All Shapes and Sizes

Kelly D. Blessinger

SUMMARY. Every type of library will inevitably have problem patrons, but this article focuses mainly on public and academic libraries. As the times have changed, so has the magnitude of the problem patrons. Problems of the past seem irrelevant compared to some of the problems we are currently facing. Discussed in this article are particular types of problem behavior, including, but not limited to anger, harassment of staff, and homelessness. The types of each category include examples to illustrate each concern, and possible remedies. *[Article copies available for a fee from The Haworth Document Delivery Service: 1-800-HAWORTH. E-mail address: <getinfo@haworthpressinc.com> Website: <http://www. HaworthPress.com> © 2002 by The Haworth Press, Inc. All rights reserved.]*

Kelly D. Blessinger is Geographic Information Systems Librarian, Middleton Library, Louisiana State University, Baton Rouge, LA 70803 (E-mail: kblessi@lsu.edu).

[Haworth co-indexing entry note]: "Problem Patrons: All Shapes and Sizes." Blessinger, Kelly D. Co-published simultaneously in *The Reference Librarian* (The Haworth Information Press, an imprint of The Haworth Press, Inc.) No. 75/76, 2002, pp. 3-10; and: *Helping the Difficult Library Patron: New Approaches to Examining and Resolving a Long-Standing and Ongoing Problem* (ed: Kwasi Sarkodie-Mensah) The Haworth Information Press, an imprint of The Haworth Press, Inc., 2002, pp. 3-10. Single or multiple copies of this article are available for a fee from The Haworth Document Delivery Service [1-800-HAWORTH, 9:00 a.m. - 5:00 p.m. (EST). E-mail address: getinfo@haworthpressinc.com].

© 2002 by The Haworth Press, Inc. All rights reserved.

KEYWORDS. Problem patrons, anger, harassment, crime, damage, property, homelessness, children, public libraries, academic libraries

PROBLEM PATRONS

A problem patron could be defined as someone who infringes on others' enjoyment of the library by displaying behavior that is deemed destructive, criminal, bothersome, offensive, or otherwise inappropriate to the norms of behavior in libraries or society. Since a librarian's role is to work in a client/patron based environment, the employee has to learn to control their immediate impulse to react to negative situations, which usually would not be a proper solution, and in many cases is a test in self-control. Employees have to keep in mind that problem patrons are usually the exception from the norm, and usually entail only a small percentage of the total client base. The negative situations are certainly the scenarios that seem to remain in our minds though, rather than those of the polite patrons. While "problem patrons" and "problem people" exist in every type of library and place where humans gather, the focus in this article will mainly be on those that exist in the public and academic domain.

ANGER

Anger usually stems from underlying feelings, whether they are frustration, lack of power, inadequacy, or feeling as though we have not been treated fairly. Anger is a reaction to these underlying feelings, and not a very constructive or positive one. As librarians, we have to do our best to defuse the patron's anger. Having people react inappropriately to situations is inevitable. We can never please everyone, but what librarians can control is our reaction to the anger in question.

As librarians, we have to rise above the negativity, and be the better person. Sometimes just having someone to listen and sympathize is all the patrons need. First and foremost, we should let the person explain why they are upset. From there, we should try to be understanding and reassure the patron that we recognize his or her problem. We should try to offer any available solutions to the problem in question, and not resort to taking the anger of the patrons personally. Usually the patron is mad at the situation, and not the person, but will become angry with anyone that represents the institution that created their anger. The old maxim, "the customer is always right," certainly is not true. However, unless patrons are physically or emotionally abusive, we should try to reason with them, and alleviate their anger without becoming emotional ourselves.

HARASSMENT OF STAFF

Although harassment of staff can tie in with anger, there are other forms of harassment as well. They can come in the forms of stalking, unwanted sexual advances, or anything that may make a staff member feel uncomfortable or in danger. Unfortunately, staff sometimes feel as if they have no power over the person that is causing them the distress, and are reluctant to inform their supervisor of the matter. Worse yet, some administrators would rather ignore the problem in the hopes that it will go away rather than confronting it head on. A lot of managers feel powerless to confront a problem, and have no legal right to do so until a crime is committed. In a survey based on public libraries in three Midwestern states in 1996-97, seventy one percent reported a problem with staff harassment leading to expulsion or arrest in the previous 12 months (Lorenzen, 135).

In 1992 a suit was filed against the Freeport Illinois Public Library regarding the expulsion of a factory worker, Leonard Brinkmeier. The defendant made an unwanted sexual pass at a female staff member by giving her a note in the library's parking lot that read "If you love me, continue wearing low cut dresses, and bending over" (American Libraries, 1993). The police issued a no trespass order against the defendant, but he continued to call her at work repeatedly and circle the library and the residence of her grandmother numerous times. The initial suit that Brinkmeier filed against the library's director stated that his first amendment rights had been violated. When this case was dismissed, he filed another suit. The second suit claimed that the library's policy of expulsion violated his First Amendment Rights. He did not seek a monetary award from the library; he just wanted to regain access. Brinkmeier's attorney, Robert Slattery, claimed that the defendant was simply expressing an interest in the woman, and did not mean any harm. Because the letter was non-threatening, the police were powerless to take any action. In the end, the court ruled to allow Brinkmeier admittance, and also ruled that the library would have to pay the defendant's attorney fees in the amount of $3,000. The defendant is continuing to use the library, so far without incident, but the female staff member decided to resign from her position (American Libraries, 1993).

CRIME

Public libraries have a greater incidence of crime, but crime can occur in any type of library. Some libraries are now forced to employ security guards to patrol the library. Installation of video surveillance equipment and other devices are also used as deterrents in many libraries. The library, once considered a safe haven, can now be a place where deviants go to find their victims. Rapes, murders, destruction of property, and other acts of violence are becoming more commonplace. In 1999 the Hamilton County Library in Cincinnati had such a problem. A man was reported to have twice attempted rape in the women's restroom and in the stairwell. An eighteen-year-old man was apprehended in the case, even though proper security measures had already been in place, with "53 security cameras in the building, 24 hour security guards, and Cincinnati police officers during public hours" (American Libraries, 2000). A spokesman for the library maintained that there were nine security guards in place when the attacker attempted rape for the second time (American Libraries, 2000). Another case in 1999 involved a Russian immigrant walking into the Mormon Church of Salt Lake City, opening fire, killing two patrons, and injuring five others before police shot him to death. The perpetrator was said to have been schizophrenic and not taking his medication (Galloway, 1999).

DESTRUCTION OF PROPERTY

Wherever there is a product there will always be the potential for the destruction of property. The damage can be caused unintentionally, by normal wear and tear, or intentionally, from theft or vandalism of materials. It is hard to estimate the loss of materials because theft and destruction are largely covert acts, and libraries may not know for years whether a periodical or book has been damaged. In a case of deliberate destruction, Belulah High School in North Dakota was a target of vandals in March, 2000. Although the whole school was defaced, the library was the hardest hit. Computers were destroyed, windows were broken, tables were overturned and books were knocked from the shelves (American Libraries, 2000). In 1999 an extremely rare book written by Galileo was to be auctioned by Christie's when it was discovered that it had been stolen from the Polish National Library. Upon investigation, the Bulgarian student who had stolen the book was said to have in his property over 60 books and materials from the library (Library Journal, 1999). Thefts in 1991 and 1992 led to the closing of the Library of Congress's open stack policy. As a result of this, security measures such as surveillance equipment, theft deterring devices and security guards were employed. It seemed as though even the most reputable people could not be trusted. A doctor, a lawyer and a rare book dealer were all found guilty of theft (Billington, 40).

UNATTENDED CHILDREN

While public libraries and academic libraries both have problem patrons, there are some problems that are unique to the different types of libraries. This is not to deny that these problems do not exist in other libraries. The fact is that the rate of the occurrence is more common in particular types of libraries. Public libraries, for example, tend to have higher rates of unattended children and homeless.

While reading and learning should be a part of every child's life, sometimes this positive experience can produce negative results. Libraries are sometimes used as daycare for unattended children. Some parents will drop off their children alone at the library, while they carry on with their lives at a different location. For children who are mature enough to independently enjoy the library's atmosphere and respect the needs of other patrons, being left on their own can have no negative implications. However, this is not always the case. As much as librarians may empathize with such situations, it may be hard for them to rightfully accept the fact that babysitting was a required component of the MLIS degree. This is where a policy manual can be put to a good use. The Fairfax County Library located outside of Washington, DC ruled that no child under seven should ever be left alone. Children seven to nine could be left alone for an hour and a half, and children aged ten to eleven were only allowed to be left alone for three hours at a time (Bang, 197). This policy could not be labeled discriminatory, because it is consistent for those children according to their age level, and not their maturity level. The blame in these scenarios has to be placed with the negligent parents, and not on the children. The parents should first be alerted to the rules of the library, and proper action should be taken if they repeatedly ignore the rules.

HOMELESSNESS

The problem of homeless patrons can occur at any library, but it is most prevalent in public libraries. This might be due to the misconception by much of the public that only faculty and students are allowed into academic libraries. Maybe some homeless people fear that they would be more apt to be noticed in academic libraries. On the other hand, everyone knows that public libraries are for the public, and everyone, even the homeless have the right to use them.

Urban areas seem to have the largest problem with the homeless, because generally, cities have a higher rate of homelessness than rural areas. Location of libraries within the cities is also a key factor. If the library is within distance of a homeless shelter, naturally the occurrence of the homeless in the library will be much higher. An example of this is the main branch of the Richland County Public Library in Columbia, South Carolina. It is located across the street from the Oliver Gospel Mission, which provides shelter and services for homeless men. While the Gospel Mission provides a great service to the community and should be commended, it also naturally tends to bring homeless people to a central location. The large majorities of the homeless are without transportation, and tend to congregate in areas within walking distance, especially those that are free. At almost any given time, there will be at least one homeless person in the Richland County Public Library.

This issue is a very hot topic within libraries today. While wanting to be sympathetic to the homeless, many people tend to be uncomfortable around them. The homeless tend to carry a stigma of either being crazy or dangerous. Whether it is their unkempt appearance, their odor, or their odd behavior, the general public and librarians often do not know how to react. Unless they cause a direct threat to another patron, or the library, they should be allowed in the library. Still, even without posing a direct threat, the homeless still may make some patrons ill at ease. A good example would be the homeless patron who makes no illusion of reading, or any use of material, and openly stares at patrons. Women patrons especially will become uncomfortable in such situations, because they are not sure if a confrontation will occur.

Another problem is homeless patrons using the libraries as a home base for sleeping, and for personal hygiene. This tends to make some of the non-homeless so uncomfortable that they will not use the public restrooms.

PAST vs. CURRENT PROBLEMS

Compared to the present, the problems libraries faced in the past seem a bit laughable. As the times have changed, so have the problems and their severity. When the largest problems of libraries in the past were noisy patrons and food in the library, librarians had much less to worry about, and they certainly never feared for their lives:

> The 'problem patron' who in the mid-70's was a mere annoyance is now often perceived as a real threat. Many of the people who walk through the doors of public libraries today are frightening in aspect and behavior and appear to be deranged. They are victims of homelessness, hopelessness, unemployment, or a mental health system that has abandoned them. (Milnor-Smith, 316)

In addition to the growing incidence of anger, violence and otherwise inappropriate behavior, the library has seen great changes with the boom of the electronic age. Recently librarians at the Minneapolis Public Library's Central Library filed a case with the Equal Opportunity Commission, stating that they felt the ease of patrons access to pornography made the work environment uncomfortable for many of the female employees (Legal Facts, 2000).

The American Library Association stands firm behind their stance that there should be free access to all materials, and no filtering software should be in place, but did they take into account how this may make some of the workers feel, and how people have been charged with harassment for far less? Since most librarians are female, a case could definitely be made regarding this issue. Where should we draw the line? Is viewing graphic material a right of anyone that comes into the library, even though the computers are intended for research? At the same library a six year old boy was observed to have been viewing and printing out pornography in the children's section. It was also found that sex offenders were starting to congregate at the library, and at certain times the librarians had reported that as many as one fourth of the computers in the library were being used to view pornography. One staff member was quoted as saying that "the only other place that resembles our environment right now is an adult bookstore" (Legal Facts, 2000).

CONCLUSION

While some of the aforementioned scenarios are extreme and uncommon, we still must be prepared to deal with problems of this magnitude arising. We must strive to make the library a welcome place for all, because if the general public is uncomfortable using the library, this could lead to the lack of funding because of a lack of public interest, or proposed need. One thing that all libraries should do to protect themselves against problem patrons is to set clear and concise guidelines in print. By doing this, the library will know what steps to take when a problem occurs. Being consistent with problems will ensure that everyone who displays the negative behavior will be treated equally, and would have no basis to claim otherwise. An attorney should read the policies to check for legality, and to make certain that the guidelines are not vague or discriminatory, so that it would hold up in a court of law. Once the document has been checked, the library should hold training sessions to familiarize all staff with the new policies. While "problem patrons" are inevitable, and often out of our control, our reactions to them, and our policies regarding them are not.

REFERENCES

Bang, Patricia. "When Bad Things Happen in Good Libraries: Staff Tools for the '90s and Beyond." *Public Libraries* 37 (1998): 196-99.

"Barred from Library, Patron Sues to Regain Access." *American Libraries* 24 (1993): 291.

"Barred Patron Regains Access." *American Libraries* 24 (1993): 696.

Billington, James H. "Here Today, Here Tomorrow: The Imperative of Collections Security." *American Libraries* 27 (1996): 40.

Galloway, Joseph L. "Shooting in the Stacks." *U.S. News and World Report* 126 (1999): 44.

Legal Facts. Ed. Janet M. LaRue. 18 May 2000 <http://www.frc.org/legal/lf00e03.html>.

Lorenzen, Michael. "Security Issues in the Public Libraries of Three Midwestern States." *Public Libraries* 37 (1998): 134-36.

"North Dakota Library Trashed." *American Libraries* 31 (2000): 27.

Rogers, Michael, and Norman Oder. "Stolen Rarities Found." *Library Journal* 124 (1999): 20.

Smith, Nancy Milnor. "Staff Harassment by Patrons: Why Administrators Flinch." *American Libraries* 25 (1994): 316.

"Suspect Held in Rape Attempts." *American Libraries* 31 (2000): 32.

The Problem Patron:
Is There One in Your Library?

Calmer D. Chattoo

SUMMARY. Library staff and other patrons encounter patrons who are one or a combination of the following: mentally ill/disturbed, homeless, street persons, angry, aggressive, unreasonable, rude. Commonly referred to as "problem patrons," they appear in any type of library: public, academic, institutional, corporate and special. Most of them behave poorly because of their own troubles. The history of "problem patrons," various types of problem patrons and their identifying behaviors are discussed in this paper. In attempting to define "problem patrons" the information provides a framework for understanding the problems of challenging patrons and for learning to discriminate between problem patrons and patrons who have problems. *[Article copies available for a fee from The Haworth Document Delivery Service: 1-800-HAWORTH. E-mail address: <getinfo@haworthpressinc.com> Website: <http://www.HaworthPress. com> © 2002 by The Haworth Press, Inc. All rights reserved.]*

KEYWORDS. Difficult patron, challenging patron, problem behavior, street people, problem patron, homeless patron, angry patron

INTRODUCTION

It is generally accepted that most human endeavor begins with a thought or an idea. That idea or thought is then put into an appropriate

Calmer D. Chattoo is Assistant Librarian, Cataloger, Charles B. Sears Law Library, University at Buffalo Law School, Buffalo, NY 14260 (E-mail: chattoo@acsu.buffalo. edu).

[Haworth co-indexing entry note]: "The Problem Patron: Is There One in Your Library?" Chattoo, Calmer D. Co-published simultaneously in *The Reference Librarian* (The Haworth Information Press, an imprint of The Haworth Press, Inc.) No. 75/76, 2002, pp. 11-22; and: *Helping the Difficult Library Patron: New Approaches to Examining and Resolving a Long-Standing and Ongoing Problem* (ed: Kwasi Sarkodie-Mensah) The Haworth Information Press, an imprint of The Haworth Press, Inc., 2002, pp. 11-22. Single or multiple copies of this article are available for a fee from The Haworth Document Delivery Service [1-800-HAWORTH, 9:00 a.m. - 5:00 p.m. (EST). E-mail address: getinfo@haworthpressinc.com].

© 2002 by The Haworth Press, Inc. All rights reserved. *11*

form such as the written word, or even a plowed field. The clarity and efficiency with which the form is produced, as it does with the clarity and structure of the initial thought, determine the success or failure of any endeavor.

The phrase "problem patrons" conjures up difficulties, trouble, or abnormal behavior from one being served–a customer, client, or user. Based on that conventional idea of the phrase, are library users who fall into that category the only problem patrons? For example, a library user with a research problem, or a challenging reference question, is he/she a "problem patron" or a patron with a problem? Or could the individual be considered both? How can we make the distinction? Certainly, the clarity and efficiency with which the phrase "problem patron" is used will determine who really is a problem patron in your library.

According to *Webster's Ninth New Collegiate Dictionary*, the word "problem" when used as an adjective, as it is in the phrase "problem patron," denotes the meaning of dealing with a problem of conduct or social relationship and "difficult to deal with." The use of the phrase, therefore, seems obscure since there are many library patrons with good conduct and good social relationships who are considered problem patrons due to the nature of their demands and or requests. And are library patrons in general "difficult to deal with?" Some have really proven to be difficult, but laws and regulations and workable strategies have been established to deal with difficult ones (Turner, 1993).

In the field of structural linguistics and structural anthropology, the meaning of a word (or phrase) is often centered on the use of the word. Patrons who are daily complainers about homeless people in the library may or may not be problem patrons. This may be determined by the context in which the nature and extent of their complaint is explained and understood. Likely you have identified several users in your library whom you consider "problem patrons." What criteria have you used to describe the patrons as such?

HISTORY OF "PROBLEM PATRON"

The challenge of dealing with problem patrons, and indeed, the problems of patrons, has become a difficult fact of library life, ever since libraries have adjusted their rules to admit the general public irrespective of age. The phrase "problem patron" has become part of the collective vocabulary of libraries to describe users such as vandals, flashers, people who smell bad, angry persons and even the homeless (Rubin, 2000).

It has been the focus of many books, videos, articles, workshops and conferences, some dating back to our earliest professional literature.

In ancient Greece as well as medieval and modern Europe, it has been found that there were rules and regulations governing library use and behavior. For example, in 1931, the Library Company of Philadelphia "promulgated a dictum which required the librarian to awake individuals who fell asleep while apparently engaged in more lively cerebral activities than snoring" (Sable, 1988, p. 169). Ann Arbor, Michigan Public Library also had to deal with a similar problem (Nelson, 1985).

Toward the end of the late 19th century and into the early 20th century, the literature indicates that both England and the United States had the problem of "library loafers" (Gross, 1913), another term used to refer to problem patrons then. Other terms such as "library pests" (Hagen, 1886; Thompson, 1985), and "idle hands and idle minds" (New York Libraries, 1913) have also been used.

WHO IS A PROBLEM PATRON?

Shuman gives an uncomfortably broad definition of a problem patron as "anyone who is doing anything illegal, immoral, annoying, or upsetting to anyone else" (Shuman, 1989, p. 6). Just as there are many potentially upsetting books in the library, so can there be many patrons whose behavior is upsetting. He explains that "a problem patron is anyone who visits the library and either breaks or flouts existing rules, or presents an actual or potential threat to other people within the building" (Shuman, 1996, p. 6). Clearly then, any patron can potentially become a problem.

In Simmon's definition of a problem patron, he includes illiterates simply seeking shelter, alcoholics, the homeless, the mentally disturbed, aggressive young people, and those with offensive odors (Simmons, 1985). In 1993 the *Eastern Region News* carried an article in which the writer defined a problem patron as "the person who gets a library staff member riled up. This obviously covers a lot of territory but can include the demanding; the emotionally disturbed; the homeless, the drunks; babblers and starers; the lonely and the angry; the liars, the exhibitionists, the sleepers and the fragrant; criminals (drug dealers, purse snatchers); unruly teens; and unattended small children" (Eastern Region News, 1993).

In their study of incidents of problem patron behavior in Illinois public and academic libraries, Brashear and his colleagues identify three types of problem patrons (Brashear et al., 1981):

Type 1: Harmless nuisances. These are persons who do not pose any overt threat or cause disruption, but may be generally regarded by staff and other patrons as offensive.

Type 2: Disruptive or threatening. These are patrons who disrupt other patrons or staff members, or who pose a threat without actually attempting to commit an act of violence.

Type 3: Violent. These are patrons who commit or attempt to commit an act of violence against a staff member or other patrons (Brashear et al., 1981).

TYPES OF PROBLEM PATRONS

Problem patrons are real humans, and human characteristics can help to identify them. Individuals who are classed as such vary greatly and the phrase is synonymous to "difficult" or "challenging patrons" (Comstock-Gay, 1995; Sarkodie-Mensah, 2000). Sable describes these patrons as:

Peace disturbers: canvassers of political, religious, social or social service causes; coughers and laughers; violent criminals; loafers; drunkards and drug-intoxicated ones. Among them are eaters and drinkers; the emotionally and psychologically disturbed; fighters; gamblers and game players; loud mouths; inconsistent users of AV materials and equipment; hostile persons; pet owners (not the seeing-eye dog); self-talkers; sleepers; hyperactives; verbal abusers; whispers who never cease.

Sexually oriented: casual daters; child molesters; homosexuals; prostitutes; sexually active couples; exhibitionists and voyeurs.

Specific categories: those emitting body and manmade odors which may be irritating to others and cause allergic reactions; demanders of special attention and services based upon their status; drug dealers; and monopolizers of librarian's time. He also includes patrons who use library facilities for unauthorized purposes; monopolize library materials and equipment; manipulate and violate rules and borrowing privileges. Thieves, pickpockets, extortionists, arsonists, mutilators, and vandals are also placed in this category of problem patrons (Sables, 1988, p. 170-171).

PROBLEM PATRONS OF THE 90s

Noisy Seniors

Retired seniors account for a large portion of most public libraries' clientele and they magnify some old problems and create new ones. When meeting as a group of about three or more they can talk as loudly as any group of teenagers, even if just a few in the group are hard of hearing. Everyone must "speak up," becoming loud and noisy. Feeling that they have passed the age to be disciplined they may become indignant if asked to "tone down a little."

Technology-Created Problem Patrons

With the rise of the information superhighway come problem patrons who live according to the times. Sarkodie-Mensah's identification of these patrons is summarized here.

> *Cellphone users (cellofites):* persons who annoy other patrons with their use of cell phones or pagers in some of the most inappropriate places in the library.

> *Persons with pagers (beepsie beepers):* similar to annoying cell phone users, with their pagers activated and in a "Quiet Study Only" area of the Library.

> *Laptop Computer Users (laptomites):* those who make noise keyboarding in study areas and disturb other patrons there.

> *Technophobes:* patrons fearful of using the computer and trying anything on their own. They call on library staff to perform basic functions for them (Sarkodie-Mensah, 2000, p. 163).

Included in the technology-created problem patrons are those who visit adult web sites at public workstations in the library, or on computers located in and around the vicinity of the children's department. Similarly, patrons who use a public workstation for e-mailing without consideration of the needs of others are classified as technology-created problem patrons.

PATRONS' PROBLEM BEHAVIOR

According to Shuman any behavior that is illegal, immoral, annoying, or upsetting is problematic (Shuman, 1989, p. 6). However, rarely is the person or *only* the person the difficulty. Instead, the situations/behaviors that patrons present may be or may become problems to library staff and others.

To elaborate on his definition of problem behavior, Shuman uses five categories–*eccentric behavior*; *noncompliance with library rules*; *harassment*; *intentional behavior* and *behavior caused by mental illness* (Shuman, 1984, p. xxvii). Sarkodie-Mensah characterized problem patron behaviors as rude, unreasonable, waiting to direct anger at library staff and needing satisfaction (Sarkodie-Mensah, 2000, p. 161). All are included in Shuman's categories.

Eccentric Behavior

Patrons with eccentric behavior talk to themselves, gesture non-threateningly at other patrons or staff, hum, wear bizarre clothes or speak in tongues. This type is differentiated from true problems basically because of the harmless nature of the activity in which the patron is engaged. Behaviors from nuisance patrons, while non-threatening, can be annoying, unpleasant or obnoxious. Students listening to music through earphones that can be heard ten feet away are considered nuisance patrons. Constant ringing of cellular phones and beepers in a quiet reference room has recently become a major problem behavior of an eccentric nature in many libraries.

Non-Compliance with Library Rules

Behaviors resulting from non-compliance with library rules range from library to library as rules and regulations vary. For example, depending on the library, sleeping and snoring may not be a problem. So while it may be expressly forbidden in one library, it may be overlooked in another, and tolerated or not discussed in another. Regarded as a problem in libraries since time immemorial, the literature reveals that librarians had to keep track of patrons dozing and snoring (Wright, 1958). But are all sleeping patrons "problem patrons?" For example, a student who stayed up all night and who is resting quietly at a section in the library may not qualify as a "problem patron" situation. However, patrons found doing it regularly, such as street people, may create problem situations.

Irate patrons are among ones showing non-compliance with library rules. Typically, these patrons dare to challenge the library's policies and will not take "no" for an answer. This characteristic would be typical of a patron who refuses to pay a fine; one who throws a book when told it cannot be renewed and a student shouting obscenities about the policy on reference materials. The technically sophisticated patron, who refuses to allow anyone else to use the computer terminal and becomes infuriated by restrictions on use, is also displaying non-compliance with library policy. In some extreme cases irate patrons may become abusive and threatening, but generally they just want to speak what's on their mind.

Cuesta places the "dignitary nuisance" (Cuesta, 1996, p. 79) in the group of patrons not complying with library rules. This group of patrons is peculiar to the academic environment. They are known to be persons in position of authority or influence and are certain that library rules apply to everyone except themselves.

Sarkodie-Mensah illustrates behaviors of patrons who use their differences to create problem situations (Sarkodie-Mensah, 2000, p. 162-163). For example, a black patron who is known for returning library materials late may be quick to accuse staff of racism when told that he/she has to pay a fine for overdue books. Similarly, an adult student may use his/her age to demand service above younger patrons waiting in line; or a gay patron accuses library staff of homophobia when told periodicals do not circulate and gay/lesbian journals cannot be taken out.

Behaviors resulting from non-compliance with library rules also include breaking the "no food in the library" policy. Some patrons barefaced bring food into the library by openly displaying the item. Others hide it in their backpacks prepared to eat it in the library. Bringing in pets (not guide pets) into the library, smoking, making excessive noise even in areas designated and clearly identified as "Quiet Study Area," or just making the library into a debating ring or an arena where public address is made, are all considered problem behaviors.

Harassment

Harassment of library staff and/or other patrons is also considered a form of objectionable problem behavior. Commonly understood to mean occasional or justifiable anger or irritation at alleged rude treatment or unusual delays, it also includes persistent badgering, verbal abuse, following, or even staring intently at library staff or patrons (Shuman, 1984, p. xxvii). But not all patrons staring intently can be guilty of harassment. According to Johnson a homeless person, or anyone, could "suffer from an ailment which makes them appear to be glaring or staring, when they are in fact just sitting quietly or possibly even experiencing seizure-related problems. Patrons with disorders such as Tourette's Syndrome may have physical spasms or shout out words or unintelligible sounds, which could be misinterpreted by staff members unfamiliar with such disorders or with the patron" (Johnson, 1996, p. 115).

Problem patrons harass in many ways: in person, by telephone, fax, and in recent times, by e-mail. Closely connected to harassment is solicitation in the library. This type of behavior affects patrons as well as library staff of both genders. Johnson classifies soliciting that leads to sexual harassment as visual, verbal, and physical (Johnson, 1996).

Visual harassment includes leering, or showing sexually oriented materials. Verbal harassment includes, but is not limited to, making sexually suggestive comments, making unsolicited comments on the recipient's appearance, and constantly asking for dates. Physical harassment involves "inappropriate touching, patting, brushing against, and physically blocking the recipient's exist" (Johnson, 1996, p. 110).

Intentional Behavior

Lincoln maintains that intentional behavior is crime and includes theft, vandalism, mutilation, drug use and/or sale, assaults, arson, and a number of other types of incidents that annoy, threaten, or victimize staff or other patrons (Lincoln, 1984). Some of such behaviors include damage to library property, destroying materials and cutting pages from books and journals, to name a few. Since the advent of the electronic age it is not uncommon for students to kick workstations, unload paper from printers, remove ink cartridges and switch power cords. Violent crimes, though unusual for libraries, are on the increase in many. California, Arizona, and Utah have had violent crimes in libraries recently (Lifer, 1994).

Other intentional bad behaviors include stalking library staff or other patrons and exposing oneself to other users. Soliciting sex on the restroom walls and on carrels and even sexual assignations in the restrooms are not uncommon problem behaviors in libraries. Many of these inappropriate public sexual activities are generally anecdotal, possibly because the subject does not seem worthy of reporting or because libraries would rather not publicize the fact.

Problems Caused by Mental Illness

Behaviors caused by mental illness create problems for library staff as well as other patrons. The majority of mentally ill persons are "homeless." Turner identifies the types of homeless persons found in the library as "street people" (Turner, 1993). He describes them as patrons who are raunchy looking, travel with most of their worldly possessions in trash bags or bedrolls, wear ragged clothes, and haven't bathed lately. This type may or may not exhibit various eccentric or anti social behaviors indicative of mental illness, alcoholism, or other substance abuse (Turner, 1993, p. 31-32). According to *U.S. News and World Report* they "exhibit bizarre behaviors, disorganized thinking, or extreme paranoia" (*U.S. News & World Report*, 1988).

While a street person's appearance is his/her defining characteristic, he/she is not a problem simply because of appearance or a putative lifestyle. It is what the "street person" does in the library that may or may not create a problem for library staff and other patrons.

Library staff and others, however, consider them nuisances. Coping with problems associated with street people such as lack of access to proper sanitation and hygiene, lack of interest in the same, and sometimes mental illness, can affect the library as well as those who spend time in it. Some street people smell so badly that they cause nausea. Sleeping street people may snore so loudly it disturbs contemplation. For hygiene reasons patrons may fear handling materials touched or used by street people. As a result many librarians classify "street people" as "problem patrons." Similarly, because of a disheveled appearance, it is easier to assume that a street person is a problem.

Certain forms of mentally disturbed behaviors can appear frightening. Salter helps us to identify some of these frightening behaviors. He and his colleague point out that patrons suffering from hallucinations may converse angrily with imaginary persons or creatures. Those with delusions may accuse library staff of being foreign spies, devils, or even creatures from other planets. Sociopaths are those with a weak or non-existent moral code, and may boldly lie about other patrons or staff (Salter & Salter, 1996, p. 18-19).

Unfortunately, street persons sometimes fall into the general classification of problem patrons along with thieves, exhibitionists, and persons whose behaviors are annoying and worrisome yet completely legal. However, it is important to note that not all street persons are problem patrons, and that not all problem patrons are street persons.

Street persons who use the library as a haven from the streets, a place with public restrooms and quiet rooms where one can read, socialize, and on occasion sleep without the requirements of paying for the privilege, are not dangerous, whatever else they may be. They do not all act, react, or think the same way. Some are, admittedly seriously and dangerously ill, and that illness may be physical, mental or even emotional. Others are quite "normal" in the sense of being average in intelligence and perception. They however, share a syndrome of human conditions from which they cannot easily escape.

CONCLUSION

Defining "problem patron" is the hardest part of the problem. The attempt in this paper to define it has in no way established a criterion. Personal definitions may vary and situational circumstances will call for alternate meanings. Most library staff members have seen "problem patrons" in library departments or branches, and may have been harassed or abused. Some have been attacked and a few even killed (Library Hotline, 1993).

There is no doubt that problem patrons will continue to be a fact of every library operation, and even more so with the introduction of new technologies. Interestingly, Stiel describes them as the spice of life. She points out that "if every customer were easy to work with, you'd be bored silly. Difficult customers [patrons] are the spice of life. Enjoy them!" (Stiel, 1995, p. 61). Understanding the diversity of personality types we encounter daily and the nature of our working environment will help us to rise above any problem and be a better public service staff.

Using the theory of anthropologists and linguists to define words, it would be important to analyze situations (the context) to determine if a patron is really a "problem patron." Are the problems always caused by "problem patrons"? Or does the knowledge and attitude of "problem" staff create the problems? Before we label all those whom we consider problem patrons, think about what bother we all are when we play the role of customer, patron, user, in our personal lives.

REFERENCES

Brashear, J. Kirk, James J. Maloney, and Judellen Thorton-Darringe. "Problem patrons: the other kind of library security." *Illinois Libraries* 63 (1981): 344.

Comstock-Gay, Stuart. "Disruptive behavior, protecting people, protecting rights." *Wilson Library Bulletin* 69 (Feb. 1995): Online Wilson Web. 15 March 2001.

Cuesta, Emerita M. "Problems with patrons in the academic library." In *Patron Behavior in Libraries: A Handbook of Positive Approaches to Negative Situations.* B. McNeil and D. J. Johnson (Eds.) Chicago: American Library Association, 1996.

Eastern Region News January/March, 1993. Quoted in Kwasi Sarkodie-Mensah, "The difficult patron situation: A window of opportunity to improve library service." *Catholic Library World* 70 (2000): 161.

Gross, C. W. F. "The reading room loafer." *Library Association Record (London)* 15 (1913): 69-70.

Hagen, H. A. "A new library pest." *Library Journal* 11, (1886): 184.

"How attempts to help the homeless can backfire." *U.S. News and World Report* 104 (Feb. 29, 1988): 33.

Johnson, Denise J. "Sexual harassment in the library." In *Patron Behavior in Libraries: A Handbook of Positive Approaches to Negative Situations.* B. McNeil and D. J. Johnson (Eds.) Chicago: American Library Association, 1996.

Lincoln, Alan J. *Crime in the Library.* New York: Bowker, 1984.

Nelson, W. D. "Ban on sleeping and smelling." *Wilson Library Bulletin* 59 (1985): 468.

New York Libraries 3 (1913): 219-221.

"Patron fatally wounds librarians in Sacramento." *Library Hotline* 22 (April 26, 1993): 1.

Rubin, Rhea Joyce. *Defusing the Angry Patron: A How-to-do-it Manual for Libraries and Paraprofessionals.* New York: Neal-Schuman, 2000.

Sable, Martin Howard. "Problem patrons in public and university libraries." *Encyclopedia of Library and Information Science* 43, New York: Marcel-Dekker, 1988, p. 169-179.

Salter, Charles A. and Jeffrey L. Salter. "Mentally ill patrons." In *Patron Behavior in Libraries: A Handbook of Positive Approaches to Negative Situations.* B. McNeil and D. J. Johnson (Eds.) Chicago: American Library Association, 1996.

Sarkodie-Mensah, Kwasi. "The difficult patron situation: a window of opportunity to improve library service." *Catholic Library World* 70 (2000): 159-167.

Shuman, B. A. *River Bend Revisited: The Problem Patron in the Library.* Phoenix: Oryx, 1984.

Shuman, B. A. "Problem patrons in libraries: a review article." *Library and Archival Security* 9, no. 2 (1989): 3-19.

Shuman, B. A. "Down and out in the reading room." In *Patron Behavior in Libraries: A Handbook of Positive Approaches to Negative Situations*, B. McNeil and D. J. Johnson, (Eds.). Chicago: American Library Association, 1996, p. 3-17.

Simmons, Randall C. "The homeless in the public library: implications for access to libraries." *RQ* 25 (1985): 110-111.

Stiel, Holly. *Thank You Very Much: A Book for Everyone Who Has Ever Said, "May I Help You?"* Berkeley, CA: Ten Speed Press, 1995.

St. Lifer, Evan. "How safe are our libraries?" *Library Journal* 119 (Aug. 1994): 35.

Thompson, Lawrence. Library pests. *Library and Archival Security* 7, no. 1 (1985): 15-24.

Turner, Anne M. *It Comes with the Territory: Handling Problem Situations in Libraries.* Jefferson, N.C.: McFarland & Co., 1993.

Webster's Ninth Collegiate Dictionary. Springfield: Merriam-Webster, 1988.

Wright, G. S. "America's first library kept patrons awake." *Wilson Library Bulletin* 32 (1958): 649.

The "Problem Patron"
Public Libraries Created

Mary K. Chelton

SUMMARY. Normal adolescents are generally suspect within public and retail settings in the U.S., thanks in part to relentless negative media coverage of the age group, and to adult fear and misreading of their appearance. These suspicions also occur in public libraries, with occasional justification, but an argument can be made that public libraries have created this problem for themselves through a set of often taken-for-granted service assumptions. This article addresses these assumptions, pointing out how they contribute to the creation of a "problem" class of users, and how they might be changed or adjusted to change the situation. *[Article copies available for a fee from The Haworth Document Delivery Service: 1-800-HAWORTH. E-mail address: <getinfo@haworthpressinc.com> Website: <http://www.HaworthPress.com> © 2002 by The Haworth Press, Inc. All rights reserved.]*

KEYWORDS. Adolescents, young adults, service assumptions, problem users, public libraries

INTRODUCTION AND BACKGROUND

While the description of problem patrons in professional literature is slowly evolving from categories of "problem people" to categories of

Mary K. Chelton is Associate Professor, Graduate School of Library and Information Studies, Queens College, 254 Rosenthal Library, 56-30 Kissena Boulevard, Flushing, NY 11367 (E-mail: mchelton@optonline.net).

[Haworth co-indexing entry note]: "The 'Problem Patron' Public Libraries Created." Chelton, Mary K. Co-published simultaneously in *The Reference Librarian* (The Haworth Information Press, an imprint of The Haworth Press, Inc.) No. 75/76, 2002, pp. 23-32; and: *Helping the Difficult Library Patron: New Approaches to Examining and Resolving a Long-Standing and Ongoing Problem* (ed: Kwasi Sarkodie-Mensah) The Haworth Information Press, an imprint of The Haworth Press, Inc., 2002, pp. 23-32. Single or multiple copies of this article are available for a fee from The Haworth Document Delivery Service [1-800-HAWORTH, 9:00 a.m. - 5:00 p.m. (EST). E-mail address: getinfo@haworthpressinc.com].

© 2002 by The Haworth Press, Inc. All rights reserved.

"problem behaviors" regardless of the people doing them (Smith, 1994), teenagers still seem to crop up frequently as an irritant to public library staff in this regard, even on professional listservs supposedly composed of librarians interested in serving youth. Despite the overwhelming presence of young people in public libraries, a lot of public library staff find ways to marginalize their importance (National Center for Education Statistics, 1995; Chelton, 2000).

Adults have been lamenting the fecklessness of the young since the time of Aristotle, but the perception of the adolescent age group that has stigmatized them as a "problem" in the United States has some specific origins. Before the shootings at Columbine High School in Littleton, Colorado in 1999, adolescents were viewed with suspicion by adults because of the long-held American myth that the age group is somehow "in crisis" and needs to be contained. This is the direct legacy of psychologist G. Stanley Hall, the so-called "founder" of the concept of adolescence, regardless of evidence to the contrary (Lipsitz, 1975, pp. iv; Kett, 1977, pp. 217-244). This suspicion is supported by ongoing and frequently biased media accounts of anti-social and self-destructive behavior by teenagers, as well as structural age-segregation within the larger culture that prevents positive interactions between adults and adolescents (Males, 1994, 1996).

After Columbine, adult suspicion changed to fear, even in the face of declining youth crime statistics. What used to be merely irritation over subculture clothing and appearance, has now become an excuse for school suspensions, punishment and censorship (*IF Newsletter*, 2000). Public librarians are not immune to these views.

HOW THE YOUNG ADULT PROBLEM PATRON HAS BEEN CREATED

Developmental Misunderstandings and the "Ideal Patron" Syndrome

Adolescence is a distinct developmental stage of human life during which many important things happen, two of the most important being reproductive maturity and the onset of formal operational thinking–that is, the ability to think about experiences hypothetically. This ability to think about problems not yet personally encountered is a precious cognitive gift. It allows people to understand alternate scenarios for decision-making and critical thinking if it is nurtured. Asking "what if?"

also leads to an intense interest in speculative stories, which is why science fiction and mysteries are so beloved by many in the adolescent age group. On the other hand, formal operational thinking can also make adolescents question or test long-established rules and become argumentative because their hypothesized alternatives often seem clearer than the old "real" reality in front of them. This can make them seem like "problems" to adults trying to control them as if they were still children.

Dichotomized Service

Adolescence is also the time during which most people make educational choices that can affect their entire working lives, such as deciding not to take advanced mathematics (Lipsitz, 1984). These changes alone might be considered important enough for special service attention; however, most public libraries make no formal recognition of this reality, opting instead to serve this group as if they were still children or already adults, when evidence of career decision-making information needs abound (Julien, 1998; Schneider and Stevenson, 1999).

The adult-juvenile dichotomy has historical roots in the development of the public library. Prior to the establishment of compulsory secondary schooling, young people went to work at age 14, so technically, they *were* adults at that age, and the organizational services dichotomy made sense. Even then, however, children's services pioneers like Anne Carroll Moore at the New York Public Library, worried about what happened to carefully nurtured patrons when they were cast upon the mercies of the adult department of the library. Out of this concern, she hired Mabel Williams, a high school librarian from New England, to begin what has become the Office of Work with Young Adults there (Campbell, 1998, pp. 7-8).

Today's adolescents prepare for work with a much longer period of schooling, and they are discouraged legally from going to work until they have completed high school, and preferably beyond that. They are not legally regarded as adults, even if they work while completing high school, as many of them do. In addition to, and in part because of this longer schooling and legally restricted social period, adolescents have become a subculture unto themselves with all the symbolic "glue" such a status entails, with their own music, dress, slang, heroes, etc. Nearly all of these symbols can appear calculated to disturb or get negative attention from adults, regardless of whether this reaction is intentionally sought or not (Chelton, 1997). Besides these different work and educational expectations, today's adolescents have also grown up with television, and many with computers, in far different family configurations with much less access to adult time and caring (Hochschild, 1989, 1997). While they may not dress or act like it, they still badly need adult support and concern, if for no other reason, that it is now so rare for them.

One of the hallmarks of adolescence is the recognition that one is part of a distinct generation. As adolescents move psychologically and socially beyond the protected arena of their families, friends become an important barometer of what is considered normal, and same-sex friendships provide a healthy developmental support system and frame of reference. In fact, withdrawal from friends is considered a risk factor in adolescent suicide and mental disorders; yet, most public libraries find adolescents in groups difficult to deal with, despite the fact that the groupings are both normal and healthy. Such groups are usually regarded as "rowdy" or likely to become "rowdy," and staff energy primarily goes toward controlling them rather than assuming such groups are normal and planning for them. The irrational assumption that a group of healthy adolescents should behave like shy, friendless, hearing-impaired seniors is rarely questioned. Whether these attitudes come from a skewed "theory of practice" that determines the worthiness of various categories of library users (Chelton, 1997, 2000), from the peculiarities of one-size-fits-all physical environments (Thomas, 1996), or from some other source, has yet to be determined.

Since adolescents of the same age mature at different rates from each other, and various maturation processes can differ in speed within the same individual, it cannot be assumed that a young person who looks "adult" will necessarily think like one. Conversely, it cannot be assumed that an immature-looking adolescent will still think like a child. Physical appearance is as highly deceptive in this age group, as is inferring anything from age or grade level. Adolescents are not homogeneous, despite surface style similarities, and it often seems that this is what makes them a difficult user group for public libraries trying to squeeze them into too narrow a category (Lipsitz, 1975, pp. 26-28, 63-66).

Resistance to Library Use and Learning as a Social Process

One of the unexamined assumptions of public librarians which affects their acceptance of and attitudes toward adolescent users is that, except for library sponsored classes and group programs (which are controlled by the library), learning in the library is expected to be a solitary pursuit. Interaction is conceptualized as something a person does with a library resource, not another person, except when asking the librarian for help. There seems to be a great ignorance or denial among public librarians about social learning, or this kind of learning is deemed so unimportant that it can be relegated to places outside the library boundaries. This flies in the face of one of the most important maturation processes of adolescence, namely, social competence. Becoming able to relate to other people, to "read" them and their reactions, and to achieve a sense of belonging is very important to the growing sense of self and identity which assumes great importance during this period, which is why doing things with friends is so essential to teenagers (Benson, Williams and Johnson, 1987, pp. 33-46).

Unfortunately, adolescents talking with their friends is actively discouraged and disparaged in public libraries in several ways–through arbitrary restrictions on the number of people who can sit at tables at any particular time, the prohibition of chat room use on Internet terminals, the absence of group study rooms, the prohibitions on meeting room reservations by age and use, and the type of architecture and furnishings chosen when libraries are being built. Thomas (1996) makes this point in her study of what library environments say about expected users and uses:

> In addition, the style, character, and arrangement of furniture which suggested formal "study halls" in all areas of the facility, actually provided support for adolescents to behave only in the same kinds of predictable, essentially passive ways as would generally be associated with "adult" library use. This approach essentially privileges users for whom learning is understood as individual and task-oriented, and disaffirms activities which could be considered as cooperative, social, or reflective. (p. 427)

These additional remarks by two public librarians reported by the author (Chelton, 1997, p. 120) capture the attitude that adolescent social interaction is not considered legitimate:

> I think they use it as an informal meeting place also, and not always necessarily to study, but just to get together and see one another and have a chance to go someplace else other than just being at home, if they're sitting at a table or whatever the case may be, just to be together to talk and spend some time exchanging ideas or telling each other what happened during the day or the week or the

weekend, or plans. I think they use it as an informal meeting place. And I've seen that, especially here, because we are lucky in that the young adults have their own separate room there as opposed to some of the other branches. It's just all together. So I've seen groups go in there, and they–there are chairs in there, and they get comfortable, and they study or have, you know . . . I know they're getting a lot of programs and stuff for them as well, and that's a social occasion for them.

While prohibitions on chat rooms using library Internet terminals seem on their face only to be promulgating rules for the most equitable use of scarce resources, they are basically more discriminatory toward adolescents than any other group since chat rooms have replaced telephones for many teens as a technologically friendly means of talking to each other about common interests.

Inadequate Assumptions About Adolescent Information-Seeking

The expressed information needs of adolescents in public libraries tend to cluster primarily around homework assignments which always seem to be a problem for public libraries because they force many teenagers to look for information on the same topic, often from more than one school at the same time. This is the so-called "mass assignments" problem. Although this is an ubiquitous problem for public libraries, many librarians merely complain about it and scapegoat school librarians for "not doing their job," with little understanding of what school media specialists actually do. Few seem to plan for it by contacting local schools for curricula, buying multiple copies of needed items, creating temporary "reserve" shelves, creating pathfinders, and calling teachers when needed, even in the face of documented public support for the public library's taking a formal educational support role (D'Elia and Rodger, 1994).

The professional literature on information-seeking behavior until recently did not acknowledge that there is a class of questions that do not originate with the person asking them, so-called "imposed queries," or that the person forced to ask may be less than interested in the topic of the query (Gross, 1995). All homework-related questions fall into this class.

Adolescents inevitably present themselves at the last minute (because they are still learning how to be future-oriented using their new thinking abilities), with homework questions on topics they do not fully understand or care about, often unprepared to find the answer without more help than most busy public librarians are prepared to give them. The idea that a public librarian should also be an information literacy instructor is just beginning to take hold in the field, because changing technology has changed the learning curve for everyone and made them all "adolescent users" in some fashion. This is why many public libraries have decided to offer homework centers or some sort of formal educational support besides one-on-one reference service which usually cannot bear the brunt of doing information literacy training in this fashion without breaking down under the numbers needing it.

The problem created by imposed queries for the reference encounter is further complicated by the lack of agreement among reference librarians on whether the librarian just gives users the desired information or whether the librarian just starts users on the path toward finding it for themselves and tries to teach users how to search for the next time they need something (Bopp and Smith, 1995, pp. 24-25). There is some hypocrisy in the way in which this unresolved dilemma is visited upon adolescents, though. Most librarians in public libraries automatically assume that all homework assignments presented by adolescents are intended to teach the user how to use the library, as opposed to any queries from adults, regardless of the fact that there is little evidence used to support this supposition. This causes the "just-get-them-started" method to be used almost exclusively (and punitively) with adolescents until it becomes obvious that the teenager does not know how, nor will be able to do the assignment without more instructional help in accessing and evaluating library resources.

Adolescent reference questions also come through surrogate users in the form of parents trying to help their children with their homework. These parents are often frustrated themselves over having to do it, and frustrating to librarians because they do not fully understand what is needed, leaving the librarian never sure whether the correct question has been answered. The situation is only worse when the parent and teenager appear together. The amount of ranting among public librarians over "parents-doing-their-child's-homework" is self-defeating and unnecessarily judgmental. Since this situation is also ubiquitous in public libraries, it seems wiser to create tools to help these parents to help their children on websites or as giveaways before they appear, rather than blame them after the fact for a family situation the librarian knows nothing about.

CONCLUSION

It is possible to hire and keep public library reference staff who like and relate to youth by making it a requirement of the job and a part of the hiring process, something long overdue in many public libraries, given the numbers (Chelton, 1997). When the message comes from the top that inequitable service to teenagers is unacceptable, things at the bottom may start to change. Administrative support is vital. There are also specific teen-friendly activities that can make adolescents less of a self-induced "problem" class of users. Luckily, exemplary models of these activities exist in many libraries already and have been documented for replication (*Excellence*, 1994, 1997, 2000).

Arranging library spaces so that self-selected groups of teenagers can work and talk together without coming under suspicion of frivolous library use would foster a sense that the institution welcomed adolescent friendship interactions, rather than scorning them. If the public library in question is limited by having only one space for everyone, that space should be subdivided into solitary and social uses (even, perhaps, by time of day) with matching signs to let users know what is expected where and when. It is also important to point out consistently to adult users who complain about teenagers in the library that all ages are entitled to use the library. It is long past time that the silent support for public libraries by parents of adolescents is acknowledged.

Accepting rather than resenting the fact that homework questions will always be part, often a *large* part, of public library reference services would go a long way toward reducing the perception that this group of users is a problem. This means doing things like keeping in touch with schools ahead of time to find out what might be required when during the school year, like preparing pathfinders on frequently requested topics (and FAQs on library web pages), and doing collaborative information literacy lessons with school library colleagues in both types of libraries. It also means changing collection development practices to purchase materials to meet school needs, and preparing handouts to help parents help their kids with homework. In some cases, it may also mean setting up a formal homework center in the public library for after-school use. Models of all of these activities exist, if only in response to a youth or public library listserv query, so asking for help from colleagues on such lists is also a good way to get access to emerging trends and ideas that are not yet documented in library literature.

It is important to realize that there is nothing startling about all this, except for the recognition that viewing teenagers as problems does not need to continue. The array of solutions just needs the kind of attention, research and caring any good professional librarian should be able to muster, unless there is some vested interest in continuing the miserable status quo.

REFERENCES

Benson, Peter, Dorothy Williams and Arthur Johnson. (1987). *Quicksilver Years: The Hopes and Fears of Early Adolescence.* San Francisco: Harper and Row.

Bopp, Richard E. and Smith, Linda C. (1995). *Reference and Information Services: An Introduction.* 2nd ed. Englewood, CO: Libraries Unlimited.

Campbell, Patty. (1998). *Two Pioneers of Young Adult Library Services.* Lanham, MD: Scarecrow Press.

Chelton, Mary K. (1997). *Adult-Adolescent Service Encounters: The Library Experience.* Unpublished doctoral dissertation, Rutgers University, New Brunswick, NJ.

Chelton, Mary K. (1997). "Three in Five Public Library Users are Youth: Implications of Survey Results from the National Center for Education Statistics," *Public Libraries 36 (2)*: 104-109.

Chelton, Mary K. (2000). "Young Adults as Problems: How the Social Construction of a Marginalized Category Occurs," *Journal of Education for Library and Information Science 42 (1)*: 6-14.

D'Elia, George and Rodger, Eleanor Jo. (1994). "Public Opinion About the Roles of the Public Library in the Community: The Results of a Recent Gallup Poll," *Public Libraries 33*: 23-8.

Excellence in Library Services to Young Adults 3: The Nation's Top Programs. (2000). 3rd ed. Mary K. Chelton (Ed.). Chicago, American Library Association.

Excellence in Library Services for Young Adults: The Nation's Top Programs. (1997). 2nd. ed. Mary K. Chelton (Ed.). Chicago: American Library Association, 1997.

Excellence in Library Services for Young Adults: The Nation's Top Programs. (1994). (2000). Mary K. Chelton (Ed.). Chicago: American Library Association.

Gross, Melissa. (1995). "Imposed Query," *RQ 35 (1)*: 236-243.

Hochschild, Arlie. (1989). *Second Shift: Working Parents and the Revolution at Home.* New York: Viking.

Hochschild, Arlie. (1997). *Time Bind: When Work Becomes Home and Home Becomes Work.* New York: Metropolitan Books.

"It's Our Bill of Rights, Too! Children, the First Amendment and America's Response to Violence," (2000). *Intellectual Freedom Newsletter 69 (5)*:130, 166-180.

Julien, Heidi. (1998). "Adolescent Career Decision Making and the Potential Role of the Public Library," *Public Libraries*, 37(6): 376-381.

Kett, Joseph. (1977). *Rites of Passage: Adolescence in America 1790 to the Present.* New York: Basic Books.

Lipsitz, J. (1975). *Growing up forgotten: A review of research and programs concerning early adolescence.* Durham, NC: Learning Institute of North Carolina.

Lipsitz, Joan. (1984). "Economic Future of Girls and Young Women," Address presented at the Conference on the Economic Future of Girls and Young Women,

Spring Hill Conference Center, Wayzata, Minnesota, May 22, 1984. Unpublished paper.

Males, Mike. (1994). "Bashing Youth: Media Myths About Teenagers," *EXTRA! The Magazine of FAIR 7 (2)*: 8-11.

Males, Mike A. (1996). *Scapegoat Generation: America's War on Adolescents*. Monroe, ME: Common Courage Press.

National Center for Education Statistics. (1995). *Services for Children and Young Adults in Public Libraries*. (NCES 95-731). Washington, DC: U. S. Government Printing Office.

Schneider, Barbara and Stevenson, David. (1999). *Ambitious Generation: America's Teenagers, Motivated but Directionless*. New Haven, CT: Yale University Press.

Smith, Kitty. (1993). *Serving the Difficult Customer: A How-to-Do-It Manual for Library Staff*. New York: Neal-Schuman.

Thomas, Nancy Pickering. (1996). *Reading Libraries: An Interpretive Study of Discursive Practices in Library Architecture and the Interactional Construction of Personal Identity*. Unpublished doctoral dissertation, Rutgers University, New Brunswick, NJ.

Historical Perspectives on Problem Patrons from the British Public Library Sector, 1850-1919

Gary Kenneth Peatling

SUMMARY. Failure to engage an historical perspective can lead to exaggeration of the novelty of the "problem patron" phenomenon in libraries. In fact, from the institutions' earliest years, there were significant levels of fear that British public libraries would be abused by their intended users. This paper examines the experience of the problem patron in British public libraries in the years 1850-1919, and the definitions and solutions suggested by supporters and staff of these libraries. Contemporary sources are used to suggest that some observations about this period may have continued relevance for present discussions of the "problem patron." *[Article copies available for a fee from The Haworth Document Delivery Service: 1-800-HAWORTH. E-mail address: <getinfo@haworthpressinc.com> Website: <http://www.HaworthPress.com> © 2002 by The Haworth Press, Inc. All rights reserved.]*

KEYWORDS. United Kingdom, public libraries, history, problem patron, order, crime, class

Gary Kenneth Peatling is Research Assistant, Department of Information and Library Studies, University of Wales Aberystwyth, Llanbadarn Fawr, Aberystwyth, Ceredigion, SY23 3AS, United Kingdom (E-mail: gtp@aber.ac.uk).

The author would like to thank Dr. Chris Baggs for his advice and assistance, and the Arts and Humanities Research Board for funding the research project during which this piece was written.

[Haworth co-indexing entry note]: "Historical Perspectives on Problem Patrons from the British Public Library Sector, 1850-1919." Peatling, Gary Kenneth. Co-published simultaneously in *The Reference Librarian* (The Haworth Information Press, an imprint of The Haworth Press, Inc.) No. 75/76, 2002, pp. 33-43; and: *Helping the Difficult Library Patron: New Approaches to Examining and Resolving a Long-Standing and Ongoing Problem* (ed: Kwasi Sarkodie-Mensah) The Haworth Information Press, an imprint of The Haworth Press, Inc., 2002, pp. 33-43. Single or multiple copies of this article are available for a fee from The Haworth Document Delivery Service [1-800-HAWORTH, 9:00 a.m. - 5:00 p.m. (EST). E-mail address: getinfo@haworthpressinc.com].

© 2002 by The Haworth Press, Inc. All rights reserved.

There is a recurrent temptation to regard current or future problems in the behaviour of library patrons as unprecedented.[1] It would be dangerous however to ignore a mass of past data relevant to issues of "problem patrons" by implicitly accepting an unreconstructed notion of a past "golden age" of orderly library use. In fact, professional anxiety about the "problem patron" is far from being an entirely new phenomenon; while contemporary changes in patterns of library use may produce a sense of stepping into an unknowable future, it is doubtful that the leap in the dark facing contemporary information professionals is quite equivalent to that made by the first generation of staff at publicly funded libraries.

In the United Kingdom, after the 1850 Public Libraries Act, staff were faced with the responsibility of library provision for the denizens of the new towns and cities created by the ongoing social upheaval of the first industrial revolution. Amidst serious fears of political uprisings, reliable sources of information about the relatively new social milieu of most patrons of the new popular libraries were undoubtedly lacking. However, supporters of the public library movement suggested that such institutions would increase social cohesion by bringing members of such social groups together with their well-to-do betters.[2] Arguably, far from Victorian library staff being assured of genteel patrons,[3] the period 1850-1919 was the public library's most significant "outreach" phase.

Historians attempting to estimate the extent of problems of order in the new libraries, and the success of librarians' efforts to control them, face numerous difficulties. On the one hand, a catalogue of types of patron misdemeanour would make the problem of order seem chronic.[4] Traditional scholarly librarians such as E. Maunde Thompson of the British Museum expected considerable problems in maintaining order and silence in the public library, especially in protecting bona fide users from "the coarse-mannered and unwashed" to emerge as the service expanded.[5] Nonetheless, statistics on tangible problems with patrons do not seem large. Inferences from such statistics, however, must be carefully drawn. Continuities can be observed in the problems experienced with patrons and the methods suggested for dealing with them, between the first seventy years of the public library on the one hand, and predictions for the twenty-first century on the other.

PROBLEMS OF ENFORCEMENT

The provision of publicly rate-funded libraries in Britain is usually dated from the 1850 Public Libraries Act, although a few such libraries did exist before this date. A "disciplinary impulse" was especially evident in features of library layout and design which maximised the possibilities of surveillance.[6] However, the practical success of any such "micro-physics of power" is questionable. One writer suggested that even staff members with a proverbial "hundred eyes" would often have been unable to detect who was responsible for deliberate damage to books and newspapers. Even law-abiding users were "problem patrons" in this analysis, since they failed to report the misdeeds of miscreants.[7] Some libraries thus assumed that the last borrower of an item was responsible for any damage–even with the evident risk of consequential injustice.[8] Other types of misdemeanour in the public library were also not infrequently found to escape detection.[9]

Successful prosecutions for theft of books, mutilation of library materials, petty thefts and other criminal misdemeanours in libraries are recorded in the professional press throughout the period 1850-1919. But even if miscreants were identified, successful prosecution was not assured. If libraries found it necessary to proceed against guarantors to recover fines from defaulting borrowers, legal technicalities could interfere.[10] Strategies of resistance by borrowers were exemplified by the individual who escaped punishment after a disorder in Stockport public library through giving a false name.[11] The uncertain outcomes of the law led libraries to organise alternative deterrents, such as posters warning about the penalties for misdemeanours, arranging for a police presence in the library, or drawing up their own regulations (which often seem pedantic by modern standards).[12]

The main national legislation passed in the period particularly to deal with misdemeanours in libraries was the Libraries Offences Act 1898. This permitted the imposition of fines of up to 40 shillings in all public libraries for disorderly, violent, or obscene behaviour, gambling or remaining after hours. However, in order to qualify as an offence, such misdemeanours had to be an irritant to another library user–disturbances affecting only members of staff were not considered sufficiently serious.[13] Comments from a parliamentary proponent of the measure suggest it was of more relevance to co-operative than public libraries.[14] Within public libraries it seems to have been useful mainly in giving staff confidence to expel troublemakers.[15] Few prosecutions seem to have resulted from this act, and local improvement acts, other laws and library procedures continued to provide recourses when problems arose.

THEFT, DAMAGE AND "PROPER" USE

There is little evidence in British public libraries of the laxity regarding thefts which some observers have found in the early twentieth-century American service.[16] The annual reports of Aberdeen public library, for instance, were distinguished by the production of a minutiae of statistics and details about the loss of books, as well as grave expressions of regret if even only a small number went missing.[17] The implementation of open access in public libraries inspired some fears (not always disinterested) that opportunities for theft would increase.[18] Defenders of open access asserted that the losses were not significantly greater than under closed access, and that in most cases a small number of isolated individuals were responsible for thefts.[19] The fact that more and more libraries adopted open access as time passed suggests that the problems resulting from the policy were not considered to be greater than the perceived benefits to patrons. Few libraries in this period followed the Bishopsgate Institute Library (not a public library) in taking the opposite step of moving from open to closed access in response to the numbers of thefts suffered.[20]

Deliberate damage to items and damage caused by carelessness were not always easy to distinguish. However, even wear and tear on items from ordinary use could entail considerable replacement costs. Fears that open access would mean increased wear and tear through greater casual contact with books by borrowers gave rise to some hesitation about the policy. Librarians' sensitivity to the issue of damage to items was suggested when Lord Rosebery made the innocent suggestion at Battersea in 1890 that " 'the thumb-mark of the artisan' would now be imprinted on the literature of the age, and would ultimately become the chief, if not the only, criterion of merit and utility."[21] Rosebery soon thought it prudent to clarify that he did not mean to condone those who deliberately damaged books.[22] Sources of damage to items included borrowers lacking clean hands and the dog-earring of pages. The influential James Duff Brown suggested inserting a bookmark in each book issued, in order to discourage this latter temptation, and to display reminders of library rules.[23] Some extreme statistics of damage to items were occasionally published by libraries, including Barrow-in-Furness's assertion that the aggregate number of repairs to items during 1896-7 was greater than the number of items in the library.[24] The implication is that such statistics depended heavily on definitions of damage–a wider definition might be politically useful in emphasising the amount of work achieved by staff.

Items returned tardily could sometimes be difficult to recover or take time (and/or require technology) to keep track of and pursue.[25] Libraries charged fines for items that were sufficiently overdue, in part to compensate library and community for the resulting inconvenience.[26] But maintaining records of unpaid fines also involved staff in labour.[27] Conversely, however, fines were a source of revenue to libraries. Statistics from Barnsley indicating that 4% of loans incurred overdue fines were probably not abnormal.[28]

Annual reports also provide general evidence as to the state of order in libraries. Many statements contained therein are formulaic, asserting that "the orderly behaviour and quietude that prevail show that [the library's] attractions continue, and justify to the full the provision that has been made for the wants of all classes."[29] Owing to the funding requirements of some libraries in their early years, any voluntary support that could be won for the library was to be valued. Thus libraries' reports emphasised the prevalence of quiet, disciplined, "proper use"[30] in order to reassure local notables that their donations and political assistance would facilitate respectable exercises in self-improvement by "the real *Working Man Class* for whom the Library Acts exist"[31] rather than the "free loaferies" sometimes depicted by the movement's critics.[32] Libraries' detailed rules could also provide politically useful safeguards against "improper" use.

FEMALE AND JUVENILE PATRONS

The homogenising elements of the "discourse" of library annual reports, which constructed a mass of orderly patrons, are clearly problematic in relation to gender differences between patrons. However, even those elements of library publicity which provide particular details about library use handle the issue of gender with unease. For instance, women are often listed as a separate category of patron distinct from breakdowns by occupation and age.[33] One reading would suggest that socially constructed visions of "proper use" of libraries tended to conceal women's use of the institutions.[34] Suggestions also emanated from certain sources that female patrons particularly tempted by fashion plates in books were responsible for a high proportion of mutilations in public libraries.[35] Even commentators who took a relatively positive view of women's use of libraries might still view women as potential sources of difficulty to be controlled: Butler Wood argued that the publications provided in his ladies' room at Bradford were sufficiently interesting "to keep in subjection the natural conversational propensities of the sex."[36] Women were also occasionally perceived as potential victims of problem patrons, and in some libraries separate rooms, entrances and/or counters for women were offered as security against improper mixing of the sexes. In 1909, however, a female librarian offered a more positive narrative of female presences in libraries: "the influence of a woman attendant in the general newsroom is often found to reduce to a minimum any disturbance, and it is rare that she has to speak twice to any of the visitors, and disrespect, even in the worst of neighbourhoods, is almost an unknown quantity."[37]

In 1901 one discontented library user suggested that much of librarians' attention was given over to the "mere discipline of unruly boys."[38] In several cases indeed the task of maintaining discipline among the more youthful of a library's patrons was the occasion for a request for police assistance.[39] There seems little reason to assume that such a police presence would have been easier to obtain in nineteenth-century Britain than in late twentieth-century America.[40] Early examples of separate facilities for young patrons might be perceived less as a far-sighted innovation by those with an awareness of the "real needs"[41] of contemporary youths, but rather as a defensive effort to neutralise disciplinary problems with juveniles. The record of success was not absolute: Leicester's juvenile library was forced to close on Sundays on account of the impossibility of keeping order.[42] But although nostalgic images of the discipline of youngsters in the "good old days" evaporate under close scrutiny, the extent of intergenerational conflict in the public library should not be exaggerated. At least some surviving accounts from users (a valuable and scarce resource for library historians) suggest that libraries were rather unusual among predominantly adult institutions of the period in the extent of the welcome they offered to juveniles.[43]

LOAFERS AND GAMBLERS

Library newsrooms (or rooms where current issues of periodicals were available to patrons) were often regarded in this period as the focus of a relatively high proportion of "improper use." The particular object of this ire was the "idle loafer who uses the reading-rooms merely as a shelter and resting-place."[44] Frustrated librarians in London and elsewhere complained that these appropriated library resources required by "the real public library public."[45] Other librarians accepted the presence of "loafers" if "they are clean and orderly."[46] Policies for removing undesired presences from libraries included removing all or the most comfortable seating, a measure which some modern libraries are reviving.[47] Some, such as Duff Brown and H. E. Johnston of Gateshead, suggested the closure of newsrooms altogether; however, Johnston's proposal found limited support in his local Library Association.[48] Herbert Jones suggested tickets should be requisite for access to newsrooms, and these could then be refused to any "questioned or questionable person."[49] However, Jones, as some of his contemporaries appreciated,[50] undoubtedly simplified the difficulties involved in discerning a "proper" from an "improper" user of a newsroom at point of entry. Members of the working class might be able to take advantage of middle-class ideals by playing the "respectable" part as occasion demanded.[51] The presence of "loafers" in libraries could be interpreted more positively, since (it was suggested) the library associated them with more wholesome moral influences than any other equally accessible arena.[52] However, most library staff seem only rarely to have felt that they could afford the luxury of such principles.

"Betting men," individuals who utilised newspapers and journals in public libraries in order to obtain information relevant to their habits of gambling, were also perceived as "crowds of undesirables" who made "it difficult for quiet and orderly readers to use these places."[53] At Wolverhampton public library, the "blacking-out" or obscuring of columns of "betting intelligence" was considered a successful discouragement.[54] "Blacking out" was a popular policy in newsrooms in the 1890s and 1900s, but was by no means introduced in every case; some library officials objected to the implicit censorship involved in the procedure, did not perceive it as a (or the most) successful way of dealing with the problem, or simply did not believe that there was a problem with gamblers in their particular libraries.[55] Those librarians' who perceived betting to be a major problem within the public library may have been subject to those exaggerated suspicions of gambling as a *social problem* also articulated in this period by "respectable" opinion in other walks of life.[56] The idea that unemployed workers looking for vacancies advertised in newspapers was "proper" use of libraries, whereas the same individuals consulting betting news was "improper" use, was not ideologically neutral. Popular gambling was in fact usually honest (if illegal), and the successful working-class gambler was no more dependent on luck in acquiring wealth than many middle-class moral reformers.[57] Librarians' hostility to "betting men" reflected the hegemonic faith (and self-justification) of the middle classes as much as real problems of order in libraries.

Encounters with aggression and discontent are difficult to quantify. The "person known as the 'grumbler,'" one writer suggested, "is a familiar figure. This estimable rate-payer–he is always a 'ratepayer,' by-the-bye: he tells you so–is one of those people who could have improved the creation, provided he had been present on that great occasion."[58] There were certainly a number of regular sources of possible confrontation, including overdue fines, damage to items, and difficulties in obtaining desired items. Ernest Savage suggested that unsatisfied patrons might prompt reforms of unnecessarily bureaucratic library procedures,[59] but it was much easier to adopt this philosophical attitude to "the problem patron" with the benefit of hindsight. Suggestions that aggression in public libraries was less prevalent in this period than in contemporary libraries are based on faith rather than the available data.

CONCLUSION

Current literature surrounding the "problem patron" underestimates the extent of the historic continuity of the issue.[60] Early public library staff were probably less affected by problem patrons than their modern equivalents, in part because problems were reduced by restrictive rules and procedures. On the other hand, coping with the problems that arose was complicated by the want of adequate technologies, political obstacles, and lack of ready knowledge about patrons. But Victorian and Edwardian librarians attempting to deal with "problem patrons" shared some difficulties with their modern equivalents. The range of problems and of local contexts meant that a formula that was successful in Wolverhampton's newsrooms, for instance, could not be applied elsewhere. Locating culprits in cases such as the mutilation of library items was certainly no easier in the past. In other cases, perceived problems were insufficiently serious or too hard to police to justify the application of much effort. Historical retrospect yields a critical attitude to the Victorian and Edwardian discursive demarcation between "the real library public" and "improper" users which may also have relevance to current debates: occasionally still today too intimate an association is drawn between socially marginalized patrons and problems in libraries, whereas in fact a significant proportion of problems has always arisen from patrons of socially comfortable backgrounds (whether "ratepayers" or "taxpayers") with unrealistic expectations of service standards. Problem patrons are socially constructed in the sense of social contexts both generating issues with which libraries have to deal, and influencing definitions of problem patrons. No period of libraries' existence, indeed, should be studied in isolation from society. The final relevant aspect of the period 1850-1919 is the germinating professional consciousness among librarians, which provided the structures for a discussion of "problem patron" issues which not only is useful to the historian of the period, but occasionally furnished contemporaries with policy options of which they may not otherwise have conceived. This is one aspect of nineteenth- and early twentieth-century practice worthy of continued imitation.

REFERENCES

1. Thomas Latuszek, Jr., "Library security: a growing awareness," *Library & Archival Security*, vol. 15, no. 2, (2000), 3-7.

2. A. Black, *A new history of the English public library: social and intellectual contexts, 1850-1914* (London, 1996), pp. 30, 38-9.

3. Betty Braaksma, "Zero tolerance at the library: the work of the Thunder Bay public library's security task force," *Library & Archival Security*, vol. 14, no. 2, (2000), 43-9, especially 43-4.

4. Black, *New history*, p. 190.

5. E. Maunde Thompson, "Some hints on the future of free libraries," *The Library*, i (1889), pp. 402-10, especially p. 410.

6. Black, *New history*, pp. 245, 247.

7. H.T.C., "Wilful damage: the general reader's responsibility," *Library World*, xv (July 1912-June 1913), pp. 206-7, especially p. 206.

8. A.W. Robertson, "Note on 'Fines' for the damage of books," *The Library*, iv (1892), pp. 115-6.

9. "Notes and news," *Library Association Record*, xiv (1912), p. 265.

10. *Library Association Record*, ii (1900), pp. 166, 608.

11. *County borough of Stockport. Parks, museum, and library committee. Reports* (1903), p. 7.

12. *The thirty-seventh annual report of the Leicester municipal libraries committee, to the town council of the borough of Leicester. 1907-8*, pp. 21-4.

13. R.J.B. Morris, *Parliament and the public libraries* (London: Mansel, 1977), pp. 98, 104, 271-2, 278.

14. *Hansard's Parliamentary Debates*, fourth series, lx (27 June 1898), c.195-6.

15. *Library Association Record*, xiv (1912), pp. 270-7, especially p. 271.

16. Ann Curry, Susanna Flodin, Kelly Matheson, "Theft and mutilation of library materials: coping with biblio-bandits," *Library & Archival Security*, vol. 15, no. 2, (2000), 9-26, especially p. 11.

17. *Aberdeen public library. Twenty-third annual report of the committee for the year 1906-1907* (1907), pp. 6-7: *Aberdeen public library. Twenty-fourth annual report of the committee for the year 1907-1908* (1908), p. 11.

18. Thomas Kelly, *A history of public libraries in Great Britain, 1845-1965*, 2nd ed. (London: Library Association, 1977, first published 1973), p. 156.

19. *Borough of Bootle. Fourth general report of the free library and museum committee* (1891), p. 3.

20. Peter Claus, "Managing boundaries: history and community at the Bishopsgate Institute," in Hilda Kean, Paul Morgan and Sally J. Morgan (eds.), *Seeing history: public history in Britain now* (London: Francis Boutle, 2000), pp. 151-70, especially pp. 162-5.

21. *The Library*, ii (1890), p. 198.

22. "Opening of the Edinburgh free public library. Speech by Lord Rosebery," *The Library*, ii (1890), pp. 265-9, especially pp. 267-8.

23. James Duff Brown, "The working of Clerkenwell public library," *The Library*, v (1893), pp. 108-19, especially pp. 114-5.

24. *Free public library, Barrow-in-Furness. Fourteenth annual report, 1896-7* (1897), pp. 5-6.

25. *Aberdeen public library. Nineteenth annual report of the committee* (1903), p. 6.

26. W. Geo. Fry, "Fines and other penalties," *Library World*, xvii (July 1914-June 1915), pp. 1-8, especially pp. 1-2.

27. *Free public library, Barrow-in-Furness. Eleventh annual report, 1893-4* (1894), p. 5.

28. *Borough of Barnsley. Free public library. Report* (1907), pp. 3-5.

29. *Rugby urban district council. Annual report of the public library committee, 1901-2*, p. 6.

30. *Library World*, viii (July 1905-June 1906), p. 15.

31. Herbert Jones, "The newsroom," *Library Association Record*, xiv (1912), p. 182-90, especially p. 187.

32. *Library Association Record*, v (1903), p. 643.

33. *The ninth annual report of the committee of the free public library, Barrow-in-Furness, 1891-2*, p. 11.

34. Evelyn Kerslake, "Constructing women in library history: responding to Julia Taylor's 'left on the shelf,'" *Libraries and Culture*, xxxiv, no. 1 (winter 1999), p. 52-63.

35. Thomas Greenwood, *Public libraries: a history of the movement and a manual for the organization and management of rate-supported libraries* (Hertford: University Microfilms Ltd for the College of Librarianship, Wales, 1971, reprint of 4th ed. first published 1894), p. 386.

36. Butler Wood, "Three special features of free library work-open shelves, women readers, juvenile departments," *The Library*, iv (1892), pp. 105-14, especially p. 108.

37. Mizpah Gilbert, "Ladies' rooms," in *Library economics* (Libraco Limited, London 1909), p. 27, pp. 26-9.

38. "Grievances of a free library reader. III," H.J. O'Brien, *Library World*, iii (July 1900-June 1901), pp. 118-20, p. 120.

39. Salford Local History Library, L/CS/C055/AM1; Corporation of Salford, Museum & Library Committee, 1849-55; pp. 99-102, especially pp. 99-100; meeting of Museum and Library Committee, 18 Feb. 1851.

40. Bruce A. Sherman, "The devious, the distraught and the deranged: designing and applying personal safety into library protection, *Library & Archival Security*, vol. 14, no. 1, (1997), 65-8.

41. Margaret Kinnell, "Managing in a corporate culture: the role of the chief librarian," in Margaret Kinnell and Paul Sturges (eds.), *Continuity and innovation in the public library: the development of a social institution*, Library Association Publishing: London, 1996, pp. 167-88, p. 182.

42. *The thirty-fifth annual report of the Leicester municipal libraries committee, to the town council of the borough of Leicester. 1905-6*, p. 6.

43. James G. Ollé, "Portsmouth public libraries: the first fifty years," *Library History*, xii (1996), pp. 201-15, especially p. 215.

44. "Obliteration of betting news," *Library Association Record*, ix (1907), pp. 24-9, especially p. 29.

45. Jones, "Newsroom," p. 185.

46. J. Minto, "Recent attacks on public libraries," *Library Association Record*, v (1903), pp. 559-68, especially, p. 562.

47. Braaksma, "Zero tolerance at the Library," p. 47: "Obliteration of betting news," *Library Association Record*, ix (1907), pp. 24-9, especially p. 29.

48. *Library Association Record*, vii (1905), pp. 44-7, especially p. 46.

49. "Newsroom," p. 189.

50. *Library Association Record*, xiv (1912), pp. 270-7, especially pp. 270-3.

51. Peter Bailey, *Leisure and class in Victorian England: rational recreation and the contest for control, 1830-1885* (Methuen, London, 1987, first published 1978), p. 185.

52. M.S.R.J., "The people's palace library," *The Library*, ii (1890), pp. 341-51, especially p. 350.

53. Thomas Green, "Obliteration of betting news" in *Library economics*, pp. 7-8: J. Elliot, "The extinction of the betting evil in public news rooms," *The Library*, v (1893), p. 193.

54. Elliot, "Extinction of the betting evil," pp. 193-4.

55. Robert Snape, "Betting, billiards and smoking: leisure in public libraries," *Leisure Studies*, xi (Sept. 1992), no. 3, pp. 187-99, especially pp. 192-3.

56. Mark Clapson, *A bit of a flutter: popular gambling and English society, c.1823-1961* (Manchester University Press, Manchester, 1992, pp. 207-10).

57. Ross McKibbin, *The ideologies of class: social relations in Britain, 1880-1950* (Oxford: Clarendon Press, 1994, first published 1990), p. 123.

58. F. Anstee, "Grievances of a free library reader. Two rejoinders," *Library World*, iii (July 1900-June 1901), pp. 65-8, especially p. 65.

59. E. A. Savage, *A librarian's memories: portraits and reflections* (London, 1952), p. 67.

60. Curry, Flodin, and Matheson, "Theft and mutilation of library materials," pp. 24-5.

Difficult Library Patrons in Academe: It's All in the Eye of the Beholder

C. Lyn Currie

SUMMARY. Difficult patrons have been considered primarily from the perspective of the problem behaviours they present in libraries. Many have attempted to define the problem patron and to provide advice and develop guidelines for frontline public service staff. To understand the difficult patron in academic libraries we need to answer three questions–How well do we know our patrons? Do we unwittingly create difficult patrons through our failure to appreciate their needs? Do we regard patrons as difficult because the way they use libraries and conduct their information research does not match our idea of how it should be done? The answers to these questions suggest that we need to reconceptualize both our patrons and the services we provide. Library staff need to see difficult patrons not as problems but as challenges to the service ideas and standards we hold. A paradigm shift is necessary if we are to reconstruct our beliefs about our patrons, their information seeking behaviours, and the services we provide to meet their needs. Some strategies for developing the skills of library staff to work effectively with difficult patrons are presented. *[Article copies available for a fee from The Haworth Document Delivery Service: 1-800-HAWORTH. E-mail address: <getinfo@ haworthpressinc.com> Website: <http://www.HaworthPress.com> © 2002 by The Haworth Press, Inc. All rights reserved.]*

KEYWORDS. Library patrons, library staff–training and development, library services, library instruction, technology and libraries, problem patron

---

C. Lyn Currie is Head, Education Library, University of Saskatchewan, 28 Campus Drive, Saskatoon, Saskatchewan, S7N 0X1, Canada (E-mail: Lyn.Currie@usask.ca).

[Haworth co-indexing entry note]: "Difficult Library Patrons in Academe: It's All in the Eye of the Beholder." Currie, C. Lyn. Co-published simultaneously in *The Reference Librarian* (The Haworth Information Press, an imprint of The Haworth Press, Inc.) No. 75/76, 2002, pp. 45-54; and: *Helping the Difficult Library Patron: New Approaches to Examining and Resolving a Long-Standing and Ongoing Problem* (ed: Kwasi Sarkodie-Mensah) The Haworth Information Press, an imprint of The Haworth Press, Inc., 2002, pp. 45-54. Single or multiple copies of this article are available for a fee from The Haworth Document Delivery Service [1-800-HAWORTH, 9:00 a.m. - 5:00 p.m. (EST). E-mail address: getinfo@haworthpressinc.com].

© 2002 by The Haworth Press, Inc. All rights reserved.

INTRODUCTION

Much of the literature on difficult library patrons describes and categorizes those patrons according to the nature of their problem behaviours–the relatively harmless nuisance, the disruptive, or the violent (Shuman, 1989, Cuesta, 1996). Shuman (1989) acknowledges that attempts to define the problem patron are elusive, imprecise, and difficult and suggests that even a comprehensive definition of a problem patron as "anyone who visits the library and either breaks or flouts existing rules, or presents an actual or potential threat to other persons" may not necessarily fit a particular person or behaviour.

In academic libraries today we need to consider more broadly the question of what constitutes a difficult patron. In my library, for example, some of the most difficult library patrons are the mature age students returning to studies after many years. What makes them difficult? For many of them the current technological environment presents a significant barrier to learning. At the other end of the patron continuum are the technologically competent high school graduates. These patrons are difficult because of their total embrace of technology–their tendency to go straight to the Web bypassing traditional methods of doing library research. Each of these patron groups are difficult for very different reasons. In an attempt to understand the "difficult" patron in academic libraries we need to address three questions:

- How well do we know our patrons?
- Do we unwittingly create "difficult" patrons through our own failure to understand and meet their needs?
- Do we regard patrons as difficult because they do not conform to our view of how information research "should" be conducted?

HOW WELL DO WE KNOW OUR PATRONS?

In academic libraries we often fail to acknowledge and therefore effectively deal with the fact that our patrons are ever-changing and constantly pose new challenges for librarians. Patrons vary considerably in their abilities and skill level to work with the technology. One of the significant challenges comes in working with the current "cut and paste generation" of library patrons (Roth, 1999). These patrons are "difficult" customers for a variety of reasons, not the least of which is their preference for conducting all their information research surfing the

Web. This "remote control/mouse click" generation is not interested in any of the conventional methods of doing library research. Students grow up with Sega, Nintendo and the World Wide Web. They tend to be familiar and comfortable with computers and expect immediate feedback from interactive systems. They certainly do not want to take time to learn–they just want to sit down and get the information.

Stoffle (1996) observes that patrons have become customers who are more discriminating and demanding. They have increasing options and alternatives such as online information systems marketed directly to the public. As a result, their expectations of library service and response times have escalated, fueled by a culture of instant gratification. We tend to regard these patrons as "difficult" because of their preference for doing all their information research via the Internet and because of their expectations of instant access to and supply of information.

At the same time we are also working with patrons who are the reluctant or inexperienced users of technology. They are faced with working in a library environment characterized by what Becker (1991) calls the pervasive effect of "creeping featurism." Databases are added, products are enhanced, sophisticated searching options are enabled or software is completely updated almost daily. Any one of these by itself may seem like a good idea but the cumulative effect of many minor improvements or the trauma of a major upgrade can be most disheartening for patrons and staff alike.

For these patrons "confronted" by the need to work with technology–library systems, electronic databases and Internet searching, for example–learning anxiety can be significant. Patron anxiety in information seeking situations is well documented (Keefer, 1993, Kuhlthau, 1991, Mellon, 1988, Ford, 1980). That anxiety interferes with the mental and creative processes required for information searching. The operational or physical aspects of the search process are also easily degraded by the stress and anxiety of learning the ropes of a new and unfamiliar system. Keefer (1993) suggests that because the affective aspects are always part of any human activity involving the learning of new skills, a large part of what we do at the reference desk in academic libraries must include helping patrons understand the normality of their frustration with the system. Letting patrons know that everybody experiences anxiety and that asking for help is an important part of the search process can go a long way toward making patrons' initial library experiences less stressful. These patrons can be seemingly "difficult" or demanding to library staff because of their expectations of or need for extensive help in working with the technology and retrieving information.

DO WE UNWITTINGLY CREATE "DIFFICULT" PATRONS THROUGH OUR FAILURE TO APPRECIATE THEIR NEEDS?

It is useful to know our patrons in terms of the various difficulties they present. We must also ask the question: how well do we design library services and implement systems based on a sound understanding of what our patrons need or are prepared to use? There are those (Lewis, 1990, Cargill, 1992) who have urged librarians to watch and listen to patrons and try to understand what their words and their actions say about how our libraries work and what they feel is important. This is necessary if we are to organize services to meet the actual information needs, habits and preferences of patrons–not what librarians think is wanted. In the context of library instruction, Bessler (1990) suggests it is time to stop trying to teach patrons and to focus more effort on listening. Instead of working to create incentives for patrons to act the way we feel is in their best interests, librarians should learn more about the value the patron places on different services and develop these accordingly.

We need to engage in an ongoing process of re-defining our patrons and be willing to examine and legitimize their needs and expectations for library service. Without this, we continue to experience patrons as difficult simply because their expectations for service are not met by our service provisions. Consider the patrons who expect to use library computers for unlimited Internet and e-mail use, to download and print full text documents, to order electronic documents online and receive them immediately. How well do our policies and services accommodate and keep pace with these and other evolving expectations of our patrons? We will be positioning our libraries and our services well if we maintain the ability and the willingness to approach patron needs and requests with an open mind and consider the merits of extending, adapting, and developing library services to meet these.

DO WE LABEL PATRONS AS DIFFICULT BECAUSE THEY DO NOT CONFORM TO OUR VIEW OF HOW INFORMATION RESEARCH SHOULD BE CONDUCTED?

In addition to rethinking and legitimizing patron needs and developing appropriate and relevant services, we need to re-examine our ideas of how information research is "best" conducted.

Are we guilty of regarding patrons as "difficult" because the way they use libraries and look for information does not match our idea of how it "should" be done in an academic library?

The debate in the literature about academic librarians immersing themselves in the cause and processes of user education (Bessler, 1990) raises important questions about why we provide library instruction and what we think patrons need to learn. Has instruction become necessary because the systems, electronic products, search software which libraries provide do not address patrons' access and content needs? Rettig (1995) describes library instruction as a remedial response to the library systems' failures or deficiencies. The present model of library instruction assumes that the library system is deficient and that patrons are not capable nor self-sufficient and are in need of remediation (Herrington, 1998). The real problem here is that while technology has thrust the library into the electronic information age our models of service delivery have not changed. What is needed is a paradigm shift–not only a change in procedures and methods but also the reconstruction of reality and beliefs–especially our beliefs about how our patrons should conduct their information research.

Rudd and Rudd (1986) discuss the tendency of patrons to only acquire a satisfactory subset of the amount of information available–Herbert Simon's (1997) "satisficing" principle. Librarians must accept that this shorthand way of finding, scanning, and organizing information is the modus operandi of the majority of our patrons. Librarians must recognize and accept this minimalist approach to information retrieval and adapt our service delivery and library instruction to accommodate this way of doing research.

RESPONDING TO THE DIFFICULT PATRON REQUIRES AN ATTEMPT TO RE-CONCEPTUALIZE OUR SERVICE

In re-thinking the difficult patron, the first step for library staff is to view these patrons not as "problems" to be tolerated but as challenges to the service ideas and standards we hold. If we focus on actual patron needs we can begin to consider alternative approaches, seek products to meet differing needs and review the effectiveness of library services for their relevance. We can consider whether the technology actually enhances our services, whether patrons are equipped to take full advantage of new services and if not, what strategies we should employ to teach their use.

To begin with we should identify where the difficult patron is the result of a failure of the library to match service to needs. We are at a point in the ongoing evolution of libraries where a reconfiguring of our services is appropriate if not mandatory. Denham (1995) comments on the tremendous changes in society which affect the entire concept of what a library is and does. Expansion in the variety of information formats, increased competition, and the impact of technologies all give libraries the opportunity to redesign their own future. Stoffle (1996) talks about the need for transformational change in libraries to achieve breakthrough performance, and claims the most fundamental change that has to occur is a switch to a focus on customers and need. All services and activities must be viewed through the eyes of the patrons, letting them determine quality by whether their needs have been satisfied. To achieve this, libraries must move away from a staff performing narrow tasks according to prescribed policies and procedures to one empowered to make daily decisions about what work to do and how to do it in a way that results in satisfied patrons and constantly improving processes. Ultimately the academic library must change because its patrons need it to change.

There are those who advocate a paradigm shift for library instruction (Rettig, 1995, Bessler, 1990) claiming we need a new model that is not based on a remedial response to the library systems' failures or deficiencies. Librarians need to design systems which give patrons a feeling of control, systems that are so easy to use there is no need for instruction. While our philosophy in academic library reference continues to be instructing the patron in how to obtain information, we teach this today in a context in which technology increasingly allows the patron to hopscotch through the mechanics of how to find the information and reach the information quickly. If we acknowledge this, we then have the opportunity to impact on our patrons' chances for success in locating and managing information. For example we can draw upon their familiarity with new technologies, with surfing the Web and teach them how to apply those "Web skills" to other resources (Curl, 2000). Using this approach we can concentrate on teaching them to effectively articulate their information need, identify appropriate resources, evaluate what has been retrieved and redirect their continued searching. Wallace (1999) observes that technology training requires an understanding of when and how to use it with patrons. It involves observing the information-seeking behaviours of our patrons and adapting our resources and services. For library staff, just having a sense of where patrons are in this process can be of immense value when planning information services.

IMPLICATIONS FOR STAFF

It is clear from these statements about the need for change, for reconceptualizing both our patrons and our service offerings, that we need to consider what this means for our library staff. For library support staff, changes in the workplace have resulted in those staff assuming an ever-increasing range of responsibilities. As Berger (1997) observes, a simple look back over the past 10 years reveals a vigorous revolution in the relationship between library professionals and their support staff in terms of the re-distribution and assignment of duties. In the digital world most of us are wrestling with the issue of getting our staff at all levels properly trained so that they feel comfortable in this new technologically advanced working environment. We recognize the "unending new technology readiness training" (Wallace, 1999) needed in the library and the role librarianship has in demystifying information technologies for patrons. It is imperative that library managers prepare these staff to work effectively in the new roles they have undertaken. Working directly with patrons, assisting them with the use of library search systems, databases and the Internet requires substantial training and skill development.

In order to develop relevant services and provide sound training for our patrons and thereby avoid situations that produce difficult patrons, we first need to develop the confidence and competencies in staff necessary to make intelligent decisions about what our patrons need to know and about effective strategies for teaching those skills. The training of competent and effective public service staff is critical to the perceived effectiveness of the library. Our patrons' perceptions of the quality and effectiveness of the library and their satisfaction with library services are based primarily on their interaction with our public service staff. Patrons who receive consistently effective service and are treated as though their needs are significant will be more likely to perceive the library as an effective, responsive organization (Hobson, 1987).

CONCLUSION:
RESPONDING TO THE DIFFICULT PATRON

So how do we ensure that our libraries are prepared and our staff are ready to respond to the difficult patrons? The unifying theme in all the writings about problem patrons is an attempt to prepare library staff for the unexpected so that when it happens, staff will have some notion of what to do about it. The first step in training staff to deal with problem patrons should be to ensure that staff are familiar with the "rules" or policies (both legal and ethical) governing the operation of the library, and that they have a general sense of what may and may not be done concerning problem patrons and behaviours of various types. Morrissett (1996) advocates the development of a patron behaviour policy, one which protects the rights of both library patrons and library staff, provides a uniform standard of behaviour and sets out clear guidelines defining inappropriate behaviour and a course of action for library staff to follow.

Secondly, it is imperative that library managers implement a training program to help staff engage in diagnosis and prevention of problem situations. The primary objective of any staff training is to bring about change, whether an increase in knowledge, the acquisition of a skill, or the development of confidence and good judgement. Knowledge is the information needed to perform a set of activities well; skills are the techniques, methods and strategies which put knowledge into practice, and abilities are intangible qualities such as cooperation, flexibility, motivation and enthusiasm (Creth, 1986). Much has been written about the knowledge, skills and abilities required of library public services staff to provide effective services to users (Conroy, 1978, Creth, 1986). To manage those interactions with difficult patrons, staff require such traits as strong verbal communication skills, interpersonal skills, good listening skills, tact, patience and perseverance as well as more specific skills such as problem solving/analytical skills, computer skills associated with database searching, and automated systems expertise and so on. Smith (1996) strongly advocates the use of active listening (hearing and responding to the feelings and meaning behind patrons' words) as a means of gaining some insight into the behaviour of the difficult or critical patron.

Hobson et al. (1987) developed a training program which provided staff with an awareness of their critical role in the overall functioning of the library, taught specific verbal and nonverbal behaviours essential in providing positive, helpful and friendly service to patrons and introduced them to interpersonal strategies and operational procedures for handling stressful situations. Effective training along these lines not only helps staff cope with patron behaviour but also teaches staff awareness of their own attitudes and encourages them to maintain a professional detached manner. Staff need to know that dealing with problem patrons requires tact, firmness, understanding, quick-thinking, resourcefulness, courage, sympathy and sometimes a sense of humour (Shuman

1989). Cuesta (1996) reminds us that in most instances it is the judgement and common sense of the staffer that will determine the outcome of any patron interaction.

Thirdly, as a management strategy the concept of staff empowerment has merit and is worthy of consideration here. Well-trained public service staff possess the flexibility needed for resolving service problems they encounter. Decision-making authority therefore should be extended to the lowest level possible so that staff involved in direct contact with patrons possess the ability to make those decisions that directly affect their operations, their patrons and themselves (Millson-Mantula,1995).

Finally we should make a conscious effort to achieve a win-win situation in all our patron interactions. This requires a focused effort to achieve an understanding of patron needs and develop services that meet those needs. All public service staff should be familiar with the best techniques for connecting patrons with what they need. Staff must be prepared to handle the vast personality differences, the various learning styles and the differing research needs of the library's patrons. Our goal is to earn the confidence of patrons through relationships built over time (Dodsworth, 1998). Ultimately our success will be measured by the disappearance of difficult patrons from our libraries.

REFERENCES

Becker, Karen A. (1994). Coralling "creeping featurism": nurturing a more human-centred technology. *Database* April, v. 17, n. 2, 8-11.

Bessler, Joanne (1990). Do library patrons know what's good for them? *Journal of academic librarianship* v. 16, n. 2, 76-77.

Berger, Marshall (1997). Technology brings challenges and opportunities for support staff. *American libraries* v. 28, March, 30-31.

Cargill, Jennifer (1992). The electronic reference desk: reference service in an electronic world. *Library administration and management* 6, Spring, v. 8, 82.

Conroy, Barbara (1978). *Library staff development and continuing education.* Littleton, Colorado: Libraries Unlimited Inc.

Creth, Sheila D. (1986). *Effective on-the-job training: developing library human resources.* Chicago: American Library Association.

Cuesta, Emerita (1996). Problems with patrons in the academic library. In McNeil, Beth and Johnson, Denise, *Patron behaviour in libraries.* Chicago, ALA.

Curl, Sheila R. et al. (2000). Reality check: asynchronous instruction works! *C & RL News* July/August, 586–588.

Denham, Rudi (1995). Strategic planning: creating the future. *Feliciter* 41, Nov-Dec. 38.

Dodsworth, Ellen (1998). Marketing academic libraries: a necessary plan. *Journal of academic librarianship* 24, 4, July, 320–2.

Ford, N. (1980). Relating information needs to learner characteristics in higher education. *Journal of documentation* v. 36, 165-191.

Herrington, Verlene J. (1998). Way beyond BI: a look to the future. *Journal of academic librarianship*. September, v. 24, n. 5, 381-386.

Hobson, Charles J., Moran, Robert F. and Stevens, Arena L. (1987). Circulation/Reserve Desk personnel effectiveness. *Journal of academic librarianship*. 13, May, 93-98.

Keefer, Jane (1993). The hungry rats syndrome: Library anxiety, information literacy, and the academic reference process. *RQ*. 32, 3, Spring, 333-339.

Kuhlthau, Carol C. (1991). Inside the search process: information seeking from the user's perspective. *Journal of the American Society for Information Science* v. 42, 5, 361-371.

Lewis, David (1990). A matter of return on investment. *Journal of academic librarianship* v. 16, n. 2 May, 79-80.

Mellon, Constance (1988). Attitudes: the forgotten dimension in library instruction. *Library journal* v. 113, September 1, 137-139.

Millson-Martula, Christopher and Menon, Vanaja (1995). Customer expectations: concepts and reality for academic library services. *College and research libraries*. January, 33-47.

Morrissett, Linda A. (1996). Developing and implementing a patron behaviour policy. In *Patron behaviour in libraries: a handbook of positive approaches to negative situations*. Chicago: ALA.

Rettig, James (1995). The convergence of Twain or Titanic collision? BI and reference in the 1990's Sea of Change. *Reference Services Review* Spring, v. 23, 7-20.

Roth, Lorie (1999). Educating the cut and paste generation. *Library journal* v. 124, Nov 1, 42-46.

Rudd, Joel and Rudd, Mary Jo (1986). Coping with information load: user strategies and implications for Librarians. *College and research libraries* July, 315-322.

Shuman, Bruce (1989). Problem patrons in libraries–a review article. *Library & archival security* v. 9, 2, 3-19.

Simon, Herbert (1997). *Administrative behaviour: a study of decision-making processes in administrative organizations*. 4th ed. NY: Free Press.

Smith, Nathan (1996). Active listening: alleviating patron problems through communication. In *Patron behaviour in libraries: a handbook of positive approaches to negative situations*. pp. 127-134. Chicago: ALA.

Stoffle, Carla J., Renaud, Robert and Veldof, Jerilyn R. (1996). Choosing our futures. *College and research libraries* v. 57, May, 213-225.

Wallace, Patricia (1999). Hurtling through cyberspace: tackling technology training. *Computers in libraries* February, v. 19, 21-25.

The Difficult Patron
in the Academic Library:
Problem Issues or Problem Patrons?

Patience L. Simmonds
Jane L. Ingold

SUMMARY. Faculty members depend on the resources and services provided by the libraries to teach, satisfy the curricular needs of the students, and conduct their research. Students need the library for many reasons, among which are to complete their assignments and to expand on what faculty covers in class. The patron/librarian relationship in the academic library is not always perfect. Issues which students and faculty face in the academic library environment are completely different from those in the public library. Identifying the characteristics of the difficult or problem patron in academia is a little more difficult than in the public library. Are what librarians face when dealing with faculty and students more issue-related than just dealing with problem patrons? The authors will identify, from the librarians' perspectives, some of these often called difficult patron issues and offer solutions to try and preempt these issues before they become problems. *[Article copies available for a fee from The Haworth Document Delivery Service: 1-800-HAWORTH. E-mail address: <getinfo@haworthpressinc.com> Website: <http://www.HaworthPress.com> © 2002 by The Haworth Press, Inc. All rights reserved.]*

Patience L. Simmonds is Assistant Librarian, Penn State Erie, The Behrend College Library, Station Road, Erie, PA 16563 (E-mail: pls@psu.edu). Jane L. Ingold is Assistant Librarian, Penn State Erie, The Behrend College Library, Station Road, Erie, PA 16563 (E-mail: jli@psulias.psu.edu).

[Haworth co-indexing entry note]: "The Difficult Patron in the Academic Library: Problem Issues or Problem Patrons?" Simmonds, Patience L., and Jane L. Ingold. Co-published simultaneously in *The Reference Librarian* (The Haworth Information Press, an imprint of The Haworth Press, Inc.) No. 75/76, 2002, pp. 55-66; and: *Helping the Difficult Library Patron: New Approaches to Examining and Resolving a Long-Standing and Ongoing Problem* (ed: Kwasi Sarkodie-Mensah) The Haworth Information Press, an imprint of The Haworth Press, Inc., 2002, pp. 55-66. Single or multiple copies of this article are available for a fee from The Haworth Document Delivery Service [1-800-HAWORTH, 9:00 a.m. - 5:00 p.m. (EST). E-mail address: getinfo@haworthpressinc.com].

© 2002 by The Haworth Press, Inc. All rights reserved. *55*

KEYWORDS. Academic libraries, faculty, students, library staff relations, problem patrons, difficult patrons, patron characteristics

INTRODUCTION

When one mentions "difficult" or "problem" patrons in libraries, many people immediately assume that one is referring mainly to patrons in public libraries. Public libraries are indeed famous for the different types of problem or difficult patrons they attract. Problem patrons come in all shapes, sizes, races and nationalities, and stretch across many boundaries of behaviors. There are the homeless, the drunks, those who are never satisfied with the provided service, the noisemakers, the mothers with crying babies and misbehaving children and those who view on-line pornographic sites. Public library staff has acquired more experience in dealing with these situations over the years. There is documented evidence of how some public libraries deal with problem patron situations. Difficult patrons are "equal opportunity" patrons. They are present in all types of libraries under different characterizations. The literature on problem patrons overwhelmingly focuses on the experiences of public library staff. Although the academic library staff may face many of the same situations, there are some other issues to be addressed that are unique to the academic library's setting and purpose. The authors will examine these unique issues, which arise among faculty, students and library staff. The emphasis of the discussion will be on circumstances or situations, which affect the provision of quality service to faculty and students. They will discuss kinds of problem patron behaviors and the conflict issues that may lie beneath them.

LITERATURE REVIEW

Sources of conflict between faculty, students, and librarians have always been present in academic institutions. Library literature, however, shows that the problem patron issue in public libraries has received more attention and discussion than the conflicts between library staff, students, and teaching faculty. Higher education and library literature have also examined these issues in many articles and books. E. J. Josey, in an article written in 1958 states, " that staff members should be sensitive to students and faculty library needs. Staff members must never forget that the library is a service agency, and therefore they are expected to be friendly, courteous, and anxious to respond in a helpful manner" (Josey, p. 193). Sources of tension, and conflict between librarians and faculty have also been researched. Mary Biggs attributes some of the sources of tension and conflict between faculty and librarians to lack of communication between teaching faculty and librarians. "Communication, cooperation, and mutual planning are needed and must be initiated by librarians, but faculty members need to listen and participate with as much energy and as broad a view as possible" (Biggs, p. 196). " Librarians need to establish effective liaison devices and keep the faculty informed of significant new publications and acquisitions and themselves up to date on curriculum content and faculty research interests" (Biggs, p. 196).

Sarkodie-Mensah advises that "mastering the techniques of not panicking in times of crisis, and concentrating on what will ultimately satisfy the customer is the trademark of the concerned service provider" (Sarkodie-Mensah, p. 160). There was not much literature on the issue of student /librarian conflict, or on the issue of students and faculty as difficult patrons in the academic library. Literature on conflict and tension between these two groups will have to be gleaned from articles written about student satisfaction with the academic library. Anne M. Turner in her book *It Comes with the Territory: Handling Problem Situations in Libraries,* states, "that people are not the problem. The problem is the situations people create. Our task is to learn how to handle problem situations, not problem people or problem patrons" (Turner, p. 5). Guy Lyle in his book, *The President, the Professor and the College Library* talks about the various roles that everybody has to play in order to make the library an effective organization. He mentions that the "formal channels of communication are not the only means of keeping in touch with faculty and administration. If anything, the librarian should make an even greater effort to know administration and faculty personally" (Lyle, p. 28).

LABELING THE ACADEMIC LIBRARY USER

To be sure, academic librarians are confronted with certain annoying behaviors: students talking loudly, bringing food and beverages into the library, falling asleep during library instruction sessions, and throwing the occasional tantrum because desired materials are unavailable (sometimes, students are not the only patrons exhibiting these behaviors). Some students also prefer to remove periodical titles from the library and pretend they did not know how these got into their book bags. These behaviors reflect what library staff usually means when they refer to problem patrons. In some of these kinds of situations, users tend to cause problems more for themselves when their actions are revealed.

Faculty user behavior is very different from student behavior in some ways, but the occasional outburst of dissatisfaction by affronted faculty because they do not receive immediate service or do not have a particular material readily available also create difficult moments in the library. How does the library staff see the user behavior of teaching faculty where the library is concerned? The majority of faculty members visit the library on a limited basis and their interactions with the library staff are also limited. Technology and easy access to library resources, both within the library and remotely, have made it possible for many students and faculty to avoid face-to-face interactions with the library staff. Faculty members are able to access almost all library resources. In some libraries, periodical articles obtained through interlibrary loan are mailed directly to faculty homes or offices. The only time that faculty members are physically required to be in the Penn State Erie library is when they pick up books requested through Interlibrary Loan. Like the students, they need to present their identification cards to the staff at the Circulation Desk. This decrease in physical contact between users and library staff does not, however, prevent the tension and the conflict, which sometimes result in users not getting the services they expect.

Are the teaching faculty and the students in the academic libraries problem patrons, or are there problems or difficult issues, which put them at odds with the library staff in the academic libraries? This paper will not deal with the academic library staff and their interactions with students and faculty the typical way some authors have dealt with "problem patrons." However, the writers of this paper will attempt to focus on and examine the issues which arise among faculty, students and library staff. Sarkodie-Mensah describes the problem patron behavior as "rude, unreasonable, wanting to direct anger at library staff and needing satisfaction" (Sarkodie-Mensah, p. 161). This definition includes two separate ideas: the outward behaviors of the patron (rudeness, unreasonableness, and even violence) and the need for satisfaction. Librarians must recognize that need and examine what role we may have played, even inadvertently, in making the need arise. In other words, instead of focusing exclusively on problem behaviors, perhaps library staff should focus on the problem situation.

Other difficult patron situations would include: lack of respect for library staff, questioning their knowledge and power, and directing their complaints to administration rather than to the librarians or the library director. For purposes of consistency, the writers will opt to address the patrons as "difficult" rather than "problem." If tensions and conflicts are present in the interaction between library staff and academic library users, mainly faculty and students, it occurs mostly through the provision or lack of provision of good service, attitude modification, absence of knowledge about the library resources, and finally the feeling of being overwhelmed by the resources available.

The academic library staff and the faculty have one thing in common, and that is the academic well-being of the student. While the faculty teaches the students, the librarian makes sure that the library satisfies the research needs of the students. The library also tries to meet the needs of the faculty where research and curricular expectations are concerned. These needs and expectations sometimes become avenues of conflict and tension between library staff, faculty and students. This paper will attempt to identify conflict issues relating to both faculty and students and will attempt to find possible solutions to improve library service. What are some of the conflict issues that confront teaching faculty, students and library staff? What are some of the characteristics of teaching faculty? In academic libraries, labeling the patron is difficult. The students in the academic library are expected to be intelligent, focused, and concerned about their academics. Academic librarians expect many things from students, but what they do not expect and often get is difficult situations and reactions from students and faculty.

ELIMINATING SOURCES OF CONFLICT AND TENSION BETWEEN FACULTY AND LIBRARY STAFF

Teaching faculty in academic institutions are powerful, and where the library is concerned, that power is clearly evident. Some of the areas in which faculty members interact with library staff, and where the most tension will arise are:

- Collection Development and Weeding
- Circulation Matters
- Reserves
- Interlibrary Loan Issues
- Purchasing of Electronic Resources

- Reference Desk Issues
- Course-Related Library Instruction Sessions
- Faculty-Librarian Working Relationship
- Student-Librarian Working Relationship.

COLLECTION DEVELOPMENT AND WEEDING

Collection development and weeding can be a sticky point between faculty and library staff. Teaching faculty would react negatively to librarians making all collection development and weeding decisions. Library budgets make it impossible and even impracticable to acquire all needed library resources. The library will need a clear and straightforward mission statement crafted by both librarians and members of the library committee to educate users about collection development and weeding. Faculty agonizing over which library materials would be cut should be educated about the availability of resources and the ease of access of these resources electronically.

CIRCULATION MATTERS

One of the focal points of the library for teaching faculty and students can be the circulation desk. The circulation desk is often the site of faculty and students objecting to library policies that do not meet with their approval or that they have violated. Changes in library policies, when not announced to all staffing levels including work-study students, could be sources of conflict at the circulation desk. Such policies written in a clear language, outlining the consequences of certain library behaviors and misdemeanors must be accessible at all times. Also, providing the same level of service at all the times the library is open can mitigate some of the conflicts that may arise. Since locating materials in the library can be a source of frustration and anger for library users, ensuring that materials are properly arranged on the shelves must continue to be a priority for libraries.

RESERVES

When professors inform students of what is on reserve before the actual placement of the materials, students who come in earlier can be irritated. It is not uncommon for professors to completely forget to put materials on reserve, or when they do, not to put the right amount. By working closely with faculty members, librarians can help both faculty and students make the most of reserve services, while at the same time eliminating any potential source of conflict, or any copyright issues that may arise.

INTERLIBRARY LOAN ISSUES

Document delivery service is an avenue many libraries use to facilitate faculty research. Even though in many instances the turn around time for interlibrary loan is very fast, there are many faculty members who seem to want on-the-spot document delivery, no matter where the materials are coming from. Libraries have to work closely with users in educating them about the amount of waiting time delivery services can involve. By also educating users on how to locate materials in the collection, instances where interlibrary loan requests are made for readily available resources can be drastically reduced.

REFERENCE DESK ISSUES

Users at the reference desk want fast, accurate information. When immediate service is not provided to the satisfaction of the users, they become impatient. Procrastination and lack of proper knowledge of how to find library materials increase user frustration. A close working relationship between instruction and reference librarians, and reinforcing the notion that it is important to start working on assignments early can be beneficial to everybody.

PURCHASING OF ELECTRONIC RESOURCES

No academic library would want to live without electronic resources now with new and better resources being developed on a regular basis. Most faculty and students love electronic resources, especially when they realize how easy it is to obtain full-text materials almost immediately. Electronic resources make a huge dent in every library's budget, and some publishers penalize libraries for switching from print resources to electronic. Sometimes, they even give the library discounts on the electronic resource if they agree to retain the print issues. Some faculty and students are more content with the print materials, and even with the easy accessibility of some electronic resources, they would still ask for print copies of their favorite periodicals. Some professors still want copies of periodicals like Chronicle of Higher Education, and other indexes and abstracts like Current Contents routed to them even though these could easily be accessed electronically. Librarians would have to educate users about the benefits of access as opposed to ownership.

COURSE-RELATED INSTRUCTION

Instruction librarians like to provide library instruction to as many of the student population as possible. Many teaching faculty appreciate librarians providing their students with instruction, but the problem arises when many faculty use the instruction sessions as babysitting sessions. Some however, enjoy sitting in on instruction classes with their students. Sometimes, they even end up learning new things about the library. Other teaching faculty would only schedule instruction on days when they would be away from the class for a conference or an important meeting. Students seem to appreciate the instruction classes more when their instructors put some value on them. In some cases, some students would not attend the classes if they knew that their professor would be absent or cause disturbances for the librarian. In other cases, teaching faculty would ask the instruction librarian to take attendance for them before the class. The students value the instruction more when the instructor is present, and even more so when the instructor emphasizes the importance and relevance of the instruction to the class subject being taught.

FACULTY-LIBRARIAN RELATIONSHIP

Communication is obviously extremely important when it comes to certain situations among library staff, teaching faculty, and students. All the situations listed above are important, and for a good working relationship between faculty and library staff, there should be librarians assigned as liaisons between the library and the different schools and departments. Faculty should know exactly which library personnel they need to deal with on issues of library policies, rather than bouncing the patron from one library staff member to the next. It is also useful to discuss with library staff reasons for policy changes so that they are able to explain them to users, and not be caught off guard by complaints. In order to prevent these unfortunate and often embarrassing situations, all new policies and changes should be circulated among all staff, including student assistants working in the library. Communication between teaching faculty can be good if there is mutual respect and trust. Librarians should try to be more approachable and friendly to new faculty. This is where they can start to build a good relationship. Once you are friendly and respectful to people, they are less likely to show antagonism towards you.

STUDENT-LIBRARIAN WORKING RELATIONSHIP

Confrontations between students and library staff in academic libraries are different from those recorded in the library literature dealing with difficult patrons in public libraries. Confrontational situations can be very stressful for the library staff and the students involved in them. Some of these confrontations occur at the circulation desk, at the reference desk, in instruction sessions, and many in other general areas of the library.

For example, at Penn State, it is not uncommon for students attending classes in a room located in the library to talk too loudly as they exit. It is so easy for them to forget that they are in the library and that their loudness can disturb others. There are also instances when students are doing group study in a public area other than those designated for such purposes. Other common student behavior includes bringing food to the library, loud sound coming from portable music devices, carrying and using cell phones. Library policies specifically stating library restrictions should be clearly written without ambiguities and visibly displayed. These policies should be easily accessible to all users. Even though these authors support the no eating rule in the library for obvious reasons, policies for drinks need to be modified. It is almost an American tradition to see people carrying bottles of drink, especially sodas and water everywhere. Recently, the policy at the University Libraries at Penn State has been modified to allow users to bring drinks in spill-proof containers into the library. The policy of no food in the library is still upheld. If users are aware that they could bring spill-proof containers to the library then they will not resort to sneaking things into the library. Designating an area for refreshments when the spill-proof option is not practical can be useful. In confronting students' library problems, library staff can use tact and reasonableness to resolve many of these conflicts. Of course contacting campus police in instances where diplomacy and common sense do not work is always the right thing to do. Library staff must also set a good example by respecting the noise levels and the no-food policy, and not engaging in activities they constantly nag students about.

STUDENT NEEDS AND PROCRASTINATION

Student procrastination is a well-known fact to library staff. There is the student wandering aimlessly about, the one unable to locate a source he had previously found, the one constantly complaining about the lack of library staff assistance, or the one who walks to the desk for help with an assignment he left at home.

There are also students who will stick to the minimum requirements of resources suggested by their professor, and thus will not welcome any additional resources recommended by library staff, even if those resources are useful. It is obvious then that librarians have to educate students on various levels: starting their work on time, making the librarian's willingness to assist them as abundantly clear as possible, assuring them that suggestions from librarians fitly supplement their professor's resources. In the age of technology where many students think that everything is on the web, and some professors are still averse to students using any type of resources, library staff should work closely with students and faculty members to find a common ground from which the advantages and disadvantages of both web and print resources can be lucidly explored.

RECOMMENDATIONS AND CONCLUSION

It is more important than ever to promote the use of academic libraries to faculty and students who are our primary customers, and for the library staff to develop relationships with as many users as possible. Librarians and other library staff, and student library assistants, should try to distinguish between problem behaviors and library-related problem issues and must admit their part in any conflict that arises. It could be quite helpful for libraries to provide staff with conflict resolution training so that they can feel confident in their dealings with difficult patrons. Library policies should be realistic, unambiguous and not open to any misinterpretation. Open communication lines, a proactive manner, mutual respect, and sense of appreciation are the keys to successfully reducing incidents of problem patron behavior in the academic library. The faculty/library relationship should be such that the faculty members do not feel that the library staff is deliberately keeping important things from them.

Both faculty and library staff should accord one another respect in their dealings. Librarians should not fear that their authority is being usurped if faculty is involved in some of the activities of the library. On the same note, faculty should accord the library staff enough respect to know that librarians and library staff are professionals and they do know their job. Friendly faculty and students are more likely not to be offensive or rude to you in the library. Difficult situations can occur in the academic library over issues which are not always easily discernable, but faculty, students and library staff can learn to appreciate, respect, and coexist so that everyone's needs and expectations will be met.

Library staff should keep library issues affecting faculty and student behaviors in perspective, and focus on the really important issues. Some behaviors are more irritating than others, but they are not that important in the overall scheme of things. Academic library users should come away from the library with the notion that the staff are available, friendly, willing to assist them, and dependable. Taking care of these problem issues will help prevent our users from becoming problem patrons.

REFERENCES

1. Josey, E. J. "Enhancing and Strengthening Faculty Library Relationships." Journal of Negro Education. Volume 33, Issue 2 (Spring 1964): 191-196.

2. Biggs, Mary. "Sources of Tension and Conflict Between Librarians and Faculty." Journal of Higher Education. Volume 52, No. 2 (1981): 157-201.

3. Ibid, p. 157-201.

4. Sarkodie-Mensah, Kwasi. "The Difficult Patron Situation: A Window of Opportunity to Improve Library Services." Catholic Library World, Volume 72, No. 7 (March 2000): 159-167.

5. Turner, Anne M. It Comes with the Territory: Handling Problem Situations in Libraries. Jefferson, North Carolina and London, McFarland & Company, Inc., 1993, pp. 5.

6. Lyle, Guy. The President, the Professor, and the College Library. New York, H. W. Wilson, 1963, p. 28.

7. Sarkodie-Mensah, Kwasi. "The Difficult Patron Situation: A Window of Opportunity to Improve Library Services." Catholic Library World, Volume 72, No. 7 (March 2000): 159-167.

8. Biggs, Mary. "Sources of Tension and Conflict Between Librarians and Faculty." Journal of Higher Education, Volume 52, No. 2 (1981): 157-201.

Personal Safety in Library Buildings: Levels, Problems, and Solutions

Bruce A. Shuman

SUMMARY. Libraries, whatever they may represent to the public, are also workplaces for their employees, and–given human nature–can become dangerous places to visit or in which to work. A recent study of violence in the workplace conducted by the National Institute for Occupational Safety and Health reveals that "workers most at risk to workplace violence are those who deal with the public, exchange money and deliver goods and services."[1] Naturally, library staff are included in this at-risk category. When people do not feel safe in public buildings, they tend to avoid them (or working in them) for fear of danger, assault, injury, or worse. Other types of workplaces often have levels of security, commensurate with their functions, features and design, but most libraries–public places, with intentionally easy (or non-existent) admission requirements–place both employees and visitors at risk of violence.

Demonstrably, there is a need for security in library buildings, but how much and what kinds of security are desirable, feasible, and affordable are subjects open to debate. As a general rule for public buildings, more is better, but such is not necessarily the case in *library* buildings, where a high level of physical security is exchanged for reasonably barrier-free access. This paper discusses seven levels of security in work-

Bruce A. Shuman is affiliated with Texas Woman's University, School of Library and Information Studies, Denton/Dallas, TX.

Readers interested in a more extensive discussion of all aspects of library security, including protecting books and other materials and the various problems of electronic security, are referred to the author's *Library Security and Safety Handbook: Prevention, Policies, and Procedures* (Chicago, American Library Association, 1999).

[Haworth co-indexing entry note]: "Personal Safety in Library Buildings: Levels, Problems, and Solutions." Shuman, Bruce A. Co-published simultaneously in *The Reference Librarian* (The Haworth Information Press, an imprint of The Haworth Press, Inc.) No. 75/76, 2002, pp. 67-81; and: *Helping the Difficult Library Patron: New Approaches to Examining and Resolving a Long-Standing and Ongoing Problem* (ed: Kwasi Sarkodie-Mensah) The Haworth Information Press, an imprint of The Haworth Press, Inc., 2002, pp. 67-81. Single or multiple copies of this article are available for a fee from The Haworth Document Delivery Service [1-800-HAWORTH, 9:00 a.m. - 5:00 p.m. (EST). E-mail address: getinfo@haworthpressinc.com].

© 2002 by The Haworth Press, Inc. All rights reserved.

67

places, ranging in description from "perfect" to "rotten," with library buildings placing low along the continuum. Because it is in the nature of public institutions to necessitate public exposure, staff and the general public are vulnerable to occasional unpleasant surprises. Library staff, however, are not helpless just because all are free to enter their institutions. A reasoned and coherent security policy consisting of preparations and countermeasures to enhance building security is essential. Forewarned is forearmed, and preparation of staff for violent incidents in the workplace and rapid response and reaction to such incidents are extremely important, and should be included in a comprehensive security plan that provides remedies to problems of personal vulnerability while maximizing security for all building occupants. *[Article copies available for a fee from The Haworth Document Delivery Service: 1-800-HAWORTH. E-mail address: <getinfo@haworthpressinc.com> Website: <http://www. HaworthPress.com> © 2002 by The Haworth Press, Inc. All rights reserved.]*

KEYWORDS. Personal safety, library security, crime and libraries

THE PROBLEM: THE PUBLIC BUILDING AS A (POTENTIALLY) DANGEROUS PLACE

I can hear nonlibrary folks now saying, "Problems? What kind of problems could those library workers have? They just sit around and read most of the time." If only the library world was as peaceful as outsiders envisioned it!

–Mark Willis[2]

This paper deals with *physical* aspects of security in public buildings, particularly with violence perpetrated by patrons who enter librarians' workplaces every day for various reasons, and sometimes, with agendas of their own. *Not* included in this discussion are such related security problems for libraries as (1) preservation and retention of books and other materials, (2) electronic security, protecting computer records and files against hackers and other cybercriminals trying to gain access to them out of motives ranging from pranks to revenge, and (3) "inside jobs," situations in which perpetrators of violence are staff members, who are people, too, with their own problems. Each of these facets of the overarching problem is important in its own right, but this discussion, because of space limitations, focuses on protecting people in the library building from aggressive or dangerous actions of *visitors*, our patrons and clientele.

Many members of any community share the notion of a library building as a refuge, a quiet, safe haven, full of dusty books containing the dead thoughts of dead writers from a dead past, and in whose halls and rooms one can let one's guard down, read and relax. It is jarring, therefore, for the average citizen to entertain the notion of such a place as occasionally dangerous. Sure, we know that bad things sometimes happen in post offices or online brokerages that cater to day traders, but the *library*? Gimme a break! Thankfully, most people do not place libraries on their lists of places to avoid for fear of being shot, stabbed, beaten or otherwise assaulted, but the potential exists all the same, merely underscoring the recommendation that in today's world, it is always prudent to watch your back, wherever you go.

Strange and troubled people have always found library and museum buildings appealing . . . and sometimes magnetic because it is so easy to gain admission. The early-twentieth-century British author G. K. Chesterton, back in 1910,[3] wrote of his firm conviction that every London-area family with a madman among its number dropped him off in the sedate precincts of the British Museum for the day; otherwise, how could so many bizarre and eccentric people manage to congregate in one spot every afternoon? Well, some things don't change. Chesterton's observation of almost a century ago speaks to us across the years. Threatening (rather than merely annoying–who come to libraries in great big bunches, like bananas), mentally-troubled and occasionally violent people enter our workplaces every day, and once inside, they are free to demonstrate that there is a dark side to human behavior. For evidence of this, consider the following recent news items, extracted from the pages of *American Libraries:*[4]

- A librarian is murdered while working alone in a small town library. The next day, a 16-year old youth from a nearby town is arrested and charged with armed robbery, murder, and felony murder. His motive, he explains, was the desire to possess the staff member's expensive jewelry.
- A patron suddenly shoots and kills two reference librarians in a branch public library. The gunman, a transient, homeless person is later described as a regular patron of the library. Witnesses say that he entered just before closing, carrying a handgun and, without warning, opened fire on several employees, fatally wounding two librarians. The assailant is described as having no criminal or psy-

chiatric history, but is subsequently revealed to have had a grudge against the County, feeling that he had suffered extreme emotional and mental distress after being falsely imprisoned for 28 days when mistaken for a fugitive from another state.

- A gunman, carrying a pistol and what he says is a bomb, takes 18 people hostage at a large downtown library in a Western city. An alert off-duty deputy, who manages to sneak in among the hostages, subsequently shoots and kills the gunman. Luckily, no hostages are hurt, despite a tense five-and-one-half-hour standoff, but the bomb found on the dead man's person proves to be "live," and big enough to have, if detonated, blown up the whole building.
- A branch library clerk working the evening shift is beaten to death by a young man who has been harassing several of the women on the library staff, making obscene phone calls, and exposing himself to female staff members. The victim had complained to police a week earlier that the man had been harassing her, but the police pointed out that, unless an actual crime has been committed, they could do nothing.

Frightening? Certainly, but it's a fair question to ask whether these are isolated incidents, taken out of context. Perhaps they are. We do not read about the thousands of domestic airplane flights that land safely every day. We only hear about disasters and mishaps that occur in the friendly skies. So even though violence in libraries and other public buildings is rare and statistically insignificant, it remains true that any public gathering area can become a setting for unpredictable behavior and violent crime. We need, therefore, to consider and do what is possible to create a strengthened security posture that will serve to deter or contain violent visitors, protect building occupants and reduce the risk of such incidents, thereby promoting in the public a general sense that they may visit and use our libraries in safety.

WHY LIBRARIES?

Whereas museums, archives and other cultural buildings usually have guards on site, alert to various dangers, libraries all too often do not, which invites trouble. But why libraries? Why does problem behavior occur in library buildings more often than it does in, say, high-rise office buildings, sports venues, or airport terminals? Perhaps it is the openness of access to library buildings together with the absence of admission fees that permits perpetrators to enter freely without explaining themselves, and, once inside, do what they please. For some, it is that the library is often the only public building open evenings and weekends, seasonally heated and cooled, and containing free public restrooms, making it attractive to people who have no place else to go. Possibly, though, the reason is that many libraries are either undefended or poorly defended, meaning that would-be aggressors feel comfortable about starting confrontations.

How do violent incidents in public buildings become possible? For a start, there are no barriers to protect staff from personal interaction with the public, which is intentional because easy interaction helps the library in meeting the community's informational and recreational needs. Barriers to personal contact in libraries are, in fact, either minimal or non-existent. Even in high-crime areas, libraries do not choose to enact stringent security measures because free and open places require free and open access. With no metal-detector at the front door, moreover, people are free to bring any weapons they choose with them, concealed or in plain sight. Oh, sure, there *is* often a barrier, a detection gate through which you must pass as you exit the building, intended to keep books not properly checked out from leaving the library. And there lies the normal extent of much library security: any barrier you encounter affects your getting *out*; getting in is, by design, a piece of cake.

One effective antidote to permitting disturbed or dangerous people to act out their hostilities in a library is hiring and training a force of trained, resourceful and seemingly-omnipresent guards. Such a remedy, however, is beyond the financial means of many smaller communities and poorer institutions. Consequently, alternative ways must be found in the absence of security personnel on the job to heighten our security posture, instilling in patrons and staff alike the idea that they are reasonably protected against the threat of violence. Sometimes, the issue comes down to money and little more. Commercial public places such as sports stadiums and office buildings can afford to have a mix of police, guards, surveillance cameras, and alarm systems to deal with problem behaviors, yet many library buildings actually do little to protect building occupants. Reasons for this vary, but may include naiveté, apathy, or misplaced trust in human nature, but the main culprit is frequently lack of funds: a budget that does not allow for normal remedies to help ensure public safety.

LEVELS OF SECURITY

Just imagine . . . What if a disturbed but clever problem patron, who knew just how far he could and could not go (meaning that his behavior, while troublesome, violated no existing rules or laws) found his way into your library building? How would you cope? What rules would you confect and have posted in advance to enable you to give this patron the old heave-ho, and how would you ensure that they were universally applied? Secondarily, how would you write a code of policies and procedures to govern ways in which staff would respond when confronted by a threatening and highly offensive person who happened not to be violating any established rules? Suppose the problem behaviors committed by your problem behavior were principally that he was extremely malodorous and leered at women: these are not, as it turns out, deemed police matters. Administrators and staff are faced with different options for dealing with such a problem, none of them ideal, and all of them controversial, but each worth considering. Here are just five:

- Have the man banned from the library, citing as your reason his foul odor and frightening behavior towards women (trap: if such things are not specifically forbidden by the present library rules, a lawsuit could be forthcoming).
- Change the rules, rewriting them such that terrible smells, stalking, and forms of sexual harassment are now proscribed and/or punishable (trap: writing the language of such rules is going to be tricky at best).
- Have someone best suited to it play "social worker," try to "reach" the offender, and persuade him to see that his odor and conduct are disruptive and upsetting. Try convincing him to attempt to reform (trap: this only works on those who actually *want* to change).
- Have guards follow the man around the building, making him acutely aware that he is under continual surveillance (trap: such a remedy is highly labor-intensive) and even if successful, will only cause him to seek out new places to bother people.
- Ignore him, as best you can, and advise patrons to do the same (trap: doing nothing about him may only embolden him, and he may spread the word that your library is an "anything goes" place to spend daytime hours).

Granted, none of these alternatives may achieve the desired result, but just wringing your hands and hoping he will go away is not a satisfactory option. Which to try first? As a suggestion: conduct a library staff day in which these options and others are considered, discussed, role-played, and (hopefully) decided upon before a problem patron of this type begins infesting your library building and terrorizing or otherwise turning off its occupants. That libraries are public places is at the same time the good news and the bad news. Freedom may be a wonderful thing, but there are limits to freedom in public buildings, and such limits must be understood by all concerned.

Security postures for various public gathering places (including libraries) vary widely, depending on many factors, and carry a considerable range of price tags. The degree of security your facility needs is a function of how much security is perceived to be necessary together with how much money is available to ensure a reasonable degree of safety. How much security is desirable and feasible for *your* facility? Consider the following seven levels of security in public places:

Level 1: Perfect Security

Perfect security cannot be attained, however hard you try. No way. Faggedaboudit! File it under "fiction." A public place with zero tolerance for problem behaviors, such that people in it are 100 percent safe from harm is not a practical possibility. Where human safety is concerned, nothing is guaranteed despite your best attempts to ensure it or strengthen security. There are, in fact, only varying degrees of *insecurity* (see Levels 2-7). Deal with it.

Level 2: Extremely Good Security

It is now increasingly possible to transact most library business (or even "visit" museums or archives) via the Internet without leaving home. Powerful search engines and millions of Websites make it possible for one to locate and browse collections, view paintings, consult specific books and/or articles, compile data, and download or print desired information, all from the privacy–and safety–of home, without even putting on your shoes! When transacting such business from home, the chances of being physically assaulted, robbed, hit over the head, or even shouted at, are virtually nil. And even better, you do not have to look your best, or worry about driving hazards, hiring a babysitter, inclement weather, parking problems, or the high cost of gasoline. Since physical exposure to other people is zero when you do research via the Web, what keeps this level of security from being perfect? Couple of things. Communication is almost always a two-way street. Electronic access may protect your body from physical harm but your computer's operating system and files are still at risk from wily and determined hackers. Once you open a channel via a modem between your computer and an Internet provider, and thence to the entire world, you risk having your private files and information read, stolen, altered, compromised, or subjected to viruses, with unpredictable and potentially unpleasant results. Ironically, the same connection that enables you to interact with remote sites from home also makes it possible for you to give up your most private and personal information without even being aware of it. Thus you are vulnerable via the Internet to an extremely virulent strain of attack: the kind where you may not even realize what has happened until later . . . if then.

Level 3: Very Good Security

Military installations have (or at least should have) very good security as do corporate entities with valuable and proprietary secrets to protect. For instance, you cannot just stroll into the Pentagon or into the Texas Instruments' Tech Center and use their computers, take pictures, or even have a look around unless you work there or take a scheduled, supervised tour. In such places, employees work in high-security areas with guards providing heightened safety for building occupants. Governmental agencies and corporations take important and costly steps to ensure that only authorized and accredited persons are allowed admission to secure facilities, and all visitors must identify themselves to the satisfaction of the protectors in order to gain access to the people, machinery and information within. Such high levels of security are bolstered by new technologies such as password access, retinal scans, palm print/fingerprint analysis, and voice recognition. These barriers are generally effective in distinguishing legitimate, authorized staff and visitors from spies, criminals, frauds, and impostors, but no security technology can lay claim to being perfect. There is always room for improvement. A clever criminal, intent on information piracy may eventually–unless stopped or deterred–succeed in breaching even the strongest electronic fortress walls. In order to get into a "hardened" workplace with a weapon and attack the people inside, however, the perpetrator must work out how to fool, bypass, disable, or defeat any electronic countermeasures in place.

Level 4: Commendable (Pretty Good) Security

A commercial restaurant of my acquaintance in the inner-city has, as its principal security problem, keeping those inside safe, and those who belong outside, outside. Workers in this popular carry-out eatery labor in a bustling kitchen separated from a storefront waiting room by a thick wall of transparent Lucite. Customers enter the waiting room, shout their orders into speakers in the bulletproof Lucite partition, pay (in advance) through small pass-through windows, and watch the skillful cooks scurry about their ovens and burners in full sight, but not within reach. Customers may thus see their food being prepared, but harming–or even touching–the preparers is impossible. Small orders, when ready, are passed through a hatch in the Lucite. Larger orders are brought out to the waiting room by a huge man, rippling with muscle and sporting a "don't-mess-with-me" face, but that is the extent of personal contact or exposure for restaurant staff. Unless you want to try overpowering the big man in order to rob or harm restaurant employees, you would have to find a way to bypass or circumvent the barrier. The Lucite is bulletproof, so even pointing a handgun at the people in the kitchen and demanding the contents of the cash register would get you nowhere, except perhaps prison.

Level 5: So-So Security

Frequent flyers spend a good chunk of their time commuting to other cities by air or loitering in airports, waiting for their flights. But just to get as far as the waiting area–let alone on the airplane–you must submit to a routine security check of both your person and your carry-on baggage, while elsewhere in the terminal, X-ray scanners (and sometimes trained dogs) presumably check your luggage for dangerous or prohibited items. To pass from the ticketing arcade into the gate area, you are scanned by a device that detects metallic items, and those found to have concealed handguns (or other metal objects that could be used as weapons) on their persons are not only forbidden to enter the concourse, but subject to arrest and hefty fines. Unfortunately, the system is far from perfect because people still do occasionally find a way to defeat security countermeasures and manage to get aboard airplanes with prohibited weapons. But metal-detectors weed out most of the desperate or deranged individuals who hope to skyjack or crash an airliner by shooting their way into the cockpit. True, there are holes in airport security, but at least the airlines are making a determined effort to cut back on crime (and terror) aloft, leaving passengers and flight crews feeling a bit more secure. And even if airport security cannot absolutely guarantee travelers' safety, it does a reasonable job of deterring and reducing life-threatening incidents.

Level 6: Token Security (Better Than Nothing)

Larger and wealthier libraries and museums may not have an array of crimestopping technology at their disposal but they do employ security forces of paid guards who are tasked with monitoring entrances and exits, patrolling public rooms and stacks, and generally keeping the peace through surveillance and deterrence. Building guards normally receive fairly extensive law enforcement training before assuming their duties, and while not normally armed, are schooled in dealing with threatening behaviors, crowd control, isolating violent people, and rudimentary psychology. Because of the normal salary scale, however, library guards, however well-intentioned, are occasionally elderly, slow, out-of-shape, poorly trained, inattentive, indifferent, or lazy, and thus likely to be of very little help when staff must deal with persons who threaten them or other building occupants. Sometimes, library guards may be observed spending most of their shifts reading newspapers or chatting up staff or patrons, and thus are inattentive to their assigned duties. Just having someone around to summon police, however, *is* a helpful start, and having *any* kind of security presence in a public building may serve to deter individuals intent on violence or other criminal activity. Frequent (but random) patrols by uniformed, serious-looking guards, equipped with communications devices, will go a long way towards deterring problem behaviors and reassuring building occupants, and is certainly better than nothing when interposed between potentially violent visitors and other building occupants.

Level 7: No Protection (Rotten Security)

People working in Level 6 milieux may count themselves luckier than some of their colleagues because all too many library staff work in Level 7 buildings–and Level 7 is as unsafe as it gets. Such institutions have no actual security (except in the sense that everyone on staff is, as one administrator put it, euphemistically, part of the "security team"). The principal reason for this lapse is sometimes because the governmental jurisdiction claims that it is not necessary (when in actuality it is usually a pragmatic budgetary decision), leaving all building occupants vulnerable to crime and violence. Denied the protection of their first line of defense–vigilant security–staff working within such places can only deal with incidents as they arise.

SECURITY MEASURES

Library employees–especially those working at public workstations–are naturally as much at risk as are the members of the public. How, then, can one anticipate an attack? It would be really great if all bad guys, criminals, perverts, and psychopaths would wear sweatshirts identifying them as such, or if someone would invent a new type of goggles that, when worn by a staff member seated at the front door, would cause dangerous people to appear to glow cherry red or pulse, when viewed through their lenses. But what about those who walk, stumble, or stagger through the front doors who happen to suffer from full-blown psychosis or are bent on mayhem or mischief and yet give no outward sign of what they are thinking until the actual moment of truth? Such visitors may *look* like normal people, but can, without warning, become dangerous to those around them, and while chances of such an occurrence are statistically negligible–even in large cities with high crime rates–the element of risk is always there.

Some libraries employ a number of security solutions to reduce crime and to create an aura of safety in their buildings. Such measures include having on-duty or off-duty police stationed inside the library, employing paid security guards to serve as unofficial "bouncers" and peacekeepers, technical solutions like security cameras, emergency telephones, and rationing keys to public restrooms. Still, a large proportion of library security efforts are aimed at keeping the books from walking away, and while protecting library property from theft and mutilation is commendable, personal safety is much *more* important for a simple reason: human lives are at stake. Books, videos, and even computers can be repaired or replaced; people cannot.

Now imagine that, for whatever reason, during your stint at a public desk, a patron produces a handgun and starts shooting, no matter why or at whom. The salient fact is that the person has a gun and gained access to the building with it unchallenged by any countermeasures. Here is the catch: The building's defenses tend to be reactive, rather than proactive. While we are entitled to require such things as shirts and shoes of our patrons, staff are not permitted to deny access to people dressed a certain way, whose looks we don't like, or just on general "suspicion."

Public means public; we are not permitted to make such distinctions. In a very real sense, "We cannot holler until we're hurt." Face it: public employees routinely work in such surroundings, vulnerable to approach or assault by anyone whose mind may be full of strange whispered voices or uncontrollable urges. They work in a combat zone (for which some believe they deserve customary hazard pay). And as bad as that sounds, it gets worse: not only are such employees at risk from possible harm that could come to them from the actions of deranged or angry people in their midst, but so are their patrons, innocently trusting their hosts, and trusting that they are safe from harm.

Are we (and our patrons) thus without protection and defenses against such actions? Security guards are hired to monitor the activities of visitors and prevent or interdict acts that are against the law, against the rules, violent, dangerous, illegal, or potentially harmful to other occupants of the building. But salaried security guards are often a luxury simply beyond the budget's financial limits. As one smug member of a staff in a medium-sized city's downtown library told me, in explaining why there were no security guards in view, "We're all security officers, here." Yeah, right.

A pair of pertinent questions arise in this regard: (1) How can public buildings bolster their security postures such that–even if they cannot erect sturdy barriers–they can create an ambiance in which both patrons and staff can feel reasonably secure? and (2) Is there necessarily a trade-off between a heightened security posture and placing annoying barriers in the path of library visitors? To help answer these questions in a way favorable to a reasonable level of personal security, you're going to need a plan.

SOLUTIONS:
A WORKABLE PLAN FOR PREVENTING VIOLENCE
IN PUBLIC BUILDINGS

As violence–and the fear of violence–increasingly disrupt our work-places and drain our resources, we must take steps to create a safer environment for staff and patrons. While no library or institution is immune to threat, prevention of most dangerous or frightening events is possible with careful planning and cooperation. Preparation and readiness are first lines of defense: there is a lot of truth in the old adage that an ounce of prevention is worth a pound of cure. The importance of a continuous posture of defensive readiness is clear. It is easier and far better to prevent attacks than it is to diagnose what went wrong later and work out an appropriate subsequent response. But while we cannot anticipate and deter all attacks, good planning will help significantly in warding them off, in damage control subsequent to the event, and in figuring what to do to prevent any "next times." The following are thus offered as candidate basic ingredients of an integrated master plan for building safety and security. Not all may be applicable to an institution's specific circumstances, and some will simply be too costly to warrant serious consideration. But including some of these steps will help anticipate, prevent, contain, deal with, and resolve some of the more common types of violent incidents that may occur:

PREPARATION: BEFORE PROBLEMS OCCUR

- Designate a staff member as "Building Security Officer," in charge of public safety, and provide for an "officer of the day" whenever the building is open to the public.
- Maintain good relations with local police and try to encourage them to include the institution's premises on their "rounds," especially during evening and weekend hours.
- Monitor crime patterns in the community continuously and brief staff on what, in particular, to watch out for.
- Perform a building security audit, in which all existing defenses and deterrents are reviewed and evaluated. Analyze your present security posture and take remedial steps to upgrade it, including justifications for requested improvements.
- Create and promulgate a comprehensive building security policy and hold meetings to explain and discuss it with all staff members.
- The public must be aware that threats, violence, and verbal abuse will not be tolerated. Post rules of conduct and unacceptable behaviors in conspicuous public places, and have paper copies for handing to patrons in case of questions.
- Where possible, purchase security equipment (e.g., surveillance cameras) to augment existing surveillance capabilities.
- Provide telephones and lists of emergency telephone numbers (e.g., police, paramedics, firefighters) at all desks. Consider silent assistance bells or intercoms.
- Hire trained security guards; train them well in procedures, crisis management, and crowd control. A uniformed guard should be at or around the front door to the building during normal hours of operation, and patrols of the building should be irregular and unpredictable.

- Emphasize the need for security to staff and make them aware that "security is everybody's business." Encourage staff to be alert and observant at all times and make them aware that human behavior is difficult or impossible to predict.
- Where funds permit, have on-duty staff work in pairs or teams.
- Provide staff training in security precautions (e.g., calm-voiced assertiveness, avoidance of overreaction, careful observation, problem recognition, description, communication skills, interpretation of verbal clues and body language).
- Establish special code words (e.g., a distinctive surname), so that staff members can communicate danger or warning signals verbally or by telephone without alerting others present to problems.
- In frequent in-service workshops, provide group exercises (drills and simulations in dealing with confrontations) designed to reduce response time to emergencies.

ACTION: STAFF RESPONSE AND REACTION

- Remember the most important goals: protect human lives and nobody gets hurt.
- Attempt to isolate a problem patron from others in the room or area.
- A calm voice and reasonable, pleasant manner may defuse tricky situations or at least buy time.
- Separate merely annoying problems from threatening or dangerous ones and act accordingly.
- Apply and enforce all rules fairly, firmly, and consistently.
- Treat homeless people as you would others, providing that they live by the rules.
- Staff response to crisis should be conditioned due to repeated drills and role-plays.
- Never be afraid to "bother" the police with a problem; that's what they are there for.

FISCAL REALITIES

Some aspects of "good security" may seem to run contrary to the nature and mission of a public building, and thus be deemed undesirable. There is unavoidable tradeoff between how much security is provided and how free of constraints building occupants are, or feel themselves to be. Ubiquitous guard presence and scanning surveillance cameras may reduce crime and promote the comforting sense of being protected, but the same security measures may also be perceived as intrusive impediments to the intellectual freedom that people expect from free institutions in a free society. From a staff point of view, a high degree of security (e.g., Lucite shields between employees and the untrustworthy public, password access) might protect employees from the potential actions of violent patrons, but it is important to think through what would be gained and what lost if such changes could be brought about.

CONCLUSION

Good building security normally entails the purchase of considerable equipment and/or a much larger payroll for guards. While it is possible to achieve consensus on the *desirability* of such measures, opinions vary considerably on which security measures are most effective and whether enhanced security is important enough to warrant the additional outlay of funds. In terms of costs, however, it is generally true that you get what you pay for; good security is expensive, and very good security runs into serious money. Marshaling arguments intended to convince the funding body (or community) that considerable additional spending for augmented security is money well spent can be a daunting task in this era of taxpayer unrest, Internet access, and dwindling inner-city tax bases. Still, you have to try. Even if you win only a small victory in the form of upgrading public safety in your library, you've accomplished something. You'll fall well short of your idealized building security posture (as every public institution must), but *any* security beats none at all, six ways from Sunday.

REFERENCES

1. *Violence in the Workplace, A Comprehensive Study.* Washington, D.C.: National Institute for Occupational Safety and Health, 1997.

2. Mark Willis. *Dealing With Difficult People in Libraries.* (Chicago, American Library Association, 1999): p. 1.

3. G(ilbert). K(eith). Chesterton (1874-1936). *What's Wrong With the World.* New York: Dodd, Mead, 1910: p. 4.

4. All incidents encapsulated here were reported during the 1990s in various news roundup sections of monthly editions of *American Libraries.*

Old Problem for New Reasons: Overcoming the Challenge Presented by Mentally Ill Library Users

Stephanie Ford

SUMMARY. Evening staff members of the Research and Information Services Department (RISD) at the North Carolina State University (NCSU) Libraries have recently noticed an apparent increase in the use of the library by people perceived to be mentally ill. RISD staff members have found themselves in some ways unprepared to respond comfortably to this change. This paper, a case study, proposes reasons for this increased visibility of mentally ill people, and describes the challenges the staff members faced and how they overcame them. The RISD staff members acquired the knowledge and confidence they need to work with mentally ill people through communication among colleagues, review of the literature, and staff training. *[Article copies available for a fee from The Haworth Document Delivery Service: 1-800-HAWORTH. E-mail address: <getinfo@haworthpressinc.com> Website: <http://www.HaworthPress.com> © 2002 by The Haworth Press, Inc. All rights reserved.]*

KEYWORDS. Mentally ill, problem patrons, problem situations, extended hours, evening staff members, public Internet access

Stephanie Ford is Reference Librarian, D. H. Hill Library, North Carolina State University, Raleigh, NC 27695-7111 (E-mail: Stephanie_Ford@ncsu.edu).

[Haworth co-indexing entry note]: "Old Problem for New Reasons: Overcoming the Challenge Presented by Mentally Ill Library Users." Ford, Stephanie. Co-published simultaneously in *The Reference Librarian* (The Haworth Information Press, an imprint of The Haworth Press, Inc.) No. 75/76, 2002, pp. 83-90; and: *Helping the Difficult Library Patron: New Approaches to Examining and Resolving a Long-Standing and On-going Problem* (ed: Kwasi Sarkodie-Mensah) The Haworth Information Press, an imprint of The Haworth Press, Inc., 2002, pp. 83-90. Single or multiple copies of this article are available for a fee from The Haworth Document Delivery Service [1-800-HAWORTH, 9:00 a.m. - 5:00 p.m. (EST). E-mail address: getinfo@haworthpressinc.com].

© 2002 by The Haworth Press, Inc. All rights reserved.

INTRODUCTION

In fall 1999 the evening staff members of the Research and Information Services Department (RISD) at the North Carolina State University (NCSU) Libraries became markedly aware of the increased visibility of people perceived to be mentally ill using the library. After much thought I have concluded that this apparent increase results from two recent changes at the NCSU Libraries: RISD staff who only work in the evenings and the availability of public access to the World Wide Web from computers in the library. This paper describes the challenges the RISD staff faced and the steps taken to overcome them. It also points out a few issues of concern for libraries with staff members who work only in the evenings: communication with supervisors and other day staff, patron familiarity (which is a natural consequence of routine and long desk shifts), and staff training.

THE PROBLEM

As an academic library, the role of the NCSU Libraries is defined. Nevertheless, as a part of the community NCSU Libraries has a mission to serve the general public. With its urban setting and proximity to downtown Raleigh and the homeless shelters, the NCSU Libraries is more likely to have mentally ill users than more isolated academic libraries.

Staff members strive to make the environment at the NCSU Libraries an inviting one for users. The RISD staff members are tolerant and patient, as most librarians seem to be, but at times they have felt overwhelmed by the nightly presence of mentally ill people in the reference department asking for assistance and using the public workstations. Some RISD staff members have felt threatened, and have worried that the atmosphere of research and scholarship will be compromised by disruptive mentally ill library users. Most of the anxiety was due to their limited knowledge about mental illness and uncertainty about the best way to interact with the mentally ill. None of them have any experience or background in psychopathology, and sadly, their limited knowledge is tainted by negative stereotypes and media representations. Instinct might tell staff members to treat a mentally ill person asking for reference assistance the same way they would treat any other library user. This approach only works sometimes. The mentally ill do not behave like other library users. Their requests for assistance are frequently repetitive and their questions are sometimes personal and inappropriate.

Evening-Only Staff

In August 1996, in response to popular request from students, the NCSU Libraries started providing twenty-four hour service, including reference service, at the main D. H. Hill Library, from Sunday through Thursday. With the extended hours came full-time and part-time RISD staff members who were hired to work only the evening or night shifts. Although day staff members who work short periods at the reference desk have occasional interactions with the mentally ill, the staff members who keep daily evening hours are most affected by the few mentally ill people who repeatedly use the library. There is not a problem with unauthorized people in the library in the middle of the night. The library policy of admittance to only NCSU affiliated users between midnight and 7 a.m. is prominently posted and strictly enforced. The uniformed security guards are a strong presence. The mentally ill people using the library do so before midnight.

Evening RISD staff members have nightly interactions with mentally ill people. I, for instance, as an evening reference librarian, work four-hour shifts at the reference desk five nights per week. Routine, multi-hour desk shifts result in patron familiarity. It is heartwarming to see the library anxiety leave a student's face when he/she recognizes a familiar friendly face in the reference department. Sometimes, however, patron familiarity can be a strain. As the mentally ill patrons become more familiar with reference staff members, they become bolder in their interactions. "Are you married?" becomes " Are you still married?" which becomes "When are you going to get unmarried?" Daily, repeated interactions and familiarity can be taxing on library staff members who are unsure of the most appropriate way to provide service to the mentally ill.

Public Access to the World Wide Web

In 1996 the D. H. Hill Library had fifty-five public computer workstations for accessing the NCSU Libraries Information System, and the majority of electronic resources in the information system were accessible through locally networked CD-ROM databases. By 1999 the D. H. Hill Library had seventy-seven public computer workstations for accessing the information system and nearly 100 percent of the resources in the information system were accessible via the World Wide Web. The change to primarily Web-accessible resources allows the library to provide many useful services, such as remote database access, online renewal, MyLibrary@NCState (a customizable interface to the library's information resources), and increased resource sharing, to name only a few. The advantages of providing public access to the World Wide Web are many and outweigh any negative consequences (Watson 1997), but this change to primarily Web-accessible resources has also resulted in free public access to e-mail, chat rooms and games. Many commercial Web sites offer free e-mail. Consequently, the public workstations are now used for much more than research. At times when there is no competition for use many people are at the workstations for hours. The intrigue of the World Wide Web reaches the mentally ill people who visit the library and word of public access seems to spread through the grapevine on the street. Many of the mentally ill people now visiting D. H. Hill Library use the public workstations to access the World Wide Web. Those that lack computer skills repeatedly ask librarians for help with simple tasks, such as logging in and free online lottery entry. Because of this repetitive need for assistance, and the proximity of the workstations to the reference desk, the presence of the mentally ill is strongly felt by the staff.

With most of the students gone during the December 1999/January 2000 holiday break, the use of the library by mentally ill people was especially noticeable to evening RISD staff members. The situation seemed to sneak up on them and they suddenly realized that they indeed had a situation. In an article published in the *Washington Post* twenty years ago, the Reading Room in the Library of Congress is described as being like "the dayroom of a state mental hospital" (Mansfield 1980). In the case of the NCSU Libraries that statement would be a gross exaggeration, but in their unpreparedness, that is how RISD staff members felt some evenings. Some were wondering if they could endure the strain.

WHAT CAN BE DONE ABOUT IT?

Communication at All Levels

First, evening RISD members talked and determined that they shared the frustrations and anxiety that this situation was causing, alleviating the feeling that, "Maybe it's just me." They apprised their supervisor of the situation and their anxiety. Good communication between evening staff members and managerial staff, who most often work during the day, is very important. Evening staff members are somewhat isolated, and therefore, must communicate with management and supervisors about problem situations, awkward situations, and evening staff member concerns. Once problems are discussed, steps can be taken to resolve them. Evening staff members must keep in mind that the responsibility for this communication is shared equally between evening staff members and management.

Familiarity with the Literature

Next, knowing that mentally ill people in libraries was not a new phenomenon, the RISD staff decided to check the library literature and see what had been written that might help them cope. The available library literature on mentally ill patrons is very helpful.

Patron Behavior in Libraries: A Handbook of Positive Approaches to Negative Situations, edited by Beth McNeil and Denise J. Johnson, is readable and practical. It served as a stopgap resource until staff training could be arranged and continues to be useful. It includes a very relevant and helpful chapter by Charles A. Salter and Jeffrey L. Salter titled, "Mentally Ill Patrons" (McNeil and Johnson 1996, 18-43). Salter and Salter answer the question, "Why are they here?" with their brief description of the move to the deinstitutionalization of mental patients that began in the 1970s (21-22). They also describe and explain the types of mental illness likely to be encountered in a library and the risk levels associated with the different types (23-27). Staff training is considered imperative, as is behavior policy documentation.

Emerita M. Cuesta's chapter in the same book, called "Problems with Patrons in the Academic Library," is also useful (Cuesta 1996, 75-83). As Cuesta points out, it is more common for libraries to have written policies pertaining to criminal types of behavior than written policies pertaining to the behavior exhibited by mentally ill people (79). The correct way to respond to criminal behavior in the library is straightforward–hit the panic button. The proper response to the behavior of the mentally ill, which may present a nuisance or make library patrons uncomfortable, but poses no serious threat, is not so clear cut. Like Salter and Salter, Cuesta emphasizes the importance of staff training. She points out that training "not only helps staffers cope with a patron's behavior, but teaches them to control their own attitudes and maintain a professional detached manner" (81). Cuesta also stresses the importance of "well-defined guidelines that address common types of disruptive behavior" (80).

Charles A. Salter and Jeffrey L. Salter have also written a full length book called, *On the Frontlines: Coping with the Library's Problem Patrons*. They remind us that a mentally ill person " . . . is more disabled than bad, more a victim than a deliberate perpetrator" and that "the mentally disturbed patron (as opposed to the career criminal) should arouse first our compassion rather than anger or punitiveness" (Salter and Salter 1988, 111). Thomas E. Hecker also reminds us that the mentally ill are disabled, like the visually, hearing, and physically impaired, and are covered by the Americans with Disabilities Act of 1990 (Hecker 1996, 6). Otto F. Wahl has written a readable and well researched book called, *Media Madness: Public Images of Mental Illness*. Wahl points out that " . . . the public continues to be exposed to repeated presentations of people with mental illnesses as comical, different, and dangerous–images that perpetuate unfavorable stereotypes which, in turn, lead to the rejection and neglect of those with psychiatric disorders" (Wahl 1995, 164). Library staff members who have at least basic factual understanding of mental illness will be less predisposed to misconceptions and will be better prepared to interact with people suffering from mental illness.

In *It Comes with the Territory: Handling Problem Situations in Libraries*, Anne M. Turner provides practical guidance on handling difficult situations with people in libraries and on preparing effective problem situations manuals (1993). The RISD staff is preparing a problem situations manual with guidelines to help library staff members respond appropriately to difficult situations for the staff information server.

Staff Training

Responding to the RISD request for help, the Mental Health Association in North Carolina (MHA/NC) provided a speaker for a staff training session on the mentally ill and appropriate ways for library staff members to respond to this particular segment of the population. The MHA/NC speaker quickly pointed out that the popular notion that mentally ill people are always violent is wrong. She talked about the types of mental illness staff members would be most likely to encounter in the library and described the behavior associated with each type, thus reinforcing what the staff members learned by reading Salter and Salter (1996). The staff members learned to watch for baseline behavior changes and mood swings. Most helpfully, staff members learned that it is okay, even advisable, to respond to inappropriate personal questions and advances with a firm, "That is not an appropriate question," or "That is inappropriate behavior, and if you don't stop I will have to ask you to leave." Such a response will most likely bring about an apology. Staff members have had the opportunity to try this firm, straightforward approach, and results have been positive. Staff members are no longer afraid to say, "That is all the help I can give you right now." The MHA/NC speaker pointed out that the mentally ill regularly visiting the library mean no harm. They like the library, and will not risk being banned. D. H. Hill Library's most frequent mentally ill visitor recently verified this when he told a RISD staff member, "I need this library right now."

Every staff member attending the training session had an experience with a mentally ill patron to relate and had questions about the appropriate way to respond to a mentally ill person's unpredictable behavior. The speaker encouraged the library staff to call The Mental Health Association in North Carolina anytime they have questions or need help. The training session was immensely helpful, and made it clear that one training session is not enough. Staff training in patron behavior will be incorporated into the RISD staff training program.

CONCLUSION

Extended hours of service and public access to the World Wide Web are two new ways the NCSU Libraries is responding to the needs of its users. Librarians have responded to many societal and technological changes in the twenty years since Stephanie Mansfield wrote the *Washington Post* article about the mentally ill people who regularly visited the Library of Congress (1980). Now as the twenty-first century begins, library staff members, as always, must be prepared to interact with a variety of humankind. The RISD staff acquired the knowledge and confidence they need to work with mentally ill people through communication with supervisory staff and colleagues, review of the literature, and staff training. Much has changed; little has changed.

REFERENCES

Cuesta, Emerita M. 1996. Problems with patrons in the academic library. In *Patron behavior in libraries: A handbook of positive approaches to negative situations*, eds. Beth McNeil and Denise Johnson, 75-83. Chicago: American Library Association.
Hecker, Thomas. 1996. Patrons with disabilities or problem patrons: Which model should librarians apply to people with mental illness? *The Reference Librarian* 53: 5-12.

Mansfield, Stephanie. 1980. Library of Congress: Accommodating the disturbed. *The Washington Post.* 28 March 1980, final edition.

McNeil, Beth, and Denise J. Johnson, eds. 1996. *Patron behavior in libraries: A handbook of positive approaches to negative situations.* Chicago: American Library Association.

Salter, Charles A., and Jeffrey L. Salter. 1988. *On the frontline: Coping with the library's problem patrons.* Littleton, Colo.: Libraries Unlimited.

_____. 1996. Mentally ill patrons. In *Patron behavior in libraries: A handbook of positive approaches to negative situations,* eds. Beth McNeil and Denise J. Johnson, 18-43. Chicago: American Library Association.

Turner, Anne M. 1993. *It comes with the territory: Handling problem situations in libraries.* Jefferson, N.C.: McFarland.

Wahl, Otto F. 1995. *Media madness: Public images of mental illness.* New Brunswick, New Jersey: Rutgers University Press.

Watson, Mark. 1997. World Wide Web public access: Notes on the debate. *Resource Sharing & Information Networks* 13 (1): 5-19.

"The Homosexual" as Problem Patron

Polly Thistlethwaite

SUMMARY. Libraries host a range of human activity, some of which is overtly and unabashedly sexual. What's a librarian to do about public displays of affection? Cruising? Public sex? First, naturally, we read up on the issue. Unfortunately, problem patron library literature is spotted with vivid illustrations of irrational bias against gay men, male-to-female transgender women, and men-cruising-men. It also discounts the private nature of most consensual sex in public places. This article discusses sex and gender biases in library literature, arguing that gender equitable, privacy-respecting practices will better serve librarians administering public space. *[Article copies available for a fee from The Haworth Document Delivery Service: 1-800-HAWORTH. E-mail address: <getinfo@haworthpressinc.com> Website: <http://www.HaworthPress.com> © 2002 by The Haworth Press, Inc. All rights reserved.]*

KEYWORDS. Sex, sexual activity, homosexuality, same sex, gay, transgender, public sex, cruising, privacy

In the library one night as I sit in the reading room surrounded by serene-masked people like relics from a distant world, a handsome young man said hello to me. He sat at the same table. Noticing that he kept smiling and looking at me–at the same time that I felt his leg sliding against mine–

–John Rechy, *City of Night*, 1963.[1]

Polly Thistlethwaite is Coordinator of Instruction, Colorado State University Libraries, Fort Collins, CO 80521 (E-mail: pthistle@manta.colostate.edu).

[Haworth co-indexing entry note]: "'The Homosexual' as Problem Patron." Thistlethwaite, Polly. Co-published simultaneously in *The Reference Librarian* (The Haworth Information Press, an imprint of The Haworth Press, Inc.) No. 75/76, 2002, pp. 91-104; and: *Helping the Difficult Library Patron: New Approaches to Examining and Resolving a Long-Standing and Ongoing Problem* (ed: Kwasi Sarkodie-Mensah) The Haworth Information Press, an imprint of The Haworth Press, Inc., 2002, pp. 91-104. Single or multiple copies of this article are available for a fee from The Haworth Document Delivery Service [1-800-HAWORTH, 9:00 a.m. - 5:00 p.m. (EST). E-mail address: getinfo@haworthpressinc.com].

© 2002 by The Haworth Press, Inc. All rights reserved.

[Tearooms] may be located in any sort of public gathering place: department stores, bus stations, *libraries,* hotels, YMCAs, or court-houses. In keeping with the drive-in craze of American society, however, the more popular facilities are those readily accessible to the roadways. The restrooms of public parks and beaches–and more recently the rest stops set at programmed intervals along su-perhighways–are now attracting the clientele that, in a more pedes-trian age, frequented great buildings of the inner cities [emphasis added].

–Laud Humphreys. *Tearoom Trade:*
Impersonal Sex in Public Places, 1970.

P****** Library. Cruisy toilet in the basement level.

. . . and for the library, well the basement bathroom is somewhat cruisy. You can leave messages with time and date there. The sec-ond floor bathroom can be somewhat cruisy.

In the men's restroom of the second floor in the Library Building, there are a couple of peep holes. I've gotten occasional action, but not too much. It's fun to watch the young studs, though!

Fort C*** Library. Cruisy toilet. "The toilets have a double door that's pretty noisy. Used to have a gloryhole but they covered it up. Best time is around noon-1 p.m. Lots of hot, young GIs. This is an open post so anyone can be on the base."

–*www.cruisingforsex.com*, December 2000[2]

Libraries host a range of clientele, some of whom arrive without liter-ary agendas.

SEXUAL DOUBLE STANDARDS
IN PROBLEM PATRON LITERATURE

To facilitate discussion of erotic activity in libraries, Bruce A. Shuman draws hypothetical scenarios of public sexual display in his 1999 Amer-ican Library Association (ALA) publication on library security. "How should library staff and security personnel deal with egregious or crimi-nal sexual behavior? After all, there is usually a delicate and rather sub-jective line between what is actually criminal and what is merely offensive or in poor taste," he writes to introduce his own opinions on the topic.[3]

"A young couple[4] sits, side by side (fully clothed), in adjacent library chairs, necking furiously . . . oblivious to the stares, sniggers, and comments of those around them." Most of my library colleagues quip something to the effect of, "That should only happen to me," but Shuman calls this window-steaming scene an example of "inappropriate behavior" and "bad taste." He recommends a "stern warning" for these presumably heterosexual love birds, guiding readers that this sort of sexual public display is "not normally punishable behavior or anything that warrants calling the cops."[5]

Next, Shuman conjures up a scenario in which "a female library patron reports that she has observed a man in the stacks, squatting down and pretending to consult books on low shelves, while actually, she believes, looking up the skirts of young schoolgirls."[6] Hyper-mindful of the slanderous implications of labeling a glance harmful or a gape solicitous, Shuman instructs, "Looking at other library patrons is no crime, even if it makes others uncomfortable. Even if a security guard sees a man looking up the girl's skirts, he is taking a considerable legal risk should he detain him and accuse him of it."[7] Shuman further suggests that the girls in this case might well be asked to help prevent or respond to the situation themselves. "In one case a discussion of the young girls of what they were innocently inviting stopped the problem cold, at least for a while."[8]

Hmmm. Compare the two examples above to Shuman's advice regarding hypothetically grown-up men subject to solicitous glances and unwelcome stares from other men.

Shuman sets the scene: "A male patron uses the library building to meet other males who may or may not be interested in his sexual passes."[9] In other words, let's say a lone man stands around the library looking hunky and interested in sex with other men. Heaven forbid, Shuman's cruiser's "gaydar" glitches, and he winks at the wrong fella. In an initial spasm of good sense, Shuman suggests that library staff might legitimately ignore such a cruiser. But then Shuman suggests that libraries might just as well prosecute a cruiser as not. "Recommendation: There are several choices: Ignore him? Evict him? Call the police? If such behavior is observed in public areas, guards may wish to speak to the man, warn him that the library is not a pickup bar and that he is under continual observation. Here, it's *all right to attempt to be intimidating* without any suggestion of threat or violence. Should the offending patron attempt to conduct his erotic business in public rest rooms or appear to be forcing his attentions on others, however, *immediate eviction is called for* [emphasis added]."[10]

The male-male cruising scene solicits an austere and hardened response from this guru of vice. Shuman suggests that library staff might expect a girl to fend off a grown man's staring up their skirts because it's not a crime just to look. But, with an extraordinary, incongruous leap, Shuman calls for institutional protections for a grown heterosexual man unable to tolerate another man looking at him, cruising him. Now it's a crime just to look, time for library staff to launch a swift and stern intervention without consideration of legal infringement imposed upon the accused. Shuman treats the man-on-man glance as an offense more heinous and threatening than man-on-girl gawking.

If Shuman expects a girl to fend for herself, certainly he might expect an adult male to negotiate an unwelcome gaze from another male. Grown men can and must bear some minimal burden of sexual unease without crying out for institutional or state intervention in response to a sidelong glance. Any nonphysical act of solicitation, if not embraced as a compliment, offers a blessed opportunity for any man to transcend his own sexual fear by feeling, for just one glorious teachable moment, what it is like to be on the receiving end of an unanticipated sexual invitation. Females consistently deal with this and worse from gawking, stalking heterosexual men. If women all of a sudden united to ask library staff to respond to every unwanted male-on-female stare or solicitation cast in a library setting, staff would accomplish little else in the way of public service. Females deal with unwanted male glances all the time. Society trains women and girls to call for intervention only in extreme situations. Men should learn the same lesson. Librarian hearts need not bleed for the grown male "victims" of anyone's raised eyebrows.

CRIME? AND PUNISHMENT

According to Shuman, same sex "erotic business," even if hidden from view, is cause for immediate eviction. Remember, the heterosexuals conducting "erotic business" in the adjacent library lobby chairs merit only a stern talking-to (only if they continue to misbehave after a tongue lashing should they be banished). Shuman further recommends that a heterosexual couple engaged in consensual sex in an unlocked conference room be chased out of the building, interrupted by throat clearing, lectured, or detained for police[11]–quite a range of options.

Shuman suggests that heterosexual "miscreants" are to desist in thinking their actions a joke, but there is substantial jocularity in the tone of his text. Shuman does not recommend the same set of punishments for discovered heterosexual acts–no intimidation, no threatened surveillance, no lecture about the library not being a singles bar. Do you see the double standard at play? Librarians will tolerate heterosexual solicitation and public displays of affection but will freak out at the discovery or complaint of same sex solicitation and consensual liaisons.

Like ALA 1986 security meister John Morris who, quoting Edward Delph, recommends same sex cruisers be subject to a traumatic, "humiliating interrogation and browbeating in a formal setting,"[12] Shuman calls for library guards to intimidate same sex cruisers.[13] Delph calls for this ordeal to be "tempered with kindness;" Shuman cautions that his intimidation is to be executed with no "suggestion or threat of violence." But how, I wonder, might any authority accomplish intimidation or traumatic humiliation without some threat of physical contact or restraint? Most reasonable patrons would opt to leave the premises rather than endure such a fiasco. This trajectory of ALA-sponsored advice about same sex cruisers is discriminatory, uninformed, and abusive.

GAY PANIC

The suggestion that male-male solicitation warrants intimidation or trauma at the hands of library staff contains the same homophobic seed as the roundly criticized "gay panic" defense invoked in the trial of Matthew Shepard's killers. The "gay panic" defense was most famously deployed as an attempt to justify Aaron McKinney's murderous response to Shepard's alleged sexual come-on. The defense framed McKinney's violent reaction to be a normative, comprehensible psychological response. It was intended to garner sympathy for the murderer by characterizing McKinney's violent response to Shepard's sexual advance as a justifiable reaction, particularly in light of McKinney's "confusing" history of childhood sex with a "neighborhood bully" and later sexual experience with "a cousin."[14]

Imagine the impossibility of a similar "heterosexual panic" defense mirroring a "gay panic" defense–lesbians, say, making a "het panic" defense for offing rogues and gentlemen who make unwanted advances. (Imaginary lesbian: "But, Your Honor, he asked me to *dance,* and *ick,* it just set me off!") Imagine the outcry if an ALA publication advised library staff to intimidate, humiliate, interrogate, browbeat, or traumatize happy heterosexuals cruising for dates in library facilities. Somehow, though, the equally offensive and bizarre homosexist line of advice about punishing same sex cruisers continues to be merrily generated and presented as common sense, even by progressive library institutions embracing "diversity" and individual liberty. It is time to stop the madness.

SEX IN PUBLIC PLACES

Laud Humphreys' classic sociological study *Tearoom Trade: Impersonal Sex in Public Places,* suggested that happily or not, being propositioned against one's will or recruited into a homosexual encounter in public places is an unlikely occurrence.[15] Cruising is ritualized, with codes of behavior and participation which establish zones of privacy within public space and screen out the uninitiated and unsuspecting.[16] Frederick Desroches' 1990 study of Canadian police cases indicated that contrary to the myth of the homosexual or cruiser as predator, interactions between men in tearooms are not coercive, but consensual. They are not known to involve youths or children.[17]

Humphreys reported that 54% of the men frequenting tearooms were married and living with their wives, contrary to the assumption popular among library vice men that tearooms are entirely populated by self-identified gay men.[18] Desroches' update reported that 58% of those arrested in his sample were married. "These men do not seek homosexual contact as such, do not involve themselves in the gay community, and hide their deviance from family and others," he explains.[19] An unpublished 1992 report by the Los Angeles Gay and Lesbian Police Advisory Task Force estimated that the majority of men arrested in Griffith Park for "lewd conduct" were married, and Clive Moore's 1995 Australian study reported that the majority of cruisers Down Under are heterosexual, too.[20] Men of all genders and sexualities cruise. A whole lot of cruisers are straight, upstanding, All-American boys. The lines dividing gay, bisexual, and straight identities among same sex cruisers are not particularly well correlated with their sexual behavior.

"Gaydar" is the popular name for sexual software operable even by self-identified heterosexual men in search of sex with other men. Like most human perception systems, it can glitch when encountering fields of deception and misrepresentation. Two killers lured college student Matthew Shepard into a truck outside a bar in Laramie, Wyoming in 1997.[21] It is reasonable to suspect that suggestions regarding consensual sexual exchange were extended, entertained, or affirmed among these men. At some point, tragically, Shepard was deceived, misled, or betrayed. He paid for his desire with his life.

CRACKING DOWN ON PUBLIC SEX

In June 1985, Kenneth Zeller, a Toronto public school librarian, was killed by a gang of youths stalking an area of High Park where cruisers hung out.[22] Where are the vice cops and the vigilant citizens protecting Kenneth Zeller and Matthew Shepard from the likes of their killers? Pat Califia puts it this way, "Society will not tolerate the possibility that a straight man might be propositioned if he walks past a group of gay men on his way to use a public john. Yet society will tolerate the possibility that a gay man could be beaten or murdered if he walks past a group of heterosexuals."[23]

90 Men Seized in Boston Library for Solicitation as Homosexuals

> *Boston.* March 24. Undercover policemen have arrested 90 men who allegedly solicited homosexual in the Boston Public Library. The library asked police to crack down after it was swamped by complaints from men who said they had been approached by homosexuals. In 10 days, the police arrested a college professor, company executives, school teachers, students and doctoral candidates. Most were charged with open and gross lewdness, but a few were also accused of prostitution. The solicitation occurred in the men's room in the basement of the library's $23 million, five-year-old addition in Copley Square. "We had a tremendous number of complaints from our users," said John J. Doherty, the assistant director. "After a barrage of telephone calls to the director, the trustees said 'Let's get this situation cleaned up.'"
>
> *–New York Times*, 24 March 1978[24]

Despite the 1978 *New York Times* report from administrators that Boston Public Library was swamped with complaints from adult men[25] offensively approached by homosexuals, there is little evidence of that phenomenon in sociological studies of tearooms. Cruisers carve out privacy for sex within public spaces–behind stall doors, in locked rooms, in parked cars–well out of view by folks in the main reading room. Sex happens in sequestered niches where there is a reasonable expectation of privacy and where detection is not easy–behind a barrier, in an out-of-the-way, unlit, low-traffic place. When a non-participant enters the area, action stops until they leave.[26]

> Yet, there are many common sense things a cruiser can do not only to improve your odds of getting d***, but also to reduce the risks of arrest and of endangering a cruise spot by getting unwanted notice from non-cruisers.
>
> *–www.cruisingforsex.com*, December 2000[27]

Despite efforts to sequester, camouflaged cruising spots can be detected sometimes by non-participants, piquing prurient and repressive interests of non-participating observers. I know of no documented accounts involving unsuspecting heterosexual men, children, or families finding themselves the sexual targets of tearoom cruisers. (Families generally do not recreate in public men's rooms.) Rarely are crackdowns and surveillance of cruising areas prompted by casual sightings of actual sexual activity. It is rather that certain citizens and police object to the *idea* of men publicly soliciting sex with other men–in the park, at the mall, or in the library. They see evidence of the action and figure that the action is going on there *somewhere they can't see,* that it is bad, and that it must be stopped, its participants punished.

And oh, the ends to which police will go to put an end to it. So impossible is it for most non-participants to witness tearoom sex that police must deceive and entrap participants in order to arrest them for "public" sex. Police must artificially insert themselves into a private act, in other words, in order to make it "public," witnessed by an uninvited, deceiving third party. Police enter tearooms as decoys, displaying the consensual codes of sexual behavior, exhibiting themselves as tearoom participants. When the plainclothes (or dolled up) cops either successfully solicit sex or accept a solicitation, WHAM BAM! on go the cuffs.

The 103 men arrested and charged with felonies over a two-week period at the Boston Public Library in 1978 were entrapped by plainclothes police officers posing as men interested in sexual conversation or acts. Undercover cops in sting operations must encourage and even engage in the behavior they are allegedly attempting to punish and eradicate. Police entrapment is deceptive, aggressive, and often targeted at a perceived class or type of library patron. This "gay profiling," if you will, is as discriminatory and inappropriate as "racial profiling."[28]

Boston's *Gay Community News* reported a particularly egregious example of gay profiling in the April 1978 Boston Public Library arrests. "Kevin Jones (not a real name) . . . was in the library for a concert and had to use the bathroom. The same young man [plainclothes officer] approached him, asked if he was interested in "fooling around," and gestured for him to come closer. Kevin said that he wasn't interested. "But aren't you gay?" the young man asked. "Yes, but I'm not interested," Kevin answered. "You're under arrest." The charge was open and gross lewdness [a felony at the time].[29]

Sometimes instead of passing as cruisers to make a bust, police employ extraordinary surveillance techniques–planting hidden video cameras and microphones, positioning themselves behind wall or ceiling vents, employing long range night spy scopes. All this is to catch and document sexual activity that no other uninterested citizen, using everyday sensory mechanisms, could possibly detect. This was how the police entrapped 20 men in September 1953 in the Atlanta Public Library, at the request of library officials: vice squad members staked out a restroom behind a one-way mirror.[30] Surveillance techniques vary, but the extreme measures employed to detect "public" sex contradicts the notion that sex performed outside the home is visible and offensive to an unsuspecting, non-invasive, non-prurient public. Citizens offended by public sex usually have to exert themselves to find it. Public sex is generally uninteresting and unnoticeable to those without a mission to shut it down.

PRIVACY IN PUBLIC PLACES

The most common way institutions and police attempt to deter sex in public spaces is to eradicate zones of privacy established there. Librarians and police remove bathroom doors and barriers, flood areas with light, and increase patrols to make the space less private and more exposed to public or third party scrutiny. This razing of private space is itself hostile to the maintenance of sexual privacy by forcing private sexual behavior into exposed public space. Librarians also force the public exposure of private acts by scrutinizing access to men's rooms, say, by doling out a single restroom key often chained to a bulky, conspicuous piece of institutional refuse. One library I worked at handed out the men's room key with a paddle-ball paddle chained to it. We make the whole process of going to the men's room very public, artificially public. Why?

Americans obsess about sex with increasing, gratuitous zeal–a modern manifestation of traditional prudishness.[31] Visibility politics, the out-of-the-closet ethic born with the Gay Liberation Movement in the early 1970s, works to increase public awareness of non-normative sexual identities and behaviors. The Gay Rights Movement's right-to-privacy politics often run in counterpoint to Gay Lib's visibility politics. The right-to-privacy ethic attempts (without much success) to keep consensual sexuality unregulated within private spheres, while conceding and even advocating for state regulation of consensual sexuality in public and commercial settings. At the same time, a small, zealous sex-aware and sex-obsessed and largely right wing constituency conflate and confuse privately conducted sex in public spaces with public exposure and sexual public display. Sustained by a larger, indifferent majority, anti-sex zealots prompt the guardians of public space (here, librarians and police) to monitor and eradicate zones of privacy within public places. The zealots have rarely witnessed the sexual acts to which they object. Their assumption that it exists, and the articulation of this assumption to authorities in the form of a complaint is generally all it takes to spark a cruising crack down in public spaces.

SEXUAL IDENTITY vs. SEXUAL BEHAVIOR

Rather than fritter away time and money probing library space to expose consenting sexual behavior of any sort, librarians will do better to re-focus library safety policies regarding sexual activity. To do this, librarians must examine and revise core assumptions about the methods and meanings of identities and gender expressions vis-à-vis their public sexual behavior. A public sexual identity (gay, lesbian, bisexual, transsexual, straight) does not translate into public or private performance of any particular sexual act. Too often non-hetero sexual identities are at once sensationalized and stigmatized, with the result that all staff eyes train on the Queer who walks in merely to browse the cook books. Consider these separate statements describing a library patron from a 1988 publication:

> He *did* make a ridiculous sight, this large man mimicking the voice and movements of a woman. Some staff believed he was a male prostitute, but he never acted such overtly in the library.

At the very least, obvious transvestites such as N.D. are nuisances in the library. They distract genuine patrons by calling attention to themselves, and they create disturbances over which bathroom to use.

When the police were called, they warned library employees that the subject was believed to have AIDS.[32]

The problems with this characterization are legion. Primary among them are the assumptions that "obvious transvestites" are inherently absurd, unreal, bothersome, and distracting for others. It assumes that "obvious" transgender folk are likely to seek sex for money and have AIDS, and because of their abnormality, they inherently create a stir among readers for which they are justifiably to blame. This piece composed during the mid-1980s reflects the particular AIDS panic of its day. Sadly, many of these hateful, dubious, and repulsive assumptions endure.

Here is a more equitable example of ALA-sponsored advice about library security, shifting focus from suspect classes of patrons to behaviors exhibited by any of patron:

People who cause problems in our facility come from every imaginable social group. What we need to do . . . is to focus on the behavior. You're also protecting yourself against legal action that way . . . If you look at a group as the problem . . . you may be accused of discriminating. As long as you've decided that a certain type of behavior isn't appropriate in your facility and you treat everyone who exhibits that behavior equally, you're going to be legally on fair ground, ethically, on fair ground and you're going to be able to maintain a reasonable standard of behavior in your facility.

–Rachel MacLachlan, Director of Security,
San Francisco Public Library, 1994.[33]

WHAT LIBRARIANS ARE SUPPOSED TO DO . . .

Librarians, and police in service of them, must be concerned with keeping libraries clean, safe, and well organized. We are obliged to create and maintain an environment where employees treat all patrons with respect for privacy, dignity, and agency. This requires particular attention for the safety of gay, lesbian, bisexual, and transgender patrons and other marginalized populations. Sexually identified people are likely to suffer from excessive social and institutional surveillance and suspicion; librarians must guard against and seek to correct that. Under no circumstances should library security staff detain, humiliate, browbeat, or otherwise harass any library patron accused of issuing an isolated, harmless signal or glance to another patron. No consensual sex act, conducted with a reasonable expectation of privacy sequestered in a public place, need be cause for arrest, detention, public exposure, humiliation, or tongue-lashing. Librarians should respond to sexually offended men using the standards applied to complaints from sexually offended women. We must recognize and diffuse over-zealous, hyper-fearful complaints about the possibilities of gay sex in public spaces, measuring them judiciously by our standards for action regarding heterosexual activity. We must understand that private, consensual, sexual acts, can and do occur in public places–*all the time*–whether we approve or not. We must recognize the inevitable, largely happy truth that libraries host a range of overt public and covert private sexual encounters. We can make sure our library collections and programs serve to educate a sexually curious and active user population. We must align library "problem patron" policies with our professional goals to provide equal treatment and meaningful service for all library patrons.

REFERENCES

1. John Rechy, *City of Night*. New York: Grove Press, 1963. p. 60.

2. www.cruisingforsex.com was recently ranked in the top 1.2% of all Web sites for traffic by webmostlinked.com with over 1,500,000 visitors monthly according to Web Trends. Reprinted with expressed permission from <www.cruisingforsex.com>.

3. Bruce A. Shuman. *Library Security and Safety Handbook: Prevention, Policies, and Procedures*. Chicago: American Library Association, 1999. p. 90.

4. With gender and sexuality unspecified, one assumes this author means this is an opposite sex couple.

5. Shuman, p. 90.

6. Ibid.

7. Ibid.

8. Ibid.

9. Shuman, p. 91.

10. Ibid.

11. Ibid.

12. "Use the occasion of detecting persons in overt homosexual activity to spread the word about the library's hostility to this abuse of the facility. This is done through a humiliating interrogation and browbeating in a formal setting, like a security office. The interrogation is traumatic, purposefully, but tempered with kindness. No arrest is made. The process is intended to get the word out to the homosexual community that the library is determined to deny them the use and abuse of the building for assignations and casual homosexual liaisons." Edward W. Delph. 1980. "Preventing Public Sex in Library Settings," *Library & Archival Security* 3 (2): 17-26 quoted in John Morris, *The Library Disaster Preparedness Handbook.* Chicago: American Library Association, 1986, p. 12.

13. Shuman, p. 91.

14. Connolly, Catherine. "Matthew's Murderers' Defense." *The Gay & Lesbian Review Worldwide* 8 (1): 22-26.

15. Humphreys, Laud. 1975. *Tearoom Trade: Impersonal Sex in Public Places.* Enlarged ed. (1st ed., 1970). Hawthorne, NY: Aldine de Gruyter. A "tearoom" is slang for a same-sex cruising area.

16. Humphreys, p. 47. Rule #3, Never force your intentions on anyone. Humphreys, p. 102. All indications of this investigation are that recruitment into homosexual activity is a rare phenomenon.

17. Desroches, Frederick J. 1990. "Tearoom Trade: A Research Update." *Qualitative Sociology* 13 (1): 39-61.

18. Humphreys, p. 105.

19. Desroches, p. 47.

20. Nardi, Peter M. "Reclaiming the Importance of Laud Humphreys' Tearoom Trade: Impersonal Sex in Public Places." In *Public Sex/Gay Space.* 1999. New York: Columbia University Press. 23-27. (p. 26).

21. Humphreys defined "trade" in various ways, e.g., "men who make themselves available for acts of fellatio but who, regarding themselves as 'straight,' refuse to reciprocate in the sexual act." p. 108. Pittsburgh, PA: Cleis Press, 1994.

22. "5 Young Toronto Killers of Homosexual Librarian Released on Day Parole." *Toronto Star.* 8 July 1988, p. A3.

23. Califia, Pat. Public Sex (1982). In *Public Sex: The Culture of Radical Sex.* Pittsburgh, PA: Cleis Press, 1994. p. 77-8.

24. *New York Times*, 24 March 1978.

25. *The Times* here assumes that all cruisers are preying homosexuals and that all complainants are heterosexuals.

26. Humphreys, p. 79.

27. Asterisks added. Reprinted with expressed permission of <www.cruisingforsex. com>.

28. The police practice of questioning and harassing people with non-white racial and ethnic characteristics more frequently than those with white characteristics.

29. Bill, David. "Boston Public Library Continues Crackdown." *Gay Community News.* 1 April 1978, p. 1.

30. Howard, John. "The Library, the Park, and the Pervert: Public Space and Homosexual Encounter in Post-World War II Atlanta." *Radical History Review* 62 (1995): 166-87.

31. See Kyle, Garland Richard. 1992. "Public Sex, Public Morality." *The Journal of Sex Research* 29 (2): 291-3.

32. Salter, Charles A. and Jeffrey L. Salter, eds. *On the Frontlines: Coping with the Library's Problem Patrons.* Englewood, CO: Libraries Unlimited, 1988. p. 60-2.

33. Rachel MacLachlan, Director of Security, San Francisco Public Library. *Be Prepared: Security and Your Library.* American Library Association. Video. Library Video Network, producer. 1994. 35 minutes.

The Difficult Library Patron:
A Selective Survey of the Current Literature

Bernice Redfern

SUMMARY. The issue of the difficult library patron has been of grow-ing concern to the library community in the last decade. A number of monographs and journal articles have been published on this topic in re-cent years. This article surveys the literature concerning the problem li-brary user including the homeless, the de-institutionalized, the mentally ill, and angry/frustrated patrons. It includes literature which discusses techniques for empowering front-line employees in handling various user behaviors and responding to patron problems. *[Article copies avail-able for a fee from The Haworth Document Delivery Service: 1-800-HAWORTH. E-mail address: <getinfo@haworthpressinc.com> Website: <http://www. HaworthPress.com> © 2002 by The Haworth Press, Inc. All rights reserved.]*

KEYWORDS. Difficult patrons, homeless, angry patrons

INTRODUCTION

The issue of the difficult or problem library patron has been of grow-ing concern to the library community in recent years. A number of monographs and periodical articles have been published on the topic.

Bernice Redfern is Reference Librarian, Clark Library, San Jose State University, San Jose, CA 95192-0028 (E-mail: bredfern@email.sjsu.edu).

[Haworth co-indexing entry note]: "The Difficult Library Patron: A Selective Survey of the Current Liter-ature." Redfern, Bernice. Co-published simultaneously in *The Reference Librarian* (The Haworth Informa-tion Press, an imprint of The Haworth Press, Inc.) No. 75/76, 2002, pp. 105-113; and: *Helping the Difficult Library Patron: New Approaches to Examining and Resolving a Long-Standing and Ongoing Problem* (ed: Kwasi Sarkodie-Mensah) The Haworth Information Press, an imprint of The Haworth Press, Inc., 2002, pp. 105-113. Single or multiple copies of this article are available for a fee from The Haworth Document De-livery Service [1-800-HAWORTH, 9:00 a.m. - 5:00 p.m. (EST). E-mail address: getinfo@haworthpressinc. com].

© 2002 by The Haworth Press, Inc. All rights reserved.

This article will selectively survey the current literature on the difficult or problem library patron such as the mentally ill, the homeless, and angry/frustrated patrons. It will not include literature which discusses crime or violence in libraries. It will focus on publications of the last decade only.

Most library staff are not prepared by their formal education to cope in situations involving difficult patron encounters. The purpose of this essay is to provide front line staff with references to recent articles and books which will empower them in responding to patron concerns and problems.

GENERAL LITERATURE

Disruptive patron concerns are common to both public and academic libraries. Large academic libraries in urban or inner city locations may be especially vulnerable. Incidents may range in importance from mildly irate users to violent outbursts by mentally deranged persons. Here are some sources which provide good overviews of various types of problem patron concerns.

Ann Curry in "Managing the Problem Patron" emphasizes the importance of staff training.[1] She has designed a workshop on the problem patron issue. She stresses that it is important to clarify the rights of both staff members and those of library users. She uses role-playing and case studies to make clear the difference between staff assertiveness and staff unhelpfulness. She outlines both the users' rights and the rights of staff members. She includes many practical tips such as a section on telephone skills and multicultural communication techniques.

Beth McNeil and Denise Johnson in *Patron Behavior in Libraries: A Handbook of Positive Approaches to Negative Situations* discuss various categories of problem patrons such as the homeless, mentally ill, older adults, and the de-institutionalized among others.[2] Practical examples of active listening responses to typical frustrated patron scenarios are given. An entire chapter discusses role playing, customer care training, assertiveness training and other techniques for defusing the angry patron.

"The Difficult Patron Situation: A Window of Opportunity to Improve Library Service"[3] discusses the situation from the historical perspective and includes an overview of the various types of problem patrons found in libraries. It also has a discussion of problems caused by inappropriate use of technology such as cell phones, pagers, loud key-ing of laptop computers and so forth. The author recommends that library administrators empower library staff to override bad rules to solve patron problems. He considers patron complaints and frustrations as a way of improving library service.

Bruce A. Shuman's book, *Library Security and Safety Handbook: Prevention, Policies, and Procedures*, is a good overview of many library security issues including the homeless, the mentally ill, sexual behavior in libraries, and electronic security issues including hackers and viruses in library computing systems.[4] Shuman has an entire chapter on "Problem Behaviors in Libraries," and he includes a section of brief case studies with recommendations for each case. He advocates a written behavior policy which will provide guidelines for managing unacceptable behavior in libraries.

Management of Library Security; a SPEC Kit compiled by George J. Soete and Glen Zimmerman has representative policies and procedures for various problem patron situations including persons who wish to monopolize the time of library staff, persons suspected of being under the influence of alcohol and/or drugs, sex offenders, aberrant behavior/emotionally disturbed persons, telephone harassment, etc.[5] The authors offer practical solutions and advice to typical problem patron situations. They have a section of sample policy manuals for various types of libraries, including policies for misuse of electronic resources.

Safe at Work? Library Security and Safety Issues is a comprehensive bibliography which includes sections on problem patrons, sexual harassment, workplace violence, collection and premise security, computer and technology security and staff wellness issues.[6] It has a substantial number of references to non-library science literature as well.

It Comes with the Territory: Handling Problem Situations in Libraries by Anne M. Turner is primarily focused on the public library.[7] She discusses situations ranging from latchkey children to sexual deviates and mentally disabled street people. Turner uses the term "street people" rather than homeless. She also includes a discussion about how to handle situations with angry patrons. She includes a section of tips for front desk staff on uncivil behaviors to avoid when interacting with the public. A large appendix section has sample policies for various problem situations in libraries.

LIBRARY POLICIES

As noted in some of the above references, a good deal of the literature on the problem patron issue focuses on the need for libraries to establish written policies and procedures which can be referred to if needed. Patricia Bangs, in "When Bad Things Happen in Good Libraries: Staff Tools for the 90s and Beyond," describes how a large suburban library system developed an effective set of procedures and a training module consisting of a series of workshops to help staff cope with a broad range of patron problems/behavior.[8]

Stuart Comstock-Guy in "Disruptive Behavior: Protecting People, Protecting Rights," recommends the establishment of a code of conduct which outlines acceptable behavior in libraries, but will not limit the civil rights of users.[9]

College and university libraries are also advised to have behavior policies or guidelines in place. An article by Linda A. Morrissett, "Developing and Implementing a Behavior Policy for an Academic Library," includes examples of such policies and outlines the need for and benefits of these policies.[10]

"Proactive Problem Patron Preparedness" by Sheryl Owens advocates that all libraries take a proactive approach to problem patrons by having a policy and/or procedure manual with patron guidelines and a building usage statement.[11] She adds that library administration must support the use of such guidelines.

"Proposed Guidelines for the Development of Policies Regarding User Behavior and Library Usage"[12] sets forth the guidelines, based on constitutional principles, recommended by the Intellectual Freedom Committee of the American Library Association.

HOMELESS AND MENTALLY ILL

A large part of the problem patron literature includes citations about the homeless in libraries. The presence of homeless people and the mentally ill in libraries has been an issue of growing concern to the library profession in the last decade. Some of the general sources already mentioned include sections on this issue. Here are some references to sources which focus directly on the issue. "Down and Out in the Reading Room: The Homeless in the Public Library" by Bruce A. Shuman outlines the causes of homelessness and provides a general overview of the challenges posed for the public library.[13] Shuman makes the point that even though the homeless are often classified as problem patrons, not all homeless people are problem patrons. He also asserts that as citizens and former taxpayers, there is no reason why they should be treated differently from other library users. A recent article by Julie

Murphy addresses some of the complex issues surrounding the home-less/mentally ill in libraries.[14] Her paper juxtaposes the rights of the homeless/mentally ill versus the rights of the staff and other library patrons. She asserts that the homeless/mentally ill population deserves the same rights and respect as any other special group of patrons such as gays/lesbians or the elderly. This article looks at the issues from both sides of the desk and also includes a good review of the relevant literature. "The Homeless and the Public Library" by Karen Venturella describes some proactive efforts taken by public libraries to provide services for the homeless population.[15] She asserts that homeless patrons should not be regarded as "problem patrons." She maintains that library staff can be trained to interact sensitively with this population of library users.

Patrons who are mentally ill often cause the most concern and anxiety for library staff. These users may be quite harmless, yet their aberrant behavior can range from a mild nuisance to very stressful incidents in which security guards or police must be called. Charles A. Salter and Jeffrey L. Salter provide a good introduction and overview to problems involving the mentally ill in libraries.[16] They include descriptions and causes of the various types of mental illnesses, as well as a section on how to confront a mentally ill patron who may become disruptive. Many of the mentally ill population are de-institutionalized persons living in group homes. Fay Zipkowitz describes how public libraries can recognize and respond to the special needs of de-institutionalized patrons.[17] Thomas E. Hecker asserts that patrons with mental disorders should be treated as patrons with disabilities who should be included under the Americans with Disabilities Act.[18] He advocates a certain amount of tolerance for the behavior of mentally ill patrons. An article by Michael Cart outlines many of the social problems which in recent years have transformed the library from a sanctuary to a shelter.[19] He concludes that the public library must be a center for diverse communities, and it can serve a new role of social cohesion during a time when other social institutions are decaying.

ANGRY PATRONS

Of growing concern to library employees who staff the front desks in libraries across the country is the patron who is considered difficult for a number of reasons other than mental illness, including expressing anger at library policies or generally being rude, uncivil or demanding. An encounter of this type may not disrupt library service as would a major incident with a mentally ill patron, but it does increase the stress level of the public service staff. Library literature of the last decade is replete with books and articles discussing the best techniques for interacting with this type of difficult library user. Many of these sources emphasize various communication techniques such as active listening, assertiveness training and an improved staff service approach.

A brief article by Jean Engler is aimed at paraprofessionals, and outlines some practical approaches to interacting with irate library users such as "switch the focus away from yourself" and concentrate on accomplishing the goal of the interaction.[20] A more in depth article by Rhea Rubin, "Anger in the Library: Defusing Angry Patrons at the Reference Desk (and Elsewhere)," gives concrete practical techniques for encounters with difficult library patrons. She maintains that rudeness, anger and violence are on the rise in society as a whole and that public places such as libraries are experiencing an increase in this type of behavior as a consequence.[21] Rubin is an authority in the field and she has given numerous workshops on the topic of defusing angry patrons. Her recently-published book on the topic, *Defusing the Angry Patron: A How-to-Do-It Manual for Librarians and Paraprofessionals*[22] is designed for library staff who are stressed from interacting with angry patrons and may need to take control of the situation. Her emphasis throughout the book is getting beyond the behavior and solving the patron's problem. She offers various practical techniques for calming upset patrons including active, sympathetic listening, treating all patrons with respect, and using deep breathing. Each chapter concludes with practical exercises to help library staff practice her suggestions. A brief article by Nicolle Steffen summarizes the active listening and problem solving techniques recommended by Rubin.[23]

Nathan Smith and Irene Addams in "Using Active Listening to Deal with Patron Problems" recommend librarians use active listening to acknowledge how the patron feels, but at the same time, not take ownership of the patron's personal problem.[24] This technique helps prevent a defensive reaction on the part of reference desk staff. Specific examples of active listening and non-active listening for several hypothetical situations are given.

Serving the Difficult Customer: A How-To-Do-It Manual for Library Staff by Kitty Smith looks at the difficult patron situation from a different perspective: one that has front line staff take responsibility for their attitudes and behavior during interactions with potentially difficult patron encounters.[25] Smith says the goal is to use assertive understanding and shared problem solving to assist the patron. The focus of this book is on communication rather than larger social problems such as homelessness, latchkey children, or the mentally ill in libraries. Smith recommends strategies and tactics staff at various levels can use to empower themselves in potentially difficult situations. Like Rubin, she includes an entire chapter on understanding anger. She also describes various personality types such as chronic complainers and offers suggestions for interacting with them at public service desks.

Communicating Professionally: A How-to-Do-It Manual for Librarians[26] has a section on problem patrons and awkward customers, which includes a discussion of unlawful, dangerous, disruptive and inappropriate behavior. It also has a section on coping with special situations such as disabled users, language and speech barriers to effective communication, problems encountered in cross-cultural communication situations, and handling complaints.

Dealing with Difficult People in the Library by Mark R. Willis also emphasizes communication skills in dealing with difficult patrons.[27] The author has a degree in communication and his work assignment includes handling patron complaints and helping with difficult situations at a public library. He includes an entire chapter on the skill of listening. He also includes a section on skills which can be used to control a difficult patron situation such as looking at the situation from the patron's point of view, listening, and acknowledging the patron's feelings, apologizing if the library is in error, and focusing on the issue at hand. Another chapter discusses how to turn complainers into happy customers.

CONCLUSION

Most library employees are not prepared by their education or training to handle the wide range of difficult patron behaviors found in twenty-first century libraries. The widespread use of new technology in today's libraries has added to the situation. This article has presented an overview of selected recent literature on the subject. It has not included literature on personal safety in libraries, workplace violence, or crime in libraries on which much has been published. Included in this paper are books and articles which provide practical tips and techniques for front line staff to use in their day-to-day work at public service desks.

REFERENCES

1. Curry, Ann. "Managing the Problem Patron." *Public Libraries* 35 (May/June 1996): 181-188.

2. McNeil, Beth and Denise Johnson. *Patron Behavior in Libraries: A Handbook of Positive Approaches to Negative Situations*. Chicago: American Library Association, 1996.

3. Sarkodie-Mensah, Kwasi. "The Difficult Patron Situation: A Window of Opportunity to Improve Library Service." *Catholic Library World* 70, no. 3 (March 2000): 159-167.

4. Shuman, Bruce A. *Library Security and Safety Handbook: Prevention, Policies, and Procedures*. Chicago: American Library Association, 1999.

5. Soete, George J. and Glen Zimmerman, Compilers. *Management of Library Security; a SPEC Kit*. Washington D.C.: Association of Research Libraries, 1999.

6. Switzer, Teri R. *Safe at Work? Library Security and Safety Issues*. Lanham, Maryland: Scarecrow Press, 1999.

7. Turner, Anne M. *It Comes with the Territory: Handling Problem Situations in Libraries*. Jefferson, North Carolina: McFarland, 1993.

8. Bangs, Patricia. "When Bad Things Happen in Good Libraries: Staff Tools for the 90s and Beyond." *Public Libraries* 37, no. 3 (May/June 1998): 196-199.

9. Comstock-Guy, Stuart. "Disruptive Behavior: Protecting People, Protecting Rights." *Wilson Library Bulletin* 69, no. 6 (February 1995): 33-35.

10. Morrissett, Linda A. "Developing and Implementing a Behavior Policy for an Academic Library." *College and Undergraduate Libraries* 1, no.2 (1994): 71-91.

11. Owens, Sheryl. "Proactive Problem Patron Preparedness." *Library and Archival Security* 12, no. 2 (1994): 11-23.

12. "Proposed Guidelines for the Development of Policies Regarding User Behavior and Library Usage." *Newsletter on intellectual freedom.* v.41 (September 1992): 135-136.

13. Shuman, Bruce A. "Down and Out in the Reading Room: The Homeless in the Public Library," in *Patron Behavior in Libraries: A Handbook of Positive Approaches to Negative Situations*, edited by B. McNeil and D. J. Johnson. Chicago: American Library Association, 1996, pp. 3-17.

14. Murphy, Julie. "When the Rights of the Many Outweigh the Rights of the Few: The 'Legitimate' versus the Homeless Patron in the Public Library." *Current Studies in Librarianship* 23, no.1-2 (Fall 1999): 50-60.

15. Venturella, Karen M. "The Homeless and Public Library," in *Alternative Library Literature*. Jefferson, North Carolina: McFarland and Co., 1992, pp. 117-122.

16. Salter, Charles A. and Jeffrey L.Salter. "Mentally Ill Patrons," In *Patron Behavior in Libraries: A Handbook of Positive Approaches to Negative Situations*, edited by Beth McNeil and Denise J. Johnson. Chicago: American Library Association, 1996, pp. 18-43.

17. Zipkowitz, Fay. "Deinstitutionalized and Disabled Patrons: Opportunities and Solutions," In *Patron Behavior in Libraries: A Handbook of Positive Approaches to Negative Situations*, edited by Beth McNeil and Denise J. Johnson. Chicago: American Library Association, 1996, pp. 65-74.

18. Hecker, Thomas E. "Patrons with Disabilities or Problem Patrons: Which Model Should Librarians Apply to People with Mental Illness?" *The Reference Librarian* no. 53 (1996): 5-12.

19. Cart, Michael. "Here There Be Sanctuary: The Public Library as Refuge and Retreat." *Public Library Quarterly* 12, no. 4 (1992): 5-23.

20. Engler, Jean. "A Matter of Focus: Customer Service to Difficult Patrons." *Library Mosaics* 3 (July/August 1992): 15.

21. Rubin, Joyce R. "Anger in the Library: Defusing Angry Patrons at the Reference Desk (and Elsewhere)." *The Reference Librarian* no. 31 (1990): 39-51.

22. Rubin, Joyce R. *Defusing the Angry Patron: A How-To-Do-It Manual for Librarians and Paraprofessionals*. New York: Neal-Shuman, 2000. See also Rubin, Joyce R. "Defusing the Angry Patron." *Library Mosaics* 11, no.3 (May/June 2000): 14-15.

23. Steffen, Nicolle. "Rising to the Occasion: Working with Angry People at the Reference Desk." *Colorado Libraries*. 23, no. 2 (Summer 2000): 11-13.

24. Smith, Nathan and Irene Addams. "Using Active Listening to Deal with Problem Patrons." *Public Libraries* 30 (July/August 1991): 236-239.

25. Smith, Kitty. *Serving the Difficult Customer: A How-To-Do-It Manual for Library Staff*. New York: Neal-Schuman Publishers, Inc., 1993.

26. Ross, Catherine S. and Patricia Dewdney. *Communicating Professionally: A How-to-Do-It Manual for Librarians*. 2nd ed. New York: Neal-Schuman Publishers, 1998.

27. Willis, Mark R. *Dealing with Difficult People in the Library*. Chicago: American Library Association, 1999.

THE PROBLEM PATRON
IN THE ELECTRONIC AGE

Do We Really Have an Internet Problem? Statistics, Credibility and Issues Concerning Public Internet Access in Academic Libraries

Charlotte Cubbage

SUMMARY. Due to the nature of the Internet, a disconnect exists between observed and actual usage in libraries. A variety of problems may arise surrounding Internet access in academic settings. However, the speed with which transactions occur, the privacy issues involved, and the

Charlotte Cubbage is Head, General Information Center and the Reserve Departments, Northwestern University Main Library, 1935 Sheridan Road, Evanston, IL 60208 (E-mail: c-cubbage@northwestern.edu).
Robert Trautvetter, a technical manager for Northwestern Library's Network User Support Services, provided invaluable technical assistance in adapting LittleBrother statistics to Excel spreadsheets, and in creating formulas to run statistical reports.

[Haworth co-indexing entry note]: "Do We Really Have an Internet Problem? Statistics, Credibility and Issues Concerning Public Internet Access in Academic Libraries." Cubbage, Charlotte. Co-published simultaneously in *The Reference Librarian* (The Haworth Information Press, an imprint of The Haworth Press, Inc.) No. 75/76, 2002, pp. 115-127; and: *Helping the Difficult Library Patron: New Approaches to Examining and Resolving a Long-Standing and Ongoing Problem* (ed: Kwasi Sarkodie-Mensah) The Haworth Information Press, an imprint of The Haworth Press, Inc., 2002, pp. 115-127. Single or multiple copies of this article are available for a fee from The Haworth Document Delivery Service [1-800-HAWORTH, 9:00 a.m. - 5:00 p.m. (EST). E-mail address: getinfo@haworthpressinc.com].

© 2002 by The Haworth Press, Inc. All rights reserved.

115

vast amounts of information and services available make it impossible to assess the extent of any problem. With Internet tracking software, librarians may acquire data that will assist them in tracking problems, and in assessing user Internet behavior. This article reports on a study conducted with LittleBrother software at Northwestern University Main Library's General Information Center. *[Article copies available for a fee from The Haworth Document Delivery Service: 1-800-HAWORTH. E-mail address: <getinfo@haworthpressinc.com> Website: <http://www.HaworthPress.com> © 2002 by The Haworth Press, Inc. All rights reserved.]*

KEYWORDS. Academic libraries, Internet access, Internet tracking software, LittleBrother software, problem patrons

INTRODUCTION

"Home-Front Horror Tales for Would-Be Public Internet Access Providers" proclaims the title of a 1998 *American Libraries* article (Nagler 40). If you work in a service area that provides Internet access to the public you probably have a few horror stories of your own. A search of the literature reveals that most articles grappling with Internet "problem patrons" focus on public libraries. In the past two years, however, a few voices from academic libraries have joined the discussion. Definitions of what constitute "problems" with public Internet machines vary somewhat by library type, but in the directions you would expect given different clienteles. However, you will not find statistics that provide numerical data on how prevalent any type of Internet activity is from public access library computers. Questions of what qualifies as an abuse of Internet privileges aside, libraries need to know more about the way patrons use the Internet to formulate use policies adequately.

In an attempt to examine the type of use public-access research machines receive at Northwestern University's Main Library, staff in the General Information Center ran an Internet tracking software on 32 PCs throughout the spring quarter of 2000. Kansmen Corporation's Little-Brother, a software generally employed by businesses to track their employee Internet use, produces reports of every Web site visited, including the URL, the time each transaction occurred and how long the patrons stayed at each site. Because Northwestern requires no patron authentication at its workstations, the study was completely anonymous. The software does not report on activity within Web sites, which adds to the protection of patron privacy rights.

THE PROBLEMS

Internet access opened a Pandora's box of censorship dilemmas for the nation's libraries. Academic libraries hold a somewhat specialized niche in the discussion thanks to their audiences and purposes. Institutions of higher education tend to be bastions of freedom of expression, and their libraries traditionally view all information as potential grist for research. In general, academic libraries serve patrons who have reached adult status. These factors distance academic libraries from the arena of debate that receives the most publicity: Internet access of pornographic materials by minors. However, the growing availability of Internet access in academic libraries has raised related problems and other issues of importance.

Kathleen Weessies and Barbara Wales conducted a study on Internet policies in mid-sized academic libraries, and identified some problem areas: the demand for workstations exceeds the supply; patrons monopolize research stations for non-research activities such as e-mail, chat rooms and games (33-41). Deborah Carver mentions other concerns for academic libraries in an article for OLA Quarterly. She points out that the delivery mechanism of computers may cut into personal boundaries in a way that print did not. For example, students cognizant of the inappropriateness of passing out racist literature on campus could utilize the library's public machines to send hate e-mail or to disseminate ideas offensive to other students. Carver also notes that there is a difference in a patron looking at pornographic material in a book or magazine and viewing the same materials on a high-definition monitor easily seen by others in a public area (11-12). Weessies and Wales focus on the individual access problems, Carver on the potential for activities conducted on public machines to impinge on the rights of others. Both types of problems stem from libraries installing a new information tool in their public areas that provide types of information and services that libraries never offered before. Our wondrous electronic resources come packaged with the loss of control over the services and the content of the information we provide.

This loss of control leads to a new problem, but one that occurs frequently in academic libraries–the patrons who, with no thought to the quality of their information resources, conduct their electronic research on unvetted Web sites. Librarians used to select the materials available in their libraries. We exercised quality control and made judgment calls based on the perceived needs of our clientele. Now we spend enormous amounts of money to provide electronic access to scholarly journals and major newspapers, only to have students focus their research on materials they happen upon surfing from page to page.

ACCESS ISSUES

Academic libraries provide public computers so that patrons may conduct research. We must also deal with the side effects of the Internet as a personal communications conduit, the Internet as shopping mall, the Internet as entertainment provider. Growing numbers of patrons tie up the computers for hours while they visit chat rooms, send instant messages, play games and listen to music.

Before publishers moved information sources onto the Web students and faculty might grumble if a local businessman or high school student monopolized a research tool. In general, academic libraries worked out ways and means to share print information resources. Internet research tools offer the potential (licensing issues aside) for many patrons to use the same resource simultaneously. However, we must now ensure that patrons have adequate access to Internet machines to use the growing number of purchased library materials available only through the Web, as well as the valuable information that can be gleaned for free. Public expectations, fueled by the proliferation of electronic publishing and Internet hype, drive libraries to emphasize full-text online resources. In a paradoxical situation, librarians purchase Internet resources to broaden access to library materials beyond the library walls, only to be faced with patrons within the library who cannot find an Internet machine available to them.

If an academic library decides to implement an Internet usage policy, the question of what constitutes legitimate research use becomes sticky. Web sites with games stand out visually and are almost always a form of entertainment, making them a possible candidate for banning. Prohibiting chat rooms, instant messaging or e-mail moves into a gray area. Many professors employ e-mail and instant messaging as communication tools for courses. Northwestern University, for example, actively promotes the use of Blackboard CourseInfo. Even libraries have begun to experiment with online reference services using chat room software.

For academic libraries open to the general public the issue becomes complicated when students and faculty find that they cannot conduct library research because a patron unaffiliated with the institution has staked out a machine for an extended chat session.

Possible solutions include time limits on machine usage, requiring the display of ID cards, employing patron authentication software on a majority of public machines, and written policies setting guidelines for public-access computers. Barbara Jones presents excellent arguments encouraging libraries to write Internet access policies in her book *Libraries, Access, and Intellectual Freedom: Developing Policies for Public and Academic Libraries*. She also provides sections that focus on academic libraries and a guide to writing a variety of policies.

NORTHWESTERN UNIVERSITY LIBRARY'S GENERAL INFORMATION CENTER

Northwestern University Main Library's General Information Center contains 32 personal computers with unlimited Ethernet access to the Internet. The computers sit in a well-lighted, large open space at the library's entrance. From 8:30 a.m. to 5 p.m. Monday through Friday and Saturday from 8:30 to noon the public may enter the library. During the non-public access hours patrons must show a Northwestern ID, or an ID from a university belonging to the Committee on Institutional Cooperation (including the University of Illinois, University of Chicago and 9 other Midwestern universities), or an Infopass (issued by other Chicago-area libraries to patrons who require access to Northwestern's libraries for research purposes) to enter. No one is asked to leave when the library closes to the general public.

In the autumn of 1999 the library instituted a policy of prohibiting game playing on library computers. The policy states:

> These workstations are provided to support the academic and research mission of Northwestern University. The primary purpose of the library's workstations is to allow library users to access library catalogs, research databases, and other resources relevant to their academic and research needs. These workstations are not for game playing.

The library instituted the policy when it became obvious that library patrons tied up General Information Center computers literally all hours the library was open playing games on the Internet. This policy is posted by all the General Information Center computers. However, it requires staff intervention to be enforced. Staff may not notice game playing, or may not want to confront a patron playing games.

Similarly, the General Information Center provides 14 lower-end computers specifically for e-mail users (with both Telnet and Internet access), as a method to free the 32 research computers for academic use. The e-mail machines do receive regular use, but patrons also routinely use the research computers to access their Internet e-mail accounts. Staff will only ask patrons to move to the e-mail machines if all the computers are in use and other patrons in the General Information Center require access to a research computer.

LittleBrother SOFTWARE

The statistics for this paper were gathered by Kansmen Corporation's LittleBrother software, an Internet tracking service primarily designed to allow businesses to assess their employee Internet usage. Northwestern University Library's General Information Center installed LittleBrother on its 32 personal computers for the purposes of gathering Internet usage information. None of the information is tied in any way to individuals as no authentication is required at public terminals. Patrons never see LittleBrother, and have no knowledge that the library tracks Web site usage. LittleBrother runs under Windows NT and keeps track of WWW, FTP and newsgroup usage by site, protocol, bytes transferred, time-of-day and time spent in each site.

By analyzing use patterns we know how much time patrons spend accessing database and library research materials versus time spent in chat rooms, accessing e-mail and viewing pornography. That data can be used to write Internet use policies, and also to form an accurate picture of the extent of problematic Internet use at public research computers.

Other Internet tracking software exists. The library's technical support department chose LittleBrother because it provides the type of information we want, runs invisibly, and because it integrates reasonably well with Northwestern's network environment.

WEB STATISTICS

In a public setting such as the General Information Center the LittleBrother software produces vast amounts of data. Because the software was not designed with libraries in mind, it helps to drop the statistics into spreadsheets so that you can manipulate the numbers to answer a variety of questions. The types of problems a library experiences would dictate the types of analysis that would be helpful.

For the purposes of this paper we focused on two separate perceived problem areas: patrons who monopolize research machines for non-research purposes; and our patron usage of unevaluated web pages instead of the high-quality research databases available (for a study that focuses on problems with student use of the Internet as a research tool, see the article by Deborah Grimes and Carl Boenig: "Worries with the Web: A Look at Student Use of Web Resources"). In both cases library staff perceive varying degrees of problems. The statistics provided by LittleBrother offer some answers to the first problem, and some guidance for the second.

WEB SITES ACCESSED

In the time period covered, April 3, 2000 to June 11, 2000, the General Information Center was open 1,037 hours. Table One shows the vast number of Web pages visited. For this analysis we also ran reports each week on the top 50 Web sites visited, in terms of the amount of time spent in individual Web pages, using those sites to generate the data in Table Two. Four of the items in Table Two are aggregate figures for all e-mail servers, banner ads, commercial databases and chat rooms that appeared in the list of top 50 sites. Table One must be taken into account when analyzing the data in Table Two, as it illustrates the predominant type of use the machines receive–accessing Web pages with commercial domain, or .com, designations. Two other factors skew the figures in Table Two. Patrons frequently leave the library catalog Web page open, and the connection does not time out for three minutes. Also, the browser's "home" button defaults to the library's homepage. Both factors artificially raise the usage numbers for those pages.

The General Information Center machines receive heavy use, in terms of time spent in individual Web sites, accessing Northwestern's online catalog, e-mail (the majority of the e-mail time logged is from Northwestern servers), and Blackboard CourseInfo. The results for specific Web sites indicate that Northwestern's library catalog received the most use, followed by Northwestern e-mail servers. The catalog is accessible without a Northwestern ID, so those statistics apply to all our users. The one other site that stands out is Blackboard CourseInfo, a

TABLE 1. Total Number of URLs by Domain Name April 3-June 11, 2000

Domain name	URLs
.com	70,206
.edu	12,301
.net	8,641
.org	7,434
.gov	1,591
other	27,441
TOTAL	127,614

TABLE 2. Top 11 Web Uses April 3-June 11, 2000

Web sites or type of web sites	Time online hours:minutes
Northwestern's library catalog	515:29
E-mail servers	391:14
Blackboard's CourseInfo	253:11
Banner advertisements	18:07
Northwestern's library's homepage	4:52
Northwestern University's homepage	2:04
Yahoo	1:32
Commercial online databases	1:11
Chat rooms	1:09
Bbsgate (China Science/Technology network)	1:00
ESPN	0:53

commercial Web-based learning, discussion, and class administration tool available to all Northwestern faculty. Each course page is password protected and accessible only to class members. Clearly the Northwestern community utilizes the machines, as two of the most frequently accessed Web pages require the entry of an ID number. Interestingly, over half of that usage is for e-mail.

Analyses of all pages searched indicate that the predominant usage of machines is accessing pages in the .com domain. While patrons do not spend a lot of time within particular Web sites, they do spend hours looking at a vast variety of pages. The .com designation in no way indicates that pages do not provide research materials. Commercial databases such as Academic Universe and InfoTrac, search engines, encyclopedias, and news agencies may have .com URLs. Further analysis of the URLs was necessary to indicate the types of Web sites being accessed.

Statistics prove that the final two weeks in any quarter see the heaviest use of the General Information Center's computers. Therefore we chose those two weeks in the spring quarter to look closely at the top 150 and the top 1,500 .com Web sites viewed–top again defined by the amount of time patrons spend within Web pages (see Tables Three and Four).

Given the nature of academia any Web page could qualify as "research." However, the breakdown for this paper classifies the following types of .com pages as potential research sites: databases, search engines, news organizations/publications, directories, encyclopedias/dictionaries, e-journals, and financial organizations. The number of potential research sites drops significantly after the top 150. Out of 1,500 .coms visited the week of May 22, 62 fall into the "research" category; for the week of May 29, 72 qualify. E-mail providers and banner ads continue to be present on the lists, though in smaller percentages than in the first 150 sites (see Table Three). The following list provides examples of other pages. They are indicative of the most common types of page sought: sports, shopping, job search, apartment hunting, chat rooms, pornography and general service sites for e-mail, Web-page building, and chat rooms.

www.apartments.com	www.partyhouse.com
baseball.fantasysports.yahoo.com	www.paypal.com
www.cameraworld.com	www.playsite.com
www.cheaptickets.com	shopping.yahoo.com
www.collegeclub.com	www.shoppinglist.com
www.cruisingforsex.com	www.soccernet.com
www.eroticism.com	spin.jobtrak.com
www.hotshotceleb.com	ticketing.ticketmaster.com
www.listbot.com	www.truckracecycle.com
www.menonthenet.com	www.ultrasexpower.com
www.nba.com	www.weddingchannel.com

As the .net and .org domains receive far fewer hits we conducted a brief analysis of the types of sites most commonly accessed. Those sites

TABLE 3. Top 150 .com Sites Visited the Last Two Weeks of the Spring Quarter

Type of Sites	Number of sites week of May 22, 2000	Number of sites week of May 29, 2000
E-mail	20	24
Databases	15	15
Web service pages*	14	15
Commercial pages**	16	11
Search engines***	11	11
Sports	8	8
News****	7	7
Chat rooms	5	8
Directories	3	3
Games	2	2
Miscellaneous	8	1
(banner ads)	41	45

*Pages similar to and including Yahoo, MSN, Burstnet, that offer users a variety of Internet services.
**Pages similar to and including ebay, Amazon, Chrysler, Jobsearch.
***Pages similar to and including Google, Yahoo search, Altavista, Lycos.
****Pages similar to and including the New York Times, CNN, NBC, Washington Post.

TABLE 4. Hourly Usage by Domain the Final Two Weeks of Spring Quarter

Domain Type	Week of May 22, 2000 hours:minutes	Week of May 29, 2000 hours:minutes
.com	15:37	17:28
.edu	12:13	10:57
.net	1:53	2:8
.org	0:59	1:3
.gov	0:11	0:12
other	5:49	4:38

within the .org domain tended to fall under the research category, while those within .net were predominantly banner ads, followed by pornography pages. The .edu usage unsurprisingly centers around Northwestern University Web pages.

STATISTICS AND CREDIBILITY

In discussions with library staff from other departments about problems with Internet access, one question reoccurred: do you have any statistics? Even the passing of a "no game playing" policy ran into some resistance from librarians who distrust any type of Internet usage limitation. While no one really wanted to fight for the right of patrons to play games on our public computers, several colleagues felt that we did not need a policy because they had witnessed no problems themselves. The issue probably would have moved more quickly had we possessed statistics on Web page usage. Even now, despite our posted policy, game sites appear each week in the list of top 150 .com sites.

Similarly, statistics may strengthen the argument that an institution should have an Internet use policy, if for no other reason than to help staff handle patron complaints. Last year, at separate times, two students complained because patrons were viewing pornography on public terminals. The students felt that this constituted sexual harassment and should be prohibited under university policy that forbids publicly displaying pornographic posters. General Information Center staff requested that some type of policy be created to deal with patron complaints about pornographic site viewing. However, the general attitude was that these were isolated incidents. LittleBrother statistics show that while pornography viewing ranks well below many other Internet activities, it does occur every day. Armed with such statistics it is now much easier to plead the case for a policy to respond to such complaints.

GENERAL INFORMATION CENTER PROBLEMS

Does the General Information Center have a problem with patrons monopolizing research work stations for non-research purposes? Based on the above statistics it would seem so. During the two heaviest research weeks of the quarter every machine is frequently in use. While database and other research-page usage is heavier during those two weeks, the non-research use of the machines far outweighs that of the research.

Public users with no university affiliation complicate this issue. The General Information Center staff does receive complaints that non-students monopolize our computers. We have no way to ascertain how much non-research use stems from non-Northwestern students. However, the preponderance of .com e-mail services suggests that much of the non-research activity comes from non-affiliates, as the Northwestern community accesses its e-mail through .edu servers. The Northwestern's Main library is located quite close to the Evanston, IL, downtown area, and does not have time limits or require patron identification, both of which are policy at Evanston Public Library.

The statistics also suggest that at this time solutions to the problem should center around 9 weeks of each year: The last two weeks and finals week of the fall, winter and spring quarters. For example, we could request that patrons display their Northwestern ID cards during those weeks, and institute a policy giving Northwestern affiliates priority at all public computers.

The very low percentages of patron access to a wide variety of research databases highlights an equally perplexing problem: how do we educate our users in the intricacies of electronic research? Anecdotal evidence tells us that patrons search the library's catalog assuming they will find individual journal articles. Statistical evidence shows that the catalog receives far more use than journal databases, even those containing mostly full text. While it is heartening to see the high use the catalog receives, it also tells us that our users still tend to see it as the gateway to all of our resources.

Knowing that such a small percentage of in-library Internet usage resides in commercial databases at least may prompt us to further examine several research issues. Remote access of commercial databases, library instruction for electronic research, redesign of library Web pages are all areas that might be addressed to assess the extent of the problem.

CONCLUSIONS

In the current technological environment there is one certainty: change. Uses of the Internet mutate rapidly and in directions we might not expect. Once we allow Internet access in our libraries, we must come to terms with the types of services and materials it provides. The responsibilities of research institutions include facilitating the use of

Internet resources for scholarly purposes, and providing an appropriate environment in which to conduct research. Those who staff areas with public access to the Internet know that problems arise both with content and access. It is, unfortunately, difficult to assess the extent of either type of problem based on anecdotal evidence. Statistical evidence can measure the extent of some problems, and also point us towards effective solutions. The information provided by tracking software tells us a lot about the way our patrons use the Internet. With hard data we gain both credibility and focus with which to deal with Internet problems.

REFERENCES

Carver, Deborah. 1998. Sex, the network, and academic libraries. *OLA Quarterly* 3, no. 4: 11-12.

Grimes, Deborah and Carl Boenig. 2001. Worries with the Web: A look at student use of Web resources. *College and Research Libraries* 62, no. 1: 11-22.

Jones, Barbara. 1999. *Libraries, access and intellectual freedom: Developing policies for public and academic libraries.* Chicago: American Library Association.

Nagler, Richard. 1998. Home-front horror tales for would-be public Internet access providers. *American Libraries* 29, no. 5: 40-41.

Weessies, Kathleen and Barbara Wales. 1999. Internet policies in midsized academic libraries. *Reference & User Services Quarterly* 39, no. 1: 33-41.

Problem or Challenge?
Serving Library Customers
That Technology Left Behind

Sara Baron

SUMMARY. Every day at reference desks, public service points, and in library instruction, librarians assist people who are apprehensive about technology. There are assumptions in academe, held by librarians, faculty and administration, regarding students' technology savvy. Many of these assumptions are unfounded and incorrect. Librarians are challenged to serve those individuals technology has left behind with the same respect as those technologically up-to-speed. This paper is a discussion about technology anxiety, technophobe myths, and a theory of technophobic learning. *[Article copies available for a fee from The Haworth Document Delivery Service: 1-800-HAWORTH. E-mail address: <getinfo@ haworthpressinc.com> Website: <http://www.HaworthPress.com> © 2002 by The Haworth Press, Inc. All rights reserved.]*

KEYWORDS. Technophobia, computer anxiety, learning theories, library instruction, information literacy

Every day at reference desks, public service points, and in library instruction, librarians assist people who are apprehensive about technol-

---

Sara Baron is Director of the Instructional Technology Center and Coordinator of Library Instruction, University of Massachusetts Boston (E-mail: sara.baron@umb. edu).

[Haworth co-indexing entry note]: "Problem or Challenge? Serving Library Customers That Technology Left Behind." Baron, Sara. Co-published simultaneously in *The Reference Librarian* (The Haworth Information Press, an imprint of The Haworth Press, Inc.) No. 75/76, 2002, pp. 129-147; and: *Helping the Difficult Library Patron: New Approaches to Examining and Resolving a Long-Standing and Ongoing Problem* (ed: Kwasi Sarkodie-Mensah) The Haworth Information Press, an imprint of The Haworth Press, Inc., 2002, pp. 129-147. Single or multiple copies of this article are available for a fee from The Haworth Document Delivery Service [1-800-HAWORTH, 9:00 a.m. - 5:00 p.m. (EST). E-mail address: getinfo@haworthpressinc. com].

© 2002 by The Haworth Press, Inc. All rights reserved.

129

ogy. There is an assumption in academe, held by librarians, faculty and administration, that students enter college already knowing how to use technology. That assumption is false on several levels. Some returning students who are changing careers, trying to get promoted, or even retiring come to the library with little or no technological experience. Transfers and international students may know about technology in general, but be oblivious to effective use of the library catalog and databases. While most primary and secondary schools are incorporating technology into the classroom, there are still some students getting an education lacking in technological skills. There are even faculty, administrators and librarians at some institutions who have put off the daunting task of becoming technologically savvy. Librarians are challenged to serve these individuals that technology left behind with the same respect as those technologically up-to-speed. This paper is a discussion about technology anxiety, technophobe myths, and a theory of technophobic learning.

FEARING TECHNOLOGY

Anxiety, confusion and frustration cause many people to fear technology. The last two decades have seen a proliferation of research on computer anxiety and technophobia in professional literature. Most researchers agree that technophobia is a physical and mental response to technology. Physically, people may sweat, breathe heavily or feel light-headed when experiencing a technological situation. Mentally, one may feel fear, anxiety, and a sense of being out of control. Whether it is referred to as technophobia, technostress, techno-anxiety, or computer anxiety, it ultimately refers to fear of technology. Worthington and Zhao broaden the definition to one of existential anxiety. They argue "computer technology is seen as a challenge to one's world view; where she once lived and worked productively in an environment that did not involve the use of computer technology, the introduction of such technology into this environment forces her to revisit and attempt to rejustify her beliefs and assumptions about the world" (1999, 301).

Librarians see fear of technology daily. It often becomes an issue when librarians spend more time teaching basic computer skills than research and information literacy skills. Furthermore, fear of technology is directly related to library anxiety. Onwuegbuzie found in one study that the greatest source of library anxiety is "caused by mechanical barriers–feelings which emerge as a result of students' reliance on library technology" (1997, 6). He defines library anxiety as "an uncomfortable feeling or emotional disposition, experienced in a library setting, which has cognitive, affective, physiological, and behavioral ramifications" (1997, 6).

There are many suggestions in the literature on ways to deal with technophobia, computer anxiety and library anxiety. Before discussing these though, we should examine who the typical technophobe is. Experience, reality, and scientific studies offer many definitions and debunk many myths.

FALSE ASSUMPTIONS

Many people will argue that technophobes are generally women, older people, international students, and Luddite faculty. Another theory is that traditionally aged students entering college have no computer anxiety. There is literature which both supports and denies each of these arguments. From a librarian's standpoint, we must serve each of these groups equally, so I will highlight the literature and arguments that disprove these generalizations.

Women. While some studies find technology more masculine (Brosnan, 1998) and argue that men are more comfortable with newer technologies than women (McDowell, 1998), most studies admit that there is little significant difference between technophobia in men and women. Scott found "minimal gender differences with regard to future use of new technologies" (54-5). Rosen and Weil, perhaps the most well-known scholars on technophobia, debunk the myths that both women and older people are more technophobic than other members of society (DeLoughry, 1993). Brosnan found that the biggest differences in technology use were related to computer games, which were typically used by men more than women (1998, 72).

Older students with a gap in education. Another myth is that people who are older or have been out of school for a while are more apprehensive about technology. While this is true for some people, it is an incorrect generalization for all. Baron and Strout-Dapaz found that the major differences with age dealt with how people initially deal with technology. While younger people "jump right in," older students prefer training first (2000, 98). In addition, regardless of age, students tend to prefer technology-based resources rather than print materials. For students returning to school for another degree or continuing education, chances are they have less anxiety than traditional students. Ellis discovered that "Higher educational attainment was related to higher levels of both computer knowledge and computer interest and lower levels of computer anxiety" (1999, 6).

As opposed to technology, many older and returning students have challenges with work and family obligations (Given, 85). Even so, Cody explains many benefits for older adults learning technology. He states that they will have the "ability to enroll in distance learning classes online for life-long education, increased knowledge of news, current events and medical/health breakthroughs, increased connectivity with family members, increased intergenerational communication, increased perceptions of social support, ability to feel mentally alert, useful and to feel younger" (Cody et al., 1999, 270). Library instruction can help older and returning students as they learn technology.

International students. International students encounter technology challenges as well. Professional literature is full of studies suggesting ways to help international students reduce library anxiety and become effective information literate researchers. Jiao and Onwuegbuzie discovered that international students are most anxious about library technology (1999, 6). Chattoo offers several excellent innovative teaching tips with international students: "avoid using approaches used for teaching children; do not isolate vocabulary; encourage discussion; provide a relaxed atmosphere; be creative, flexible and resourceful; encourage group work; be a good role model; think positively; and use sophisticated graphic aids" (2000, 355-357).

Strout-Dapaz and Baron discovered that the major challenges international students face in American higher education are: language/communication problems; adjusting to a new educational/library system; and general cultural adjustments (2001). Language and library systems are issues when international students approach a new online catalog, new databases and a new library culture. Library anxiety and computer anxiety can be reduced with "effective reference and instructional services that help international students find assistance and raise their comfort levels" (Strout-Dapaz and Baron, 2001).

Traditional students and transfers. A huge myth in higher education today is that students entering academia already know about computers because they learned it in high school or at their last institution. All high schools and universities are not created equal. Onwuegbuzie suggests that library anxiety may be a result of "inexperience, since these resources (library technologies) often were not available to (students) in their public school or even local libraries" (1997, 7). Robertson's study showed "that students who have grown up with technology are not completely comfortable with it" (1999, 63). With an information culture that changes dramatically with each passing month, we are all challenged to maintain proficiency with technology. The technology resources will change from year to year, and from institution to institution. Lee warns "increasingly, parents expect their students to have exposure to and training in the use of technology . . . more students will begin selecting universities with the best computer facilities and faculty who use technologies to provide innovative instruction" (1998, 13).

Faculty. While some faculty embrace educational technology as an integral component of their curricula, others are reluctant to change. Another generalization about technophobes is the Luddite faculty member who refuses to face technology. Bollentin humorously quotes one professor who states "faculty say two prayers a day: one for the parking god to find a spot near their building and the other for the PC god so that their computers will boot for word processing and e-mail" (1998, 51). In actuality, there are many faculty who are comfortable learning and using new technologies. These are the people driving the instructional technology industry today. Bollentin continues, "educators, administrators, policy makers and learners offer innumerable perspectives on what makes for quality education, drawing from both personal and professional experiences. Technology is a fact of life, as evidenced by the vociferous objections of the neo-Luddite movement, and it will more and more become a fact of learning" (1998, 54).

Administrative support is essential to faculty success with technology. Regardless of the time and energy faculty spend incorporating technology into their classes, lack of administrative and institutional support puts a cloud over technology in the classroom. Mecklenburger states that only the administration can " . . . plan for, budget for, purchase carefully, install properly, maintain dutifully, schedule adequately, distribute appropriately, and replace systematically the electronic technology suited for their (faculty) needs" (Lee, 1998, 15). Goldman echoes the sentiment more explicitly: "The easiest way for change to occur is for administrators to take the lead by indicating that faculty pioneers will be rewarded for the work they do in IT. Absent such a move, it will take a generation of faculty to retire or die before any real shifts occur" (Bollentin, 1998, 51).

Faculty are extremely influential with their students when it comes to technology anxiety. A teacher who is anxious about using computers will pass that anxiousness on to students. Whether it is in primary or secondary education, technology anxious faculty "may actually promote the continuation of negative reactions to computers" (Brosnan,

1998, 73). Brosnan argues that as "the primary introducers of technology," teachers have an obligation to learn new skills (1998, 73). At the collegiate level, faculty are somewhat obligated to prepare their students for the real technological world. Because faculty issues with technology affect their students, I think it is important to examine why some faculty are resistant to technology. Tables A, B, and C present a brief literature review of reasons faculty give for avoiding technology, ways faculty can learn technology skills, and benefits of faculty learning technology skills.

TABLE A. Reasons Faculty Give for Avoiding Technology

Citation	Reasons faculty give for avoiding technology
Guernsey, Lisa. "Scholars Who Work with Technology Fear They Suffer in Tenure Reviews." *Chronicle of Higher Education* 43, no. 39 (June 6 1997): A21-22.	• tenure and promotion committees treat technological projects with confusion and suspicion • faculty may be marked as innovators or no longer to communicate the value of their accomplishments to their colleagues (A21) • some departments resist because they are threatened by the new literacies (A22)
Lee, Judy Raven and Chris Johnson. "Helping Higher Education Faculty Clear Instructional Technology Hurdles." *Educational Technology Review* (Autumn/Winter 1998): 13-17.	• disincentives and lack of rewards or incentives for using IT • inadequate understanding, misunderstanding, and lack of awareness about IT • resistance to give up the traditional teacher-to-pupil classroom lecture model • lack of access to resources • potential hardware and software problems • outdated institutionalized traditions (14-15)
Robertson, Lona J. and Nancy Stanforth. "College Students' Computer Attitudes and Interest in Web Based Distance Education." *Journal of Family and Consumer Sciences* 91, no. 3 (1999): 60-64.	• distance learning students will have little interaction with professor or classmates • too many technical skills are needed by faculty and students on distance learning classes (61)
Worthington, Valerie L. and Yong Zhao. "Existential Computer Anxiety and Changes in Computer Technology: What Past Research on Computer Anxiety Has Missed." *Journal of Educational Computing Research* 20, no. 4 (1999): 299-315.	• fear of appearing inept in front of students or peers while using computers • being forced to sacrifice personal interactions with students in favor of having them sit in front of computers • perceived inability to protect students from incorrect or inappropriate information on the Internet • having their jobs replaced either by computers or teachers more familiar with computers (303)

TABLE B. Ways Faculty Can Learn Technology Skills

Citation	Ways faculty can learn technology skills
Hogan, Kevin. "Technophobia: Fear of Technology." *Forbes*, February 1994, S116.	• ask advice • educate yourself • practice
Ike, Chris A. "Development through Educational Technology: Implications for Teacher Personality and Peer Collaboration." *Journal of Instructional Psychology* 24, no. 1 (1997): 42-49.	• determination to make the necessary adjustment in their personal and professional behavior (42) • collaborative autobiographies–work with peers to share both negative and positive experiences (47)
Lee, Judy Raven and Chris Johnson. "Helping Higher Education Faculty Clear Instructional Technology Hurdles." *Educational Technology Review* (Autumn/Winter 1998): 13-17.	• administrative support • campus technology plan • collaboration with other faculty • access to resources • access to technological support
Robertson, Lona J. and Nancy Stanforth. "College Students' Computer Attitudes and Interest in Web Based Distance Education." *Journal of Family and Consumer Sciences* 91, no. 3 (1999): 60-64.	• use software packages to create course websites in a reasonable amount of time and build in communication technologies (60)
Zeszotarski, Paula. "Computer Literacy for Community College Students." *ERIC Digest* (January 1, 2000) ED438010.	• collaborative learning • professional development workshops • personal initiative to contribute to the teaching of courses that integrate computer and information literacy

A TECHNOPHOBE'S TECHNOLOGY LEARNING THEORY

There are numerous learning theories in professional literature that can be applied to technology training, library instruction and information literacy education. Three I will mention cover a teaching theory, learning theories for information professionals, and a learning model for computer anxious people. Harrison recently outlined library instruction using the 4MAT model developed by Bernice McCarthy in 1972. This model presents four quadrants that help "teachers organize teaching based on the way people learn" (2000, 291). The four areas are: connections, concepts, applications, and creation. Roy and Novotny discuss behavioral and cognitive learning theories, recommending that information professionals: incorporate multiple teaching methods in instruc-

TABLE C. Benefits of Faculty Learning Technology Skills

Citation	Benefits of faculty learning technology skills
Ike, Chris A. "Development Through Educational Technology: Implications for Teacher Personality and Peer Collaboration." *Journal of Instructional Psychology* 24, no. 1 (1997): 42-49.	• beneficial to students • offer teachers an opportunity to grow educationally and intellectually (42) • improvement intellectually, psychologically and professionally (47) • information technology knowledge helps teachers embrace computer literacy, computer-assisted instruction, computer-managed instruction, and the design of teaching materials (Forcier, 44) • students use computers in creating, accessing, retrieving, manipulating, and transmitting information in order to solve a problem (Forcier, 44)
Lee, Judy Raven and Chris Johnson. "Helping Higher Education Faculty Clear Instructional Technology Hurdles." *Educational Technology Review* (Autumn/Winter 1998): 13-17.	• supports learning by creating longer, stronger attention and concentration • enhances educator's delivery of information, ideas, and experiences • customize content for different learning styles (Cummings, 15) • provides motivation for students to spend time on task • increases likelihood of learning • increases learning retention (Berger, 13)
Wilson, Brian. "Redressing the Anxiety Imbalance: Computerphobia and Educators." *Behaviour & Information Technology* 18, no. 6 (1999): 445-454.	• a role in a technologically advanced adult society • usefulness in the administrative and production tasks of education • facilitation of the teaching/learning process within the curriculum
Zeszotarski, Paula. "Computer Literacy for Community College Students." *ERIC Digest* (January 1, 2000) ED438010.	• improving instruction • increasing productivity • expanding access to more instructional technologies • facilitating participation in distance learning • elevates teaching role to designer of learning rather than dispenser of information • facilitates integration of new knowledge • faculty become learners as well as teachers (4)

tion to reach all learners; use different learning strategies; adjust to the learner's level of need; understand that humans have difficulty transferring knowledge; provide learners with an opportunity to share knowledge; and learning can be learned (2000, 136-138). From a general learning theory to a theory for information professionals, McInerny et al. present a learning theory for anxious learners. Their theory is a

"Model of Computer Anxiety for Beginning Adult Learners" and includes four major components: gaining initial computing skills, sense of control, computing self-concept, and anxiety in computing situations (1999, 466).

I propose an alternative learning theory for technophobes (Figure 1). This is a circle of factors influencing when and why people are apprehensive about learning technology. This model was developed through personal observation, personal experiences, informal interviews, and professional discussion. It has not been scientifically studied or proven. However, I believe it illustrates phases and factors of an anxious learner. I posit that there are eight phases an anxious learner passes through while learning about new technologies: fear, need, time, patience, learning, practice, questioning, and exploring. Learners may then reenter the fear phase as they come across something new.

CIRCLE OF FACTORS
REPRESENTING A TECHNOPHOBE'S LEARNING PROCESS

Fear. Fear of the unknown causes anxiety and resistance to change. Technology is not new to society, however aspects of it are new to many people. Alan Kay, a leader in the technology industry, argued that technology is anything created after you are born (Hawley). To people liv-

FIGURE 1. Circle of Factors Representing a Technophobe's Learning Process

ing in the 50s and 60s, videocassettes, color TV and space travel were new technologies. The 70s and 80s brought VCRs, camcorders, the microcomputer, CD-ROMs. In the 90s and 00s, technology has grown to include digital sound and video, streaming images, instantaneous worldwide communication and the Internet as a fact of life. To many children born in recent years, all of the above "new" technologies are history. They do not know life without television, CDs, and the Internet. However, that does not mean they all are proficient with technology, especially educational and communication technologies.

Many people learn about technology from the media and popular press, which has both positive and negative portrayals of technology. On the positive side, we see many commercials a day with people happily communicating around the world via the Internet. On the negative side, we hear stories about the Internet being a well of debauchery. Bollentin agrees that the popular press paints pictures that tap "into the greatest fears of learners, their parents or guardians, regulating agencies and taxpayers" (1998, 50). Furthermore, she argues that we are still at the beginning of this technological revolution and "there is a danger that fear will warp the process" (1998, 50). Gregory Rawlins provides an interesting response to this: "Our love for technology is a fatal attraction. We can't live without it, and we sometimes fear we can't live with it. As for fatal–it may not end our lives, but it will end them as we know it . . . Technology is part of evolution, of adapting, of remaining the fittest for survival" (Pascarella, 1997, 44).

Another cause of fear is mentioned by Comaford: "Fear stems primarily from not knowing what the latest trend is really about . . . and in part from people thinking their skills are no longer useful" (1996, 56). This is sometimes why faculty are fearful about their perceived onslaught of technology into academia. Instructional technology brings up a myriad of issues, including copyright of online course materials, adoption of online courses created by faculty from other campuses, funds shifted from academic programs to technology, and job security in a technological age. Typically, faculty and students overcome their fears when they have to. This necessity to use technology and face fears takes us to the second factor influencing when and why people apprehensive about technology learn.

Need. Necessity often causes people to learn something they may be avoiding, whether it is writing a paper in a word processor, using the Internet to find books in the library, putting a course on the web, or going online to communicate with friends and relatives around the world. People will learn the technology when they need to do these things. In the library, we see this need when students approach the reference desk with an assignment. Their demeanor and nonverbal communication tells a sad story–they are desperate.

Instructional and reference needs must be met immediately to assuage technology anxious people. Onwuegbuzie suggests "some students become so anxious about having to collect information in a library that they are unable to approach the task in a systematic manner" (1997, 6). Often they have overcome fear and library anxiety on the road to the reference desk. Now if only they had more time.

Time. Learning something new takes time. Lack of time is a major reason people do not learn new technology skills. This was apparent in my informal interviews with people and also in the literature (Cody, 1999, Lee, 1998, Ellis, 1999). One faculty member I spoke with said she could not be bothered "wasting time" trying to learn new technologies, when she should be researching and writing. Cody found that 26% of the people in his study of older adults' Internet use withdrew due to time factors (1999).

Considering that technophobia has a "tangible impact on productivity" (Hogan, 1994), it is in one's best interest to try to learn some basic skills. Some faculty are afforded release time, equipment, staff or monetary incentives to incorporate technology into their curriculum. During my discussions with faculty, time is usually mentioned as the most appreciated and needed support. For students and staff, time off is probably not an option. It is a challenge for these people to realize that simply taking some time to learn basic technology skills does wonders for one's self-efficacy. McDowell's study proved that the more experience someone has, the less computer anxiety (1998). Regardless of someone's circumstances, facing technology fears to accomplish a task takes time and patience.

Patience. Learning something new can be frustrating. We have all experienced a computer beeping, error messages, and maybe even erroneously losing a document. But the ability to try something with an expectation of future learning and knowledge is essential to learning new skills. Time and patience are factors closely linked, but I argue that patience is an attitudinal factor that can be changed through the behavior and motivation of librarians.

At the reference desk, we often see people with little time and patience for learning something new. Many students today demand full-text online articles. The research process is arduous from the first step of locating a source to photocopying the needed information. Sometimes we see students use the books or articles on the very first page of a list of retrievals, because they do not have the patience to look through several pages to find the best resources. Zeszotarski found that students lack computer literacy skills due to a lack of patience or experience (2000). Indeed, how many times have we been helping a student who makes the search take longer by clicking the mouse 10 times?

Faculty voice frustration when they inform instruction librarians that their students are writing papers that cite only websites, some of which are inappropriate. Their implication is that students who do this are not researching effectively. However, teaching students research skills often requires more than a 50 minute class session, which many faculty do not have the time or patience to relinquish. Ike notes that impatience is extremely damaging to teachers (1997). He states that some teachers "develop computer avoidance behaviors. Their impatience results in frustration, shame, and emotional pain associated with repeated failures in getting the computer to work for them" (1997, 45).

As reference and instruction librarians, we have an opportunity to help faculty and students see the importance of spending a few extra minutes searching for resources or providing alternative forms of library instruction to compensate the 50 minute class. Through communication and positive results, we may be able to persuade our customers that their patience now will bring learning later. Trial-and-error, repetition, and step-by-step tutorials all take a little time, a little patience and a willingness to learn.

Learning. Learning, defined as "the observation, study and instruction that leads to acquiring skill and knowledge," takes time and patience (New Illustrated Webster's Dictionary of the English Language). Once skills are learned, people are empowered to manipulate technology to meet their needs. This is very important to technophobes, who often feel out of control. Wilson notes " . . . students' fears . . . seemed to be largely the result of computer ignorance, and the acquisition of some knowledge, together with rudimentary skill, helped to remove much of the excessive nature of their condition" (1999, 449). Working with both faculty and students, it is rewarding to see the moment they learn something–that AHA moment when something finally clicks. Much of the literature on technophobia, computer and library anxiety offers useful advice for reference and instruction librarians teaching anxious learners. Table D offers a brief literature review of tips for librarians teaching people with technology apprehension.

The environment in which someone attempts to learn technology skills is vital to success. Positive support and energy, in addition to the many suggestions in Table D, calm the anxious learner. Both faculty

TABLE D. Tips for Librarians Teaching People with Technophobia, Computer Anxiety or Library Anxiety.

Citation	Tips
Baron, Sara and Alexia Strout-Dapaz. "A Close Encounter Model for Reference Services to Adult Learners: The Value of Flexibility and Variance." *Reference Services for the Adult Learner: Challenging Issues for the Traditional and Technological Era*, ed. Kwasi Sarkodie-Mensah, 95-102. Binghamton, NY: The Haworth Press, Inc., 2000.	• offer more classes which focus on one major electronic resource and print alternatives • offer classes which will accommodate beginners and novices • offer hands-on classes covering major databases • offer improved and additional helpsheets for all databases • offer more personalized, one-on-one instruction with nontraditional students • offer walk-in instruction sessions in departmental locations outside the library (101-2)
Ellis, R. Darin and Jason C. Allaire. "Modeling Computer Interest in Older Adults: The Role of Age, Education, Computer Knowledge and Computer Anxiety." *Human Factors* 41, no. 3 (September 1999): 345.	• increase computer-related knowledge • decrease levels of computer anxiety
Harrison, Lucy. "Stress Relief: Help for the Technophobic Patron from the Reference Desk." *Reference Services for the Adult Learner: Challenging Issues for the Traditional and Technological Era*, ed. Kwasi Sarkodie-Mensah, 31-47. Binghamton, NY: The Haworth Press, Inc., 2000.	• present a demeanor of listening, understanding, empathizing • calm, clear, open to questions • nonjudgmental and non evaluative • set time limits • limit number of topics covered • limit use of jargon • peak interest • help them to help themselves • say it, show it, have them do it • offer semester long classes or workshops • make sure the library is a comfortable, non-threatening place (35-44)
Onwuegbuzie, Anthony J. "The Role of Technology on the Library Anxiety of Arkansas College Students." *Arkansas Association of Instructional Media Quarterly* 30, no. 3 (Spring 1997): 6-8.	• familiarize students with the array of library equipment and resources as early as possible • incorporate information about library anxiety into presentations • monitor library equipment for proper functioning and maintenance • proactively provide assistance • introduce LI at high school and grade school levels–collaboration among librarians (8)

TABLE D (continued)

Citation	Tips
Presno, Caroline. "Taking the Byte Out of Internet Anxiety: Instructional Techniques That Reduce Computer/Internet Anxiety in the Classroom." *Journal of Educational Computing Research* 18, no. 2 (1998): 147-161.	• play, hands-on practice, unpressured instruction (150-1) • teach students about the "living Internet" • provide detailed instruction regarding Internet searching • provide ample practice time on the Internet • welcome spontaneous questions and address concerns and anxiety immediately • encourage peer help • allow play on the Internet • flexible and adaptable regarding course procedures and requirements • model non-anxious behavior • carefully define and describe evaluation procedures • do not overuse jargon • limit self-regulated learning (156-7)
Quinn, Brian. "Overcoming Technostress in Reference Services to Adult Learners." *Reference Services for the Adult Learner: Challenging Issues for the Traditional and Technological Era*, ed. Kwasi Sarkodie-Mensah, 49-62. Binghamton, NY: The Haworth Press, Inc., 2000.	• pace the instruction carefully • look for behavioral cues • encourage active learning • encourage use of help screens and tutorials • repetition, simplicity and humor
Robertson, Lona J. and Nancy Stanforth. "College Students' Computer Attitudes and Interest in Web Based Distance Education." *Journal of Family and Consumer Sciences* 91, no. 3 (1999): 60-64.	• incorporate Internet activities, projects, and curriculum content into resident instruction (63)
Wilson, Brian. "Redressing the Anxiety Imbalance: Computerphobia and Educators." *Behaviour & Information Technology* 18, no. 6. (1999): 445-454.	• have user-friendly computers • WYSIWYG interface • simple, concise written instructions for various software packages • demonstrate best uses for computer software (448-449)

and students want to know that their efforts to learn technological skills are worthwhile; that they will make their daily lives easier. Ike states teaching dynamics "center around the design, development, and the creation of teaching materials that . . . increase the propensity of acqui-sition of information" (1997, 44). Lee argues that learners need a vision similar to early adopters "of how they can make their teaching better and create new learning environments" (1998, 15). And for students, they need a learning environment where they can "go much farther much faster and have more fun at the same time" (Bollentin, 1998, 52).

Practice. Once a skill is learned, technophobes (and everyone else) should practice. When a skater learns to skate, she practices to improve that skating. When someone learns how to create a website, they practice building bigger and better sites. When people learn to use computers for research, practice helps hone and build on those early skills. Practice leads to experience which leads to reduced technology apprehension. In addition, as people gain more experience, their self-image changes. They realize "I CAN do this!"

Self-efficacy is a "person's judgment about his or her ability to perform a task within a specific domain" (Presno, 1998, 149). Several of the studies on computer anxiety and technophobia discuss self-efficacy. It is important for technology anxious people to feel that they can accomplish a task with technology and also know where to get help. Ingram discusses this concept in terms of self-actualization and states: "Competence is increased through practical application and guided practice" (2000, 147). Hemby found in her study that "self-directed subjects had less computer anxiety than other subjects" (1998, 306). At both the reference desk and in library instruction, we have an opportunity to tell people that they can do this–they can get the information they need by practicing their new information-seeking skills.

Questioning. At some point, as what we have learned becomes knowledge, we may begin asking questions. How do I do it *this* way? How do I make it do *that?* Now that I know how to record on this VCR, how do I set the timer to record when I am away from home? Transitioning from mastering the basics to exploring new possibilities brings learning to a new level. A study in *Techniques* found that most campuses use e-mail and web pages more than any other technology (1999, 14). During the questioning phase, one might ask questions about increasing productivity with e-mail, and learn about filters, folders and discussion lists. Or possibly someone might try to build a website, and need help getting started. Trying new things and asking for help may increase productivity and experience, which may reduce anxiety.

Exploring. Exploration of the wild unknown may be some people's perception of the Internet. But it is exploration that gets people surfing, searching, and reading about a multitude of topics. McInerny states "it seems reasonable to assume that computers will cause less anxiety when they are a source of self-directed exploration or diversion than when they are part of formal instruction" (Hemby, 1998, 305). As people become more familiar with technology and the Internet, they will enter a whole new world of information seeking, entertainment and communication. And the more people manipulate technology to find the sports scores, or stock tips, or recipes, the better prepared they will be to use technology when there is an information need.

FUTURE RESEARCH

As the gap between technology haves and have-nots grows, studies of computer, technology and library anxieties will continue to be important. As a follow-up to this article, I am interested in seeing more information correlating library anxiety and technology anxiety. Studying "technophobes" may be difficult, since I have found that people do not like to define themselves with that term. However, an analysis of the effects of library instruction and information literacy training on technology apprehension would be interesting. I also wonder if librarian collaboration assists faculty with technology anxiety. On a self-reflective note, a study of technophobia in librarianship may guide continuing education and professional development programs. Librarians' attitudes towards technophobes would also be interesting, in light of the ongoing discussion regarding computer training at the reference desk and in library instruction. There are countless other ways these topics could be studied in a way beneficial to the library profession.

CONCLUSIONS

People with technophobia and computer anxiety are challenging library customers. Some library staff may see computer anxious patrons as problems. They may require hand-holding, one-on-one assistance and time. Sometimes they learn a few skills and sometimes we see the same people asking the same questions year after year. By raising our awareness of what technophobia is and the learning phases through which technophobes pass, we are better able to understand and assist our library users. They are not problems. Technology anxious people are one of the reasons librarians exist–they need help finding information, and that is what we do.

REFERENCES

Baron, Sara and Alexia Strout-Dapaz. "A Close Encounter Model for Reference Services to Adult Learners: The Value of Flexibility and Variance." In *Reference Services for the Adult Learner: Challenging Issues for the Traditional and Technological Era,* edited by Kwasi Sarkodie-Mensah, 95-102. Binghamton, NY: The Haworth Press, Inc., 2000.

Bollentin, Wendy Rickard. "Can Information Technology Improve Education? Measuring Voices, Attitudes and Perceptions." *Educom Review* 33, no. 1 (January-February 1998): 50-54.

Brosnan, Mark J. "The Impact of Psychological Gender, Gender-Related Perceptions, Significant Others, and the Introducer of Technology Upon Computer Anxiety Students." *Journal of Educational Computing Research* 18, no. 1 (1998): 63-78.

Chattoo, Calmer D. "Reference Services: Meeting the Needs of International Adult Learners." In *Reference Services for the Adult Learner: Challenging Issues for the Traditional and Technological Era,* edited by Kwasi Sarkodie-Mensah, 349-362. Binghamton, NY: The Haworth Press, Inc., 2000.

Cody, Michael J., Deborah Dunn, Shari Hoppin, and Pamela Wendt. "Silver Surfers: Training and Evaluating Internet Use Among Older Adult Learners." *Communication Education* 48, no. 4 (October 1999): 269-286.

Comaford, Christine. "The Pain and Heartache of Technophobia." *PC Week* 13, no. 21 (May 27, 1996): 56.

"Collegiate Technophobia." *Techniques* 74, no. 2 (February 1999): 14.

DeLoughry, Thomas J. "2 Researchers Say Technophobia May Affect Millions of Students." *Chronicle of Higher Education* 39, no. 34 (April 28 1993): A25-26.

Ellis, R. Darin and Jason C. Allaire. "Modeling Computer Interest in Older Adults: The Role of Age, Education, Computer Knowledge and Computer Anxiety." *Human Factors* 41, no. 3 (September 1999): 345.

Guernsey, Lisa. "Scholars Who Work with Technology Fear They Suffer in Tenure Reviews." *Chronicle of Higher Education* 43, no. 39 (June 6 1997): A21-22.

Harrison, Lucy. "Stress Relief: Help for the Technophobic Patron from the Reference Desk." In *Reference Services for the Adult Learner: Challenging Issues for the Traditional and Technological Era,* edited by Kwasi Sarkodie-Mensah, 31-47. Binghamton, NY: The Haworth Press, Inc., 2000.

Harrison, Naomi. "Breaking the Mold: Using Educational Pedagogy in Designing Library Instruction for Adult Learners." In *Reference Services for the Adult Learner: Challenging Issues for the Traditional and Technological Era,* edited by Kwasi Sarkodie-Mensah, 287-298. Binghamton, NY: The Haworth Press, Inc., 2000.

Hawley, Michael. 2001. Presentation at the Association of College and Research Libraries Annual Convention. Denver, CO., 15 March.

Hemby, K. Virginia. "Self-Directness in Nontraditional College Students: A Behavioral Factor in Computer Anxiety?" *Computers in Human Behavior* 14, no. 2 (1998): 303-319.

Hogan, Kevin. "Technophobia: Fear of Technology." *Forbes,* February 1994, S116.

Ike, Chris A. "Development through Educational Technology: Implications for Teacher Personality and Peer Collaboration." *Journal of Instructional Psychology* 24, no. 1 (1997): 42-49.

Ingram, Dorothy S. "The Andragogical Librarian." In *Reference Services for the Adult Learner: Challenging Issues for the Traditional and Technological Era,* edited by Kwasi Sarkodie-Mensah, 141-150. Binghamton, NY: The Haworth Press, Inc., 2000.

Jiao, Qun G and Anthony J. Onwuegbuzie. "Library Anxiety Among International Students." *ERIC Document* (November 18, 1999) ED437973.

Lee, Judy Raven and Chris Johnson. "Helping Higher Education Faculty Clear Instructional Technology Hurdles." *Educational Technology Review* (Autumn/Winter 1998): 13-17.

McDowell, Earl. "An Investigation of the Relationships Among Technology Experiences, Communication Apprehension, Writing Apprehension and Computer Anxiety." *Journal of Technical Writing and Communication* 28, no. 4 (1998): 345-355.

McInerney, Valentia, Herbert W. Marsh, and Dennis M. McInerney. "The Designing of the Computer Anxiety and Learning Measure (CALM): Validation of Scores on a Multidimensional Measure of Anxiety and Cognitions Relating to Adult Learning of Computing Skills Using Structural Equation Modeling." *Educational and Psychological Measurement* 59, no. 3 (June 1999): 451-470.

New Illustrated Webster's Dictionary of the English Language. 1992. New York: PMS Publishing Company, Inc.

Onwuegbuzie, Anthony J. "The Role of Technology on the Library Anxiety of Arkansas College Students." *Arkansas Association of Instructional Media Quarterly* 30, no. 3 (Spring 1997): 6-8.

Pascarella, Perry. "Spinning a Web of Technophobia." *Management Review* 86, no. 3 (March 1997): 42-44.

Presno, Caroline. "Taking the Byte Out of Internet Anxiety: Instructional Techniques that Reduce Computer/Internet Anxiety in the Classroom." *Journal of Educational Computing Research* 18, no. 2 (1998): 147-161.

Quinn, Brian. "Overcoming Technostress in Reference Services to Adult Learners." In *Reference Services for the Adult Learner: Challenging Issues for the Traditional and Technological Era*, edited by Kwasi Sarkodie-Mensah, 49-62. Binghamton, NY: The Haworth Press, Inc., 2000.

Robertson, Lona J. and Nancy Stanforth. "College Students' Computer Attitudes and Interest in Web Based Distance Education." *Journal of Family and Consumer Sciences* 91, no. 3 (1999): 60-64.

Roy, Loriene and Eric Novotny. "How Do We Learn? Contributions of Learning Theory to Reference Service and Library Instruction." In *Reference Services for the Adult Learner: Challenging Issues for the Traditional and Technological Era*, edited by Kwasi Sarkodie-Mensah, 129-150. Binghamton, NY: The Haworth Press, Inc., 2000.

Scott, Craig R. and Steven C. Rockwell. "The Effect of Communication, Writing, and Technology Apprehension on Likelihood to Use New Communication Technologies." *Communication Education* 46, no. 1 (January 1997): 44-62.

Strout-Dapaz, Alexia and Sara Baron. "Bonjour, Ni hao, Hola, Konichiwa: Communicating with and Empowering International Students with a Library Skills Set." *Reference Services Review* 29, no. 4 (1 December 2001): 314-326.

Wilson, Brian. "Redressing the Anxiety Imbalance: Computerphobia and Educators." *Behaviour & Information Technology* 18, no. 6 (1999): 445-454.

Worthington, Valerie L. and Yong Zhao. "Existential Computer Anxiety and Changes in Computer Technology: What Past Research on Computer Anxiety Has Missed." *Journal of Educational Computing Research* 20, no. 4 (1999): 299-315.

Zeszotarski, Paula. "Computer Literacy for Community College Students." *ERIC Digest* (January 1, 2000) ED438010.

E-Problems, E-Solutions:
Electronic Reference and the Problem Patron in the Academic Library

Jacqueline Borin

SUMMARY. Problem patrons are not a phenomenon exclusive to the public library arena. Academic libraries have throughout time had their own share of difficult patrons. This article focuses on problem patrons and reference staff in the academic library with a particular focus on electronic equipment and resources, particularly the Internet. Issues include viewing of pornographic images by patrons, plagiarism and the librarian's role, use of e-mail and chat, and cell phone use in the reference area. *[Article copies available for a fee from The Haworth Document Delivery Service: 1-800-HAWORTH. E-mail address: <getinfo@haworthpressinc.com> Website: <http://www.HaworthPress.com> © 2002 by The Haworth Press, Inc. All rights reserved.]*

KEYWORDS. Libraries and readers–United States, academic libraries–security measures, academic libraries–public relations

INTRODUCTION

Although problem patrons have been around for as long as libraries have existed the issues connected to problem patrons have developed

Jacqueline Borin is Coordinator, Reference & Electronic Resources, Library and Information Services, California State University, San Marcos, San Marcos, CA 92096-0001 (E-mail: jborin@csusm.edu).

[Haworth co-indexing entry note]: "E-Problems, E-Solutions: Electronic Reference and the Problem Patron in the Academic Library." Borin, Jacqueline. Co-published simultaneously in *The Reference Librarian* (The Haworth Information Press, an imprint of The Haworth Press, Inc.) No. 75/76, 2002, pp. 149-161; and: *Helping the Difficult Library Patron: New Approaches to Examining and Resolving a Long-Standing and Ongoing Problem* (ed: Kwasi Sarkodie-Mensah) The Haworth Information Press, an imprint of The Haworth Press, Inc., 2002, pp. 149-161. Single or multiple copies of this article are available for a fee from The Haworth Document Delivery Service [1-800-HAWORTH, 9:00 a.m. - 5:00 p.m. (EST). E-mail address: getinfo@haworthpressinc.com].

© 2002 by The Haworth Press, Inc. All rights reserved.

149

and grown. Early articles on the topic range from those on "library loafers" published in the late 19th century and early twentieth century to others on patrons' use of periodical reading rooms to get racing news information and for illegal gambling (Sable, 1988). Newer articles have a heavier focus on library security and teaching of techniques for listening and calming. Most of these articles focus on the problem patron in the public library arena; only a few identify the kinds of problem patrons that academic libraries face. Most recently articles have begun to look at the new problems brought to us by the proliferation of electronic equipment and resources, particularly the Internet. However, even these tend to focus on the issues as they relate to public libraries, for example, the access to children of pornographic web sites in a public library Internet area.

THE INTERNET AND E-MAIL/CHAT

New technology has brought us more complex issues to deal with than those associated with just books. Willis (1999) notes three issues that need to be addressed in regards to the Internet: sharing the resource in demand with all those who want to use it (availability), addressing the controversial material available, and providing training to users unfamiliar with technology. These issues, while also apparent in academic libraries, have a different emphasis and in regards to problem patrons we will look at just the first two–availability of resources and controversial material available.

First let us look at availability of resources. Public libraries may employ such practices as time limits and sign in sheets to restrict the amount of access that they can provide each user. In an academic library setting, where patrons may spend longer focused periods in term paper and dissertation research, this does not work as well and tends to be a less positive move in terms of good patron relations. Some possible solutions for academic libraries in terms of availability are:

- Restricting use to the primary user clientele, their faculty and students. In practice, libraries may simply post signs stating that the primary user group has priority on using the machines, giving the staff permission in busy times to ask outsiders to relinquish the machine. While some institutions may request IDs, many simply rely on the honesty of the patron in their response. Other libraries may require users to sign in at terminals with their campus user name and password. This is effective in restricting usage to institutional users but requires a staff member to override when a legitimate outside user wishes to access information (for example, a community member looking for government document information). A compromise between the two extremes would make most of the machines require a log-in while a few, perhaps those closest to an information point, would be open for public access (Still, 1997).

- Looking at *what* people are doing, and asking those using a workstation for personal interest rather than research purposes to give up the computer at busy times. This technique is used more often in smaller libraries with a limited number of computers. This may violate a patron's right to privacy, however most users will respect the need to vacate their workstations under the circumstances described above.

Secondly, in addressing the issues of controversial material available over the Internet we will consider specifically the area of pornography, although other issues related to material available via the Internet, i.e., chat, e-mail and the concerns about plagiarism are also problems. In 1996 the Association of Research Libraries (ARL) reported in their SPEC Flyer #218 on a survey of 119 institutions to gather information on policies related to the use of electronic information. Thirty-nine institutions responded. Although a small sample, the majority of the respondents indicated they had knowledge of problems with computer usage at their institution. Twenty respondents cited knowledge of harassment incidents (e-mail, unsolicited sending of pornography, etc.), 15 mentioned incidents of pornography and 7 noted incidents related to freedom of speech. Comments indicated people were concerned with the use of computers for other than the posted educational purposes, i.e., chat rooms, e-mail and the viewing of pornography.

E-mail and chat have become a thorny issue in the academic library due to the difficulty of distinguishing between personal use and scholarly communication (i.e., chatting with friends versus participating in a chat required of an online course). In many cases, the only recourse is a policy stating that machines are to be used for course related research and communication. Other libraries simply decide they do not want to be in the position of judging whether a patron's use of e-mail or chat is appropriate and simply accept it as a "legitimate use of the technology" (Guernsey, 1998). Where e-mail becomes more of a concern is where it is used to send harassing or threatening messages to others. This is generally covered by an institution's speech code and harassment rules rather than specific library policies and procedures.

PORNOGRAPHY

Academic institutions and their libraries are beginning to develop policies to address the issues that the varieties of sexually explicit material available over the Internet bring forth. An American Association of University Professors (AAUP) report published in 1997 stated that, "An appropriate institutional policy would ensure that access to sexually explicit and other materials through university computing networks and systems would be limited to no greater degree than access to print and visual materials in library collections is limited." It did, however, recognize that as libraries limit their print collection according to curriculum and budget needs, so might they do the same for their electronic collections. AAUP also goes on to state that if certain material is already illegal, such as child pornography, "then such material may be banned or removed from a computing network or system" (AAUP, 1997).

Interpretations of the Library Bill of Rights tend to recommend that libraries develop policies that will place the fewest restrictions on those accessing material. However, in allowing users to decide for themselves what material is appropriate we do not then take into account the rights of other patrons who may not wish to be exposed to materials they feel are inappropriate (Young, 1997). While academic libraries do not in general cater to minors, in reality many college freshmen may be minors. Additionally, children of students, faculty and staff often spend some time on campus and in the library. Organized groups on campus for educational or sports camps who are likely to come to the library as a group for instruction may not be as much of a problem as the casual individual user (Peace, 1997).

In cases of minors using computers in the library who are not part of an organized group (i.e., they may be waiting for a parent in class) some libraries may find their institution has a Dependent Children on Campus Policy. Such policies generally provide for campus security to pick up unsupervised children and locate their parents. This policy usually applies whether or not the children are behaving appropriately, as libraries can not ensure the safety of young children left alone without adult supervision. For example, the California State University, San Marcos policy states:

Dependent children on campus property shall be:

- participating in a supervised University sponsored or authorized program; or
- under the direct supervision of their parent/s or legal guardian/s while attending a non-academic University sponsored or authorized event; or
- under the direct supervision of their parent or legal guardian who is attending class or work, and is unable to obtain child care for the day. Prior approval by Instructor/s or employee's supervisor, or both, is required.

Dependent children who are found unsupervised on campus property are to be reported to Public Safety Services who will attempt to locate the child/ren's parent/s or legal guardian/s to remedy the situation.

Allowing users open access also does not take into account the exposure of library staff to sexually explicit images that may be interpreted as sexual harassment. For some people the presence of sexually explicit materials being displayed on a library computer will meet the definition of a hostile environment constituting sexual harassment (coming under the category of visual harassment, the showing or displaying of sexually oriented material). Public educational institutions have limited responsibility for third party sexual harassment, i.e., the behavior of people who are not their employees, but they are expected to comply with Title VII of the Civil Rights Act of 1964 and Title IX of the Education Amendments of 1972 to provide a work and educational environment that is non-discriminatory and provides freedom from harassment (Johnson, 1996).

For example, a recent issue of the Newsletter on Intellectual Freedom reported that in May 2000 a grievance was filed with the Minneapolis Public Library Board and the Equal Employment Opportunity Commission citing a hostile and offensive work environment. The suit was brought in response to, what the librarians stated, were constant problems with viewing of pornographic web sites in the library and printing out of sexually explicit material. In response to the grievance, changes to the library's Internet policy were made. This situation should be a warning to all libraries to review their Internet policies to see what protection they provide for staff.

While some libraries' policies explicitly mention issues such as sexual harassment, many others do not. One example that does is the policy at Appalachian State University Library that reads, "Users are reminded that the library is a public place and are strongly encouraged to be considerate and not expose others to material and images that might be considered offensive. Indeed, so exposing others to such materials could violate state or Federal law or University policies, including the University's 'Policy Prohibiting Sexual Harassment' and the aforementioned 'Computer Usage Policy.'" Other libraries' policies place the responsibility on the patron. For example, Idaho State University's policy states: "The Library does not censor access to materials nor protect patrons from information they may find offensive or inaccurate."

Both the library and the university need to take a proactive role in developing the policies that address these issues. As stated by Rezmierski (1999):

> The university's proactive role begins by aggressive protection against censorship and by reinforcement of First Amendment rights for its community of faculty, staff and students . . . The university's proactive role must continue, however, by raising awareness to the effects of unintentional intrusion by one individual upon another. Its role in discipline and intervention increases significantly when acts of purposeful intrusion and harassment occur.

While academic libraries generally do not use filtering software to the extent of public libraries, the problem can be approached in other ways. Libraries can attempt to define the scope and space of an individual workstation to restrict content viewing by the use of such items as privacy screens. When a computer is equipped with a privacy screen you generally have to stand directly behind the person using the computer to really see what they have on their screen. This, in turn, limits complaints by patrons about their exposure to images they may find uncomfortable.

Staff can also use the basic rules of etiquette to encourage patrons to think about how the material they are viewing will affect others who may have differing values and who also have the right to a non-threatening environment. The patrons may be asked to move to a more private area to view the material (Rezmierski, 1995). Asking a patron to move to a less "open" workstation preserves both the patrons right to access the information as well as others right to not feel threatened or harassed. The question is often raised as to why libraries allow access to material over the Internet that would not be purchased for the print collection because of curriculum needs or budget restraints. Open dialog with staff is necessary to enumerate the reasons for providing open access and to explain print and electronic collection development policies, as well as appropriate use policies in detail.

PLAGIARISM

Plagiarism has been an ongoing problem in education and while the actual rate of plagiarism is hard to determine, it is widely acknowledged to be both widespread and on the increase. While some may not see this as a problem patron issue I believe there is a need to define problem patron on a broader level. While the patrons may not themselves be an immediate problem in terms of objectionable behavior, it may become a problem patron issue in several ways. First the patron may become angry or confrontational when the staff member informs them of copyright rules and the definition of plagiarism and discourages them from cutting and pasting documents to their paper. Another situation that has occurred in my own library is one where professors have come to the library to question library staff about a student's paper because the student has said "but the librarian told me" to use this information. Staff members then have to reassure, explain and in some cases calm an upset faculty member. Dealing with this issue at the source prevents further problem patron issues down the road.

While students used to copy whole passages from books, they are now more likely to download whole sections from websites or complete term papers from one of the many available term paper mills. Web sites such as schoolsucks.com and cheathouse.com post hundreds of term papers that students can download, usually for a fee. Their claim is that it is the problem of those professors who give broad based assignments and who give the same assignment semester after semester. Working to combat these sites are others such as plagiarism.org which reviews papers submitted by teachers suspecting plagiarism and highlights passages which either match or have been partly altered from the original (Kopytoff, 2000).

How educational institutions define plagiarism varies widely but it is generally seen as part of academic honesty and integrity. In the Academic Honesty policy of California State University, San Marcos, for example, plagiarism is defined as, "Intentionally or knowingly representing the words, ideas, or work of another as one's own in any academic exercise." Reference librarians and reference staff have a role in combating plagiarism because libraries "provide and promote the Internet as a research tool" (Gresham, 1996). When helping students to locate and review information over the Internet it is a good time to also remind them that the information they locate and use must be cited correctly and that no difference exists between a printed essay and a document on the web in terms of plagiarism (Stebelman, 1998).

Students need to be taught that they can incorporate web pages into their term papers as long as they provide attribution for their sources. It is not so important whether it is their professor or the librarian who teaches them this as long as the message gets through. Libraries are used to teaching students how to cite the information they find in different style formats and that role is easily extended to incorporate why citing is important and how lack of citation leads to plagiarism. In doing this, it is important to recognize how the Internet makes it difficult in many cases to cite correctly because of difficulties in locating individuals or organizations responsible for authoring the content, difficulty in relocating something found previously on the Internet and the lack of permanence of URLs, to list just a few examples.

Instruction librarians can work into their instruction sessions information on the definition of plagiarism and how to avoid it. Also, when working with faculty on bibliographic instruction for a class, the librarian can make suggestions to help avoid plagiarism in the assignment. For example, having a narrowly focused rather than broad based topic makes it harder for students to find a ready-made paper on the web. Additional suggestions might include having students turn in a thesis statement early on (identifying the students writing style) and providing an early bibliography, an outline, a first draft and revisions as they complete the assignment. By providing interim evidence of their work on the assignment it is less likely they will have the opportunity to utilize sites such as those mentioned above. In addition libraries can make available books and other materials for faculty that will help them to develop different kinds of assignments and to develop assignments that require critical thinking, decision making, problem solving and analysis (Austin, 1999).

A recently published book on plagiarism and the Internet (Lathrop, 2000) offers some additional suggestions for librarians that, while aimed at school librarians, are also valuable for academic librarians. It emphasizes working with faculty to: (1) help them avoid topics that will lead to frustration and thereby cheating; (2) explore different presentation ideas (oral reports, web pages, etc.); (3) develop workshops on effective use of the Internet for both faculty and students; (4) document and draw attention to Internet plagiarism on the library's web site and (5) widely disseminate information and ideas on the topic. Given the library's central role in term paper creation, it is essential for librarians to be active participants in the process of teaching students about citing sources and plagiarism.

CELL PHONES

Apart from computers there are other electronic devices that may also be a source for problem patron issues in the academic library. Cell phones are one example. Nowadays many people walk around with cell phones and with a desire to be reachable wherever their location. Therefore they are often reluctant to turn them off or even move them into silent (vibrate) mode while in the library. Patrons checking their stocks on the Internet while conducting business over their cell phones are not uncommon. Newer libraries with steel-framed construction may have fewer problems with this than older libraries as the building itself and the fixtures inside may hamper the signal (Rogers, 1999). However, in academic libraries where students are protective of a quiet environment to study in, patrons can quickly become upset at phones ringing and people talking.

As interest in policies regarding use of cell phones within libraries grows, so does the use of surveys. One informal e-mail survey of California State University (CSU) Libraries found that of the 12 CSUs that responded, one used signage to restrict cell phone use, two had policies being approved and two others cited their student code of conduct as the source they used to control cell phone use. The other seven libraries had no policy but were interested in the results of the survey for possible policy development (Kong, 2001). Another such survey resulted in Cell Phone Courtesy Week, held in San Diego, CA in July 2000. The Courtesy Week was a result of a survey question posted on the Mayor's web wherein 73% of the respondents said they would favor restricting the usage of cell phones in public places (Carpenter, 2000).

In dealing with cell phones in academic libraries there appears to be a definite split between developing new policies and signs and utilizing those already in existence (such as codes of conduct). While some libraries utilize newly developed and strategically placed visual signs, others argue that cell phones are no different than any other distracting noise in the library and that existing policies on noise or behavior are sufficient. Existing noise policies are probably sufficient for some issues such as beepers where the noise is transitory and limited, however, cell phones generally provide more of a distraction due to length and loudness of conversation (Karuhn, 1999). Expansion of existing policies may therefore be necessary to completely address the problem.

Signage and a well written policy will help to alleviate the problem. Typical cell phone policies such as the one written by the University of Hartford contain reminders about the distraction caused by noise as well as requests to turn off (or turn down) the ringer on the phone and to step outside (or to a designated place) when making or receiving a call. Other suggestions include creating bookmarks to be handed out as necessary. The bookmarks could include reminders about courtesy to other patrons as well as tips about how to avoid disturbing others who are studying (Rogers, 1999).

TRAINING

While written policies are important, equally important is the training of the people who have to enforce those policies. Training should concentrate on educating front line staff on policies, issues and customer relations. Once empowered with information on "how" to deal with situations as well as being knowledgeable on the policies backing them up, front line staff are better able to cope with patron conflict. Policies, especially those related to cell phones and computer usage, need to be visibly posted so that staff can immediately point them out to patrons. In addition, staff should be able to immediately report a problem to a supervisor and ask for help in resolving it if they do not feel comfortable approaching a patron. This applies particularly to student information workers who provide assistance with the databases and may not feel comfortable confronting their peers about a problem, especially when it relates to issues such as pornography. In many cases it is enough to teach staff to simply "hover" and ask if the patron is finding what they need, or if they need help. However, in doing this we need to be mindful of privacy concerns and the right of the patron to work without intrusion.

In addition to the "in-house" training cited above, more formal training might consist of workshops in negotiation techniques with a focus on practice through the use of situational questions and role-playing (Rubin, 2000). Especially important is training for all staff in active listening and problem-solving skills aimed at defusing a patron's anger before it escalates, as well as the procedures for contacting campus police or public safety if the situation warrants.

CONCLUSION

The issue of problem patrons appears to be similar no matter what type of library we are talking about. The similarities are even more compelling with technology-related problems. While some academic libraries might consider restricting access to the general public to reduce the amount of unrelated e-mail usage and viewing of questionable images, it is certain that students are as responsible for these issues as community users. In addition, many academic libraries are government document repositories and have an obligation to make these available to the public, and a library's mission statement may also identify additional groups eligible for service. The use of outreach and instruction librarians to provide instruction to groups such as high school students, lower division community college students, and other unaffiliated library groups helps provide access to information by matriculated students (Still, 1999).

What is necessary as a starting point is effective, clearly written policies that are conspicuously posted and readily available. An effective policy should take into account your institutional and community culture, needs and expectations, as well as those issues that are most important for your library (a good policy does not necessarily mean all-encompassing). The policy should focus generally on the behavior of patrons rather than on the individual. A list of rules has to be clearly understood at all levels, be kept current by frequent revisions and be worked on in conjunction with the frontline staff who will be called on to enforce them (Willis, 1999). While signage and policy documents help provide a framework for what is permitted within the library, they are no substitute for ongoing training and education for both staff and patrons. Patron education and staff training together will provide a solution to the difficult issues raised by technology as well as providing a way to redirect and inform the angry and/or frustrated patron.

REFERENCES

American Association of University Professors (1997), *Academic Freedom and Electronic Communications* <http://www.aaup.org/statelec.html>, accessed 12/15/00.
Association of Research Libraries (1996), *SPEC Flyer 218: Information Technology Policies*, <http://www.arl.org/spec/218fly.html>, accessed 12/15/00.

Austin, M. Jill and Brown, Linda, D. (1999), "Internet plagiarism: Developing strategies to curb student academic dishonesty," *The Internet and Higher Education* 2 (1): 21-33.

California State University San Marcos (1995), *Academic Honesty Policy* <http://www.csusm.edu/student_affairs/Policies/academic_honesty.htm>, accessed 12/15/00.

Carpenter, Dave (2000), "Cell phones: they're all the rage," *USA Today Tech Reviews* (August 1) <http://www.usatoday.com/life/cyber/tech/review/crh366.htm>, accessed 12/15/00.

Gresham, Keith (1996), "Preventing plagiarism of the Internet: teaching library researchers how and why to cite electronic resources," *Colorado Libraries* 22 (Summer): 48-50.

Guernsey, Lisa (1998), "Off-campus users swamp college libraries, seeking access to web and e-mail," *Chronicle of Higher Education* 44 (47): A17.

Idaho State University, Eli M. Oboler Library (1999), *Internet public use policy.* <http://www.isu.edu/library/internet/policy.htm> (revised 09/27/00). Accessed 12/15/00.

Johnson, Denise J. (1996), "Sexual Harassment in the Library," In: McNeil, Beth & Johnson Denise J. *Patron Behavior in Libraries: a handbook of positive approaches to negative situations*, 106-21. Chicago: American Library Association.

Karuhn, Carri (1999), "The silence of cell phones now playing: library officials aim to curb usage," *Chicago Tribune* (December 17) <http://chicagotribune.com/news/metro/northwest/article/0,2669,SAV-9912170275,FF.html>, accessed 12/15/00.

Kent, Allen and Lancour, Harold (Eds.) *Encyclopedia of library and information science.* New York: M. Dekker [1968]-<2000>.

King, Les (2001), *Cell Phone Use Survey Summary.* E-mail: calyx@listproc.sjsu.edu. Sent 01/30/01. Accessed 02/19/01.

Kopytoff, Verne G. (2000), "Brilliant or plagiarized? Colleges use sites to expose cheaters," *New York Times* (January 20), Section G: 7.

Lathrop, Ann and Foss, Kathleen (2000), *Student cheating and plagiarism in the Internet era: a wake-up call.* Englewood, Colorado: Libraries Unlimited, Inc.

"Librarians file porn grievance," (2000) *Newsletter on Intellectual Freedom* 49 (4): 97.

Peace, A. Graham (1997), "Academia, Censorship and the Internet," *Journal of Information Ethics* 6 (Fall): 35-47.

Rezmierski, Virginia (1995), "Computers, pornography, and conflicting rights," *Educom Review* 30 (March/April): 42-44.

Rogers, Michael (1999), "Communication overload," *Library Journal* 124 (July): 66-7.

Rubin, Rhea Joyce (2000), *Defusing the Angry Patron: a how-to-do-it manual for librarians and paraprofessionals.* New York: Neal-Schuman Publishers, Inc.

Sable, Martin (1988), "Problem Patrons in Public and University Libraries," In: *Encyclopedia of Library and Information Science* 43: 169-91. New York, M. Dekker [1968]-<2000>.

Stebelman, Scott (1998), "Cybercheating: Dishonesty goes digital," *American Libraries* 29 (8): 48.

Still, Julie and Kassabian, Vibiana (1999), "The Mole's Dilemma: ethical aspects of public Internet access in academic libraries," *Internet Reference Services Quarterly* 4 (3): 7-22.

University of Hartford, Libraries & Learning Resources (2000), *Cell phone policy.* <http://libaxp.hartford.edu/llr/cellphon.htm> (Modified 11/18/2000). Accessed 12/15/00.

Willis, Mark R. (1999), *Dealing with Difficult People in the Library.* Chicago: American Library Association.

Young, Sherry (1997), "Sexually-explicit materials via the Internet: ethical concerns for the library profession," *Journal of Academic Librarianship* 23 (January): 49-50.

The Problem Patron
and the Academic Library Web Site
as Virtual Reference Desk

Daniel Taylor
George S. Porter

SUMMARY. Emerging technologies continue to offer librarians new opportunities to improve user services. Comment and query links on some library web pages are absorbing a significant share of the customer service workload previously handled by traditional reference desks. Familiar types of patron problems of course continue to crop up at the "virtual reference desk." New and different aspects of patron problems also appear. Originating with the experiences of a research university library's web group in dealing with incoming user messages, this study examines the challenges as well as advantages of dealing with "problem patron" phenomena in a virtual environment. *[Article copies available for a fee from The Haworth Document Delivery Service: 1-800-HAWORTH. E-mail address: <getinfo@haworthpressinc.com> Website: <http://www.HaworthPress. com> © 2002 by The Haworth Press, Inc. All rights reserved.]*

KEYWORDS. Email, problem patrons, reference services, virtual library, World Wide Web

Daniel Taylor is Biology Librarian, Caltech Library System 1-32, California Institute of Technology, 1200 East California Boulevard, Pasadena, CA 91125 (E-mail: danielt@caltech.edu). George S. Porter is Engineering Librarian, Caltech Library System 1-43, California Institute of Technology, 1200 East California Boulevard, Pasadena, CA 91125 (E-mail: george@library.caltech.edu).

[Haworth co-indexing entry note]: "The Problem Patron and the Academic Library Web Site as Virtual Reference Desk." Taylor, Daniel, and George S. Porter. Co-published simultaneously in *The Reference Librarian* (The Haworth Information Press, an imprint of The Haworth Press, Inc.) No. 75/76, 2002, pp. 163-172; and: *Helping the Difficult Library Patron: New Approaches to Examining and Resolving a Long-Standing and Ongoing Problem* (ed: Kwasi Sarkodie-Mensah) The Haworth Information Press, an imprint of The Haworth Press, Inc., 2002, pp. 163-172. Single or multiple copies of this article are available for a fee from The Haworth Document Delivery Service [1-800-HAWORTH, 9:00 a.m. - 5:00 p.m. (EST). E-mail address: getinfo@haworthpressinc.com].

© 2002 by The Haworth Press, Inc. All rights reserved.

163

INTRODUCTION

Variations on the idea of the problem or difficult patron have become a standard component of librarianship in recent decades. More recently, the ubiquity of the World Wide Web has resulted in many libraries having a virtual reference desk, and many librarians being involved in providing electronic reference service either informally or by design. Surprisingly, however, little if any work has been done on the relevance of the problem patron concept in this electronic/virtual milieu. This article addresses this apparent neglect. Experiences relevant to the problem patron concept are explored.

THE PROBLEM-PATRON CONCEPT–
SELECTIVE LITERATURE

Was a problem patron really " . . . standing outside, grinning, and waiting impatiently to get in" when the hypothetical first public library opened its doors, as Shuman jokingly asserts in his 1989 review article on problem patrons (Shuman, 1989)? Perhaps, considering the measure of concern that the library community has focused on dealing with problem patrons in recent decades. The ancient practice of chaining down manuscripts to prevent their theft indeed points to a centuries-old lineage for problem patrons. Contemporary treatments of the concept encompass not only theft but a myriad of other facets as well: safety concerns, rights issues, legal considerations, and a host of interpersonal dimensions. In recent decades, increased attention has been devoted to strategies for interacting productively with patrons who have mental or emotional problems.

Individuals who challenge the coping skills of librarians are not, of course, restricted to the mentally ill. Cuesta (1996), Harrison (1996), and Owens (1994), among others have applied the problem-patron concept to the academic library world with its specialized student-faculty population and eccentricities of the academic environment.

Various limitations on the usefulness of the problem-patron concept have been articulated. In her 1994 book *Serving the Difficult Customer*, Smith asserts that " . . . we are much more likely to experience an effective and mutually satisfying resolution to the problem by shifting our frame of reference from the problem-patron approach to the difficult-customer approach, from a position of defensiveness and blame to one of assertive understanding and shared problem-solving" (Smith,

1994). Hecker suggests that "rather than applying the label of problem patron to persons with mental illness, librarians must recognize people with mental illness as people with disabilities who ought to receive a measure of understanding and accommodation" (Hecker, 1996). Regardless of one's preferred terminology and paradigm, however, librarians continue to encounter those who challenge their coping skills.

THE VIRTUAL REFERENCE DESK CONCEPT

Leaders and participants explored many important issues at "Facets of Digital Reference: The Virtual Reference Desk 2nd Annual Digital Reference Conference" in Seattle, October 16-17, 2000. Application of the difficult or problem patron concept within the digital environment appeared not to be among those issues, aside from questions raised a few times by one of this paper's authors. Initial skepticism by respondents gave way to acknowledgment that the implications may well be worth exploring. The only previous example anyone could think of, however, is the Internet Public Library's "category for weirdos and nuts." The problem patron concept similarly appears to be lacking from the papers presented at the initial Virtual Reference Desk Digital Reference Conference (Lankes, 2000). Examination of Sloan's excellent "Digital Reference Services: A Bibliography" <http://www.lis.uiuc.edu/~b-sloan/digiref.html> reveals the same pattern (Sloan, 2000).

The authors' experience in a research university library's web group indicates that it may indeed be useful to consider the relevance of the difficult or problem patron concept in the virtual environment.

CALTECH LIBRARY SYSTEM'S WEB
http://library.caltech.edu/

The University Librarian of the California Institute of Technology created and charged a web committee early in 1996 to "provide clear and up-to-date web-based access to library system products and services for the Caltech community"(Buck, 1996). The team structure, rather than a webmaster approach, continues now. Team membership has varied between 4 and 5 people, generally including at least 2 subject specialist reference librarians and at least one library systems staff member. Web team efforts are an important part of each person's work, but they do not constitute the primary portion of anyone's job duties.

The Caltech Library System's website did not initially include separate links for a virtual reference desk or other department specific questions, but instead channeled all questions and comments through a CGI-based (Common Gateway Interface) comments form. Currently all pages throughout Caltech Library System's (CLS) web have this comments form as well as an email link. Comments submitted through these mechanisms are distributed via email to all members of the web team. Dealing with an incoming message may involve several, non-exclusive processes including answering the respondent directly, forwarding the query to the appropriate subject librarian (but only if that librarian is known to be on duty that day), and editing web pages.

Use of the comment form and email links has increased gradually but progressively to the point where their use constitutes a substantial proportion of the Caltech Library System's reference service. The evolution of the library's web has alleviated early 1990s worries about getting users to accept email reference and making effective use of the Internet in reference service. CLS's web has become a very popular and highly functional virtual reference desk. And yet, patron problems persist in this new milieu–some similar to those experienced in the traditional environment, and some quite different.

PATRON PROBLEMS IN THE VIRTUAL MILIEU

Greater Attractiveness to Potential Nuisances Due to Global Visibility and Access

The global visibility inherent in the *World Wide Web* is both a blessing and a curse. The 24 hours a day, seven days a week presence provided by a website alleviates some of the temporal and logistical constraints of the physical library. The CLS website is an extension of the systems and services of the library. For example, patrons can, and do, initiate interlibrary loan or document delivery requests <http://library.caltech.edu/ibid/> from all over the world at any time of the day or night, without overt intervention by library staff. CLS was a pioneer in the field of patron-initiated online document ordering and in coordinating ILL/DD with locally mounted bibliographic databases (Douglas, 1997). The current state of library services delivered through IP-based technologies (web, email, telnet, SciFinder Scholar, Beilstein Commander) is a logical extension of local services developed in the 1980s, taking advantage of technological advances in the broader community.

Although many websites are unidirectional broadcast efforts, the addition of email links and the CGI-based comments forms enable two-way interaction with clientele. This allows for website suggestions, book purchase recommendations, problem reports, and reference queries, to name just a few of the possibilities.

However, a down side exists to the bi-directional communications concept. The existence of the email reference service is readily seen by anyone in the world visiting the library's website. Not all email queries will come from a library's primary clientele. This increases the likelihood that questions will be received through the system which cannot be handled in a routine manner, or which fall outside the scope of the library's primary mission. Different libraries will need to examine their mission statements and possibly develop significantly different policies about the level of assistance that they can provide within their current staffing levels and in accordance with the mandates of their funding bodies. Email traffic at Caltech has not risen to a level where it threatens to be onerous, although the level of traffic has risen steadily, month to month, for over three years.

Problematic email can fall into a couple of major categories. SPAM, unsolicited bulk commercial email, is one of the banes of existence of all Internet email users. Therefore, it comes as no surprise that the first SPAM to the generic email address <library@caltech.edu>, used by CLS to facilitate email from our user community, arrived within a week of the introduction of mailto: links on the library website. As with the rest of the email traffic, SPAM has exhibited an inexorable upward climb.

Another category of problem email arises when patrons with mental or emotional problems, who may be outside of the library's primary clientele, identify the library's website as an attractive way to interact with the library. In some cases, what may at first appear to be an information need, is later revealed to be an attempt to achieve some other type of interaction, made easier by the accessibility of the website. The high name recognition of Caltech and of some of its historically significant faculty and visitors contribute to this phenomenon. For instance, it is not unreasonable to suppose that Caltech has an extensive collection in relativity theory. Einstein collaborated with a number of Caltech faculty and was a visiting professor immediately prior to the outbreak of World War II. So it is unexceptional for the library to receive email like the following:

URL: einstein-bose time bridge theory

E-Mail: <deleted>

Comments: was interested in reading more about any up to date literature, but as you know, every body and their dog, seems to have a book now. can you suggest some origional texts, and the names of any one who has looked into this matter, recently. (7 April 1998)

The email address, deleted for privacy, indicated the inquirer was not in the local area, making physical access to the library's collections impractical. A response was prepared, in consultation with the physics librarian, suggesting a specific university library collection in the inquirer's city for the pursuit of additional reading material. The acknowledgment of the reply follows:

thanks george

I've been reading old billboard magazines and find that they were a means for the carnival industry, among other things. I wrote some comedy, as usual and dun some political satire magazines in england. I always get a "good yeild" an amusment park in denmark was consumeed in flames, although the wooden coaster remained unscathed. Reading physics for thirty years now has proved to be extremely satisfying, and of course, thee last four yeears of math. . . . .

Well I'm starting on my time machine (9 April 1998)

Six months later:

does putting looted treasure into the atlantic count as a credible time experiment

[they never told us about the 'neutrality' in school]

yours truly, in particle physics (1 October 1998)

Ease of Accelerating and Escalating Difficult Situations

A primary function of a library website is to clearly set out policies and restrictions in an easily accessible manner. The Caltech Library

System employs some of the broadcast techniques made possible by the World Wide Web. Policy documents, including the access policy <http://library.caltech.edu/publications/rulesaccess.htm> and an explanation of borrowing privileges <http://library.caltech.edu/publications/borrowing.htm>, are available online. The hours of operation of various CLS facilities are posted <http://library.caltech.edu/about/hours.htm> as well. Despite the effort expended making the rules and hours easily accessible, issues occasionally develop when someone wishes to have a greater level of access than that to which they are entitled. When this happens, electronic communication increases the likelihood that the problem may escalate out of control. Traditionally, a library user might plead her or his case with circulation staff and on up the library's administrative chain of command, proceeding one level at a time. With each unsuccessful appeal the situation escalates, until one reaches the university librarian, the provost, or other similarly august individual whose decision cannot be appealed.

Email makes escalation much easier. In a memorable recent event, an undergraduate at a neighboring college sought advice from a prominent faculty member at our university, on how to increase a classmate's access to our university's library facilities.

> [my classmate at neighboring college] would like to use [your university's] library but he's had trouble in the past getting in at certain hours, later on in the day and at night. Do you have influence over library policies? Thanks for your prompt reply. (5 April 2000)

Ever helpful, the professor was forthcoming with advice.

> I think your friend should consult <http://library.caltech.edu/about/hours.htm> and then complain to <web@library.caltech.edu>. If that doesn't work, he should email our undergrad dean. (5 April 2000)

Emails of this advice went not only to the student, but also to our library's email address, a member of our library's administrative team, and to our university's undergraduate dean. Through the simple magic of email, a routine request for additional library privileges for a student at another college instantly and effortlessly became an issue in the undergraduate dean's email.

Related Considerations

Problematic aspects of patron encounters in the virtual milieu may, of course, be multiplied and amplified by well-documented characteristics of the electronic environment itself. Email is an extraordinarily poor communications medium for deciphering information needs, particularly if the request is not clearly stated. The reference interview, in a traditional setting, permits the librarian to perceive many more cues than the mere words alone convey. Even telephone reference, lacking the visual cues of body language and facial expression, delivers inflection in the voice. Plain text, in an email message, is a barren wasteland when looking for additional clues to the meaning of phrases, in comparison to the richness of the personal encounter.

ADVANTAGES IN THE ELECTRONIC ENVIRONMENT

Many of the challenges associated with providing reference service in a virtual milieu also have advantageous counterpoints. There is a potential for better pacing of staff responses than with walk-in and telephone queries. There may be a calmer opportunity to determine how extensively to respond to a query, if indeed, a response is needed at all; with SPAM, none may be appropriate. More opportunities for better quality control may be available than with telephone and in person reference encounters. Assessment of potential political sensitivities may be facilitated. There may be greater opportunities for thorough and in depth responses, including diplomatic flourishes and helpful pointers even with negative responses. The virtual environment has greater potential for wordsmithing and vetting responses if needed. Websites can be referenced with hypertext links, and files can be embedded in a message, further enhancing an answer to patron queries. When dealing with problematic questions in an electronic setting, it may be easier for the librarian to maintain emotional detachment, and construct a response that provides appropriate closure to the interaction.

CONCLUSION

Problem patrons may be defined by the category of person or the category of request. Patrons often are problematic because they are simply not part of the library's clientele, and are requesting services to which they are not entitled or services that drain staff time away from other priorities.

Problem patrons may also be recognized by the type of interaction they initiate. Often, their primary needs are not really informational (although the initial query is often disguised as an information request). For example, in a chat reference service, some patrons may not want to terminate the session because their real need is continual human interaction rather than an identifiable piece of information. Some people need other types of social services more than they need services traditionally provided by libraries. The librarian may need to try to focus the patron's attention on any actual information needs, and then, in some cases, carefully refer elsewhere for other types of needs.

The above categories exist both in traditional and electronic environments. A significant downside within the electronic environment is that institutional visibility and accessibility is greatly increased, thus attracting the attention of many outside (and potentially problem) users. Particularly when a library is initiating a new service, there may not be an easy mechanism for verifying legitimate users. There may even be a lack of desire to do so, since most new services get low use initially, and libraries may be trying to promote use in general.

Librarians providing digital reference services enjoy several advantages compared to their traditional counterparts. When dealing with problem patrons electronically, it is easier to consult with other staff, control your response, maintain emotional detachment, and send a response that attempts to provide some resolution or closure to the situation.

REFERENCES

Buck, Anne. 1996. Caltech Library System internal document.

Carparelli, Felicia. 1984. Public library or psychiatric ward? It's time for administrators to deal firmly with problem patrons. *American Libraries* 15 (4): 212.

Chadbourne, Robert. 1990. The problem patron: how much problem, how much patron? *Wilson Library Bulletin* 64: 59-60.

Clark, Georgia Ann. 1979. The problem patron. *Law Library Journal.* 72 (1): 52-57.

Cuesta, Emerita M. 1996. Problems with patrons in the academic library. In *Patron Behavior in Libraries: A Handbook of Positive Approaches to Negative Situations*, Beth McNeil and Denise J. Johnson, eds. Chicago: American Library Association. pp. 75-83.

Douglas, Kimberly, and Dana Roth. 1997. TOC/DOC: "It has changed the way I do science." *Science & Technology Libraries* 16 (3/4): 131-145.

Dowding, Martin. 1985. Problem patrons: what are they doing in the library? *Quill & Quire*. 51 (11): 4, 6-7.

Facets of Digital Reference: The Virtual Reference Desk 2nd Annual Digital Reference Conference. 2000 (October 16-17), Seattle, Washington.< http://www.vrd.org>.

Gothberg, Helen M. 1987. Managing difficult people: patrons (and others). *Reference Librarian* 19: 269-283.

Grotophorst, Clyde W. 1979. The problem patron: toward a comprehensive response. *Public Library Quarterly* 1 (4): 343-353.

Harrison, Mary M., Alison Armstrong, and David Hollenbeck. 1996. In *Patron Behavior in Libraries: A Handbook of Positive Approaches to Negative Situations,* Beth McNeil and Denise J. Johnson, eds. Chicago: American Library Association. pp. 87-94.

Hecker, Thomas E. 1996. Patrons with disabilities or problem patrons: which model should librarians apply to people with mental illness? *Reference Librarian* 53: 5-12.

Lankes, R. David, John W. Collins III, and Abby S. Kasowitz, eds. 2000. *Digital Reference in the New Millennium: Planning, Management, and Evaluation.* New York: Neal-Schuman.

Owens, Sheryl. 1994. Proactive problem patron preparedness. *Library & Archival Security* 12 (2): 11-23.

Problem Patron Manual. 1981. Compiled by Marion Brown et al., Schenectady County (New York) Public Library.

Rubin, Rhea Joyce. 2000. *Defusing the Angry Patron: A How-To-Do-It Manual for Librarians and Paraprofessionals.* New York: Neal-Schuman.

Salter, Charles A., and Jeffrey L. Salter. 1988. *On the Frontlines: Coping with the Library's Problem Patrons.* Englewood, Colorado: Libraries Unlimited.

Shuman, Bruce A. 1989. Problem patrons in libraries–a review article. *Library & Archival Security* 9 (2): 3-19.

Smith, Kitty. 1994. *Serving the Difficult Customer: A How-To-Do-It Manual for Library Staff.* New York: Neal-Schuman.

Sloan, Bernie. 2000. *Digital Reference Services: A Bibliography.* Graduate School of Library and Information Science, University of Illinois at Urbana-Champaign. <www.lis.uiuc.edu/~b-sloan/digiref.html>.

Vocino, Michael, Jr. 1976. Overdue: the library and the problem patron. *Wilson Library Bulletin* 50 (5): 372-373, 415.

Managing the Use of Cellular Phones in a Small College Learning Resource Centre

Christopher M. Hall

SUMMARY. Seventy-five per cent of young people in Britain own a cell phone. In a survey of sixth form college (small college) Learning Resource Centres (LRCs), cell phone usage occurred regularly and was occasionally a serious problem. LRC Managers need to decide whether to ban cell phone usage or not. Disruptive behaviour in libraries is defined as any behaviour that disturbs other users. Using this criterion, cell phone use should be banned in the LRC. Policies on cell phone use need to be clearly displayed and enforced tactfully and consistently. College management support will increase the effectiveness of any ban. *[Article copies available for a fee from The Haworth Document Delivery Service: 1-800-HAWORTH. E-mail address: <getinfo@haworthpressinc.com> Website: <http://www.HaworthPress.com> © 2002 by The Haworth Press, Inc. All rights reserved.]*

KEYWORDS. Problem patron, cell phones, learning resource centres, sixth form colleges, colleges, England, disruptive behaviour, young people, rules and regulations

INTRODUCTION

Over the last decade many traditional small college libraries in England have changed from being a purely book-based resource into multi-

Christopher M. Hall is Learning Resources Manager, Shena Simon Sixth Form College, Manchester, England (E-mail: christoff_hall@yahoo.com).

[Haworth co-indexing entry note]: "Managing the Use of Cellular Phones in a Small College Learning Resource Centre." Hall, Christopher M. Co-published simultaneously in *The Reference Librarian* (The Haworth Information Press, an imprint of The Haworth Press, Inc.) No. 75/76, 2002, pp. 173-180; and: *Helping the Difficult Library Patron: New Approaches to Examining and Resolving a Long-Standing and Ongoing Problem* (ed: Kwasi Sarkodie-Mensah) The Haworth Information Press, an imprint of The Haworth Press, Inc., 2002, pp. 173-180. Single or multiple copies of this article are available for a fee from The Haworth Document Delivery Service [1-800-HAWORTH, 9:00 a.m. - 5:00 p.m. (EST). E-mail address: getinfo@haworthpressinc.com].

© 2002 by The Haworth Press, Inc. All rights reserved.

media Learning Resource Centres (LRCs). An LRC in the context of this article can be defined as an integrated service including Information Technology Centre, Reprographics and Library or a Library with multi-media resources.

The potential for more noise in the LRC has increased with the expansion in non-book materials and, in particular, the increase in use of IT. In the last few years a new technological phenomenon has entered libraries in ever-increasing numbers: the cell phone or mobile phone. In a recent survey regarding cell phone usage in Britain it was found that 54% of adults, or approximately 31.8 million people owned a mobile phone. In addition 75% of young people aged 15-24 years own a cell phone (Office of Telecommunications 2000). The main client group for small colleges in Britain is young people aged 16-19.

The cell phone has the potential to be disruptive in an LRC in three ways:

- The ringing tone often plays a tune and can be clearly heard.
- Talking on a cell phone may disturb other users.
- Text messaging in itself is usually not disruptive, however young people often gather round to read or write messages. This may become a noisy activity, as the messages are often light-hearted, humorous or offensive.

The aim of this article is to examine cell phone use in small college LRCs and to evaluate measures to manage such behaviour. The paper will first examine what is meant by a 'small college.'

SMALL COLLEGES

In the context of this article, 'small colleges' are defined as English sixth form colleges. In England there are 107 sixth form colleges catering mainly for 16-19 year old students. These colleges range in size approximately from five hundred to two thousand students. Since 1993 sixth form colleges have become independent colleges, although funded by the British Government through the Further Education Funding Council. Levels of funding are dependent on the number of students recruited by the colleges. As a consequence, some colleges have had problems with funding. Some colleges also found that their accommodation could not cope adequately with the extra number of students they recruited to keep funding levels high (Ainley and Bailey 1997 and

Mitchell et al. 1998). In addition, colleges were encouraged to recruit 'non-traditional' students, i.e., students who do not usually participate in further education and students with learning difficulties. This resulted in some students entering colleges with little motivation to study and the potential to be disruptive (Mitchell et al. 1998).

WHAT IS DISRUPTIVE BEHAVIOUR IN AN LRC CONTEXT?

Before deciding whether to ban or allow mobile phone use to any degree in an LRC it is important to be clear what constitutes disruptive behaviour in a library context.

Schenectady County Public Library defines disruptive behaviour as: "Problem behaviour is any behaviour which either consciously or unconsciously violates or restricts the rights of others to use the library" (Brown et al. 1982, p. 9). In the 1980s there were two major studies of American, Canadian and British public libraries which looked at disruptive behaviour by library patrons (Lincoln 1984 and Lincoln and Lincoln 1987). Again, disruptive behaviour was seen as behaviour which deliberately or unintentionally disturbs other users. Turner (1993) sees disruptive behaviour not as physically threatening behaviour but that which disturbs other users. Jones (1996, p. 50) states succinctly: ". . . if a behaviour disrupts others, then that behaviour is inappropriate."

In a college context, disruptive behaviour is defined as: "The term disruptive behaviour here describes patterns of repeated behaviour, which significantly interrupt the learning of others or threaten their personal security or well-being, or bring the organisation into disrepute" (Mitchell et al. 1998, p. vi). Although this differs from the library definition, the emphasis is again on disruptive behaviour being behaviour which disturbs the learning process.

It is clear from the literature that any behaviour, whether deliberate or not, which impedes people's learning is disruptive and needs to be dealt with in an appropriate manner. In this respect the literature supports the banning of cell phone use in an LRC.

CELL PHONES IN EDUCATIONAL ESTABLISHMENTS

The problems of school children using cell phones and text messaging in schools has been highlighted several times in the British press

(Brockes 1999 and Elderkin 1999). Many 16-19 year olds perceive cell phone use as natural and not as deliberately disruptive behaviour. To many young users in a busy LRC, cell phones ringing and people talking are as natural as printer and photocopier noises are to LRC staff. A modern LRC is much noisier than was a library ten years ago (Rogers et al. 1999).

The LRC users' views on cell phone use could be an important factor in whether to ban its use. But if even the learning of one user is disturbed by cell phone use then a policy concerning cell phone use in the LRC needs to be drawn up.

THE SURVEY

Research undertaken in 1999-2000 (Hall 2001) identified disruptive user behaviour in sixth form college LRCs, evaluated measures to manage such behaviour and made recommendations for best practice. One of the objectives of the questionnaire was to identify the extent and different types of disruptive behaviour found in sixth form college LRCs.

To gather further information on personal and LRC strategies on managing disruptive behaviour, 15 LRC Managers were interviewed from LRCs suffering varying levels of problem behaviour. The Critical Incident Technique was used to gather in-depth data, and in particular perceptions and feelings of the interviewees (Flanagan 1954). In addition, 12 College Managers were interviewed to discover college-wide policies on managing disruptive behaviour.

CELL PHONES IN THE LRC

Data collected concerning the frequency of disruption caused by cell phones in the LRC showed that:

- Daily 52 (62.7%)
- Weekly 15 (18.1%)
- Monthly 6 (7.2%)
- Rarely 9 (10.8%)
- Never 1(1.2%)

The results showed that mobile phone use in LRCs occurred frequently in most of the LRCs surveyed.

Although there were no further questions on cell phone use, it was commented on several times. When asked to define disruptive behaviour some respondents included cell phone usage in this category. Others commented on cell phone usage when talking about user behaviour. Another respondent saw mobile phone usage as irritating rather than disruptive, while other LRC Managers saw it as a noise problem. When asked about time spent managing disruptive behaviour, some commented on cell phone usage. A respondent stated that there were problems hourly, another mentioned having to make constant requests to users to switch off cell phones and others stated that there were constant or frequent problems with mobile phone use. Some LRC Managers stated that cell phones are confiscated if they are used in the LRC, and at one college, students were banned from bringing cell phones into the college.

All LRC Managers who were interviewed said that cell phone use was not allowed in the LRC. Some interviewees said there was a 'zero tolerance' policy on cell phone use. When asked to relate a serious incident of disruptive behaviour, three LRC Managers included an incident concerning a mobile phone.

In the interviews with College Managers there were no questions relating to cell phone use. An interviewee did state that there were problems with cell phone use in the LRC. This was the same college as one of the LRC Managers who related an incident of disruptive behaviour that included mobile phone use.

MANAGING THE USE OF CELL PHONES IN THE LRC

Most LRCs in sixth form colleges are small in size and often overcrowded (Mitchell et al. 1998 and Further Education Funding Council 2000). In practical terms, allowing cell phone use will disturb some users, even if most users are unconcerned. If there are students who are disturbed by cell phone usage the LRC policy must be to ban its use. In some bigger LRCs which have a separate IT Centre, group working area and a silent area, mobile phones could be allowed except in the silent area.

Young people tend to use mobile phones for non-academic activities so a ban would help to promote an academic ethos in the LRC. Any LRC rules, including those concerning cell phones, need to be concise and unambiguous and clearly displayed (Huntoon 1985 and Rogers et al. 1999). To gain acceptance of any ban on cell phones in the LRC, the

LRC Manager should try to gain student support through involving users in the drawing up of any rules. This will give the users a sense of
ownership (Ayers et al. 1995 and Pritchard and Barker 1996). Once the
rules have been agreed upon and then displayed, they need to be enforced tactfully, quickly and, most importantly, consistently (Huntoon
1985 and Rogers et al. 1999).

Penalties would depend on the frequency of cell phone usage. A single incident where the user has forgotten or did not know about the rule
should need no more than a mild request to switch off the phone and a
brief statement of LRC policy on cell phones (Rogers et al. 1999). More
severe penalties could be introduced for constant abuse of the no-use
rule. These could include temporary confiscation of cell phones, as happens in many schools (Elderkin 1999), although this action may throw
up legal issues or lead to a problem encounter if the user refuses to hand
over the phone. Another possibility introduced at one college to cope
with eating and drinking in the library was a fine system (Weaver-Meyers
and Ramsay 1990). This system could be used for cell phone misuse.
More conventionally the user could have lending rights temporarily
suspended and ultimately could be banned from the LRC.

A manual for all types of disruptive behaviour should be developed
and should include cell phone usage (Brown et al. 1982, Turner 1993
and Morrissett 1996). The manual would instruct LRC staff how to
tackle cell phone use in the LRC, how to deal with any incident and how
to log it. The manual should also include emergency phone numbers
and named contacts, so that when an incident escalates to a level that is
problematic, appropriate support is available for front-line staff.

Colleges could follow the line taken by some schools and one sixth
form college and ban cell phones in college (Elderkin 1999). The college needs to have an academic ethos to encourage all students to learn
(Elton 1989). Instilling this ethos into students should prevent cell
phone misuse in academic areas like the LRC. The LRC needs to be part
of any college-wide disciplinary system (Mitchell et al. 1998) so students do not perceive the area as a place where rules may be ignored
with impunity. Without access to college disciplinary procedures the
LRC staff would be powerless to prevent cell phone users from habitu-
ally ignoring LRC rules.

CONCLUSION

Cell phone use amongst young people in England is likely to continue to increase in the future. This means that in the near future nearly

every user in a sixth form college LRC is likely to have a mobile phone. It thus becomes essential to have a policy on cell phone use in the LRC. Currently cell phone use and text messaging by 16-19 year olds tends to be social. In this respect it is not an academic pursuit, and so in a college LRC it should be banned in the same way that games and chatrooms on the Internet are banned. Sixth form college LRC Managers who were interviewed were unanimous that cell phone usage was not allowed in the LRC. LRC staff need to have rules in place that can be easily used and have access to back-up systems if a situation escalates. Consistent enforcing of rules forbidding cell phone usage should lead to a decline in its occurrence. Currently cell phones have no place in academic libraries; however the development of WAP (Wireless Application Protocol) and other technologies means that mobile phones could become an educational tool (Wainwright 2000). If this happens then current thinking on cell phone usage in the college LRC will need to be reviewed.

REFERENCES

Ainley, P. and Bailey, B. (1997) *The Business of Learning: staff and student experiences of further education in the 1990s.* London: Cassell.

Ayers, H. et al. (1995) *Perspectives on Behaviour.* London: David Fulton.

Brockes, E. (1999) *Look Who's Talking: you gave them a mobile phone for use in emergency but what are they really doing with it?* Guardian, 22 Sept 1999, G2 Section, pp. 11. [online]. Internet. 21 June 2000. (URL: http://proquest.umi.com/qdweb).

Brown, M. et al. (1982) *Comps Problem Patron Manual.* New York: Schenectady County Public Library.

Elderkin, J. (1999) *When Lessons Interrupt an Important Call.* Times, 2 April 1999, Features Section, pp. 47. [online]. Internet. 21 June 2000. (URL: http://proquest. umi.com/pqdweb).

Elton, L. et al. (1989) *Discipline in Schools: report of the Committee of Enquiry chaired by Lord Elton.* London: H.M.S.O.

Flanagan, J. C. (1954) *The Critical Incident Technique.* Psychological Bulletin, 51 (4), pp. 327-358.

Further Education Funding Council. (2000) *Individual College Inspection Reports.* [online]. Internet. 2 Feb. 2001. (URL: http://www.fefc.ac.uk).

Great Britain. Office of Telecommunications. (OFTEL) (2000) *Consumers use of Mobile Telephony.* [online]. Internet. 2 Feb. 2001. (URL: http://www.oftel.gov.uk// cmu/research/mob1100.htm).

Hall, C. M. (2001 pending) *Managing Disruptive Behaviour in Sixth Form College Learning Resource Centres.* MA dissertation, Department of Information and Communications, Manchester Metropolitan University, England.

Hart, T. L., ed. (1985) *Behaviour Management in the School Library Media Center.* Chicago: American Library Association.

Huntoon, E. (1985) *When it Seems the Kids are Taking Over.* In: Hart, T. L., ed. (1985), pp. 119-124.

Jones, P. (1996) *Opposites Attract: young adults and libraries.* In McNeil, B. and Johnson, D. J., eds. (1996), pp. 44-54.

Lincoln, A. J. (1984) *Crime in the Library: a study of patterns, impact and security.* New York: Bowker R. R.

Lincoln, A. J. and Lincoln, C. Z. (1987*) Library Crime and Security: an international perspective.* New York: The Haworth Press, Inc.

McNeil, B. and Johnson, D. J., eds. (1996) *Patron Behavior in Libraries: a handbook of positive approaches to negative situations.* Chicago: American Library Association.

Mitchell, C. et al. (1998) *Ain't Misbehavin: managing disruptive behaviour.* Bristol: Further Education Development Agency.

Morrissett, L. M. (1996) *Developing and Implementing a Patron Behavior Policy.* In: McNeil, B. and Johnson, D. J., eds. (1996), pp. 135-149.

Pritchard, B. and Barker, K. (1996) *Negotiating a Classroom Contract.* Modern English Teacher, 5 (1), pp. 45-47.

Rogers, M. et al. (1999) *Communication Overload.* Library Journal, 124 (12), pp. 66-67.

Turner, A. M. (1993) *It Comes with the Territory: handling problem situations in libraries.* Jefferson: McFarland.

Wainwright, M. (2000) *Hi Honey, I'm still at School.* Guardian, 20 July 2000, Online Section, pp. 8. [online]. Internet. 2 Feb. 2001. (URL: http://proquest.umi.com/pqdweb).

Weaver-Meyers, P. L. and Ramsay, S. D. (1990) *Fines for Food: a citation system to control food and drink consumption in the library.* College Research Library News, June 1990, pp. 536-538.

PROVIDING SOLUTIONS TO THE PROBLEM: IDEAS FROM OTHER PROFESSIONS AND THE WORLD OF LIBRARY AND INFORMATION SCIENCE

How Psychotherapists Handle Difficult Clients: Lessons for Librarians

Brian Quinn

SUMMARY. Although librarians occasionally encounter difficult patrons in the course of their work, psychologists work with difficult clients much more frequently. This raises an interesting question–how is it that psychologists are able to manage these trying individuals, and in some instances even help them improve? This study attempts to answer that question by investigating how psychotherapists define, cope with,

Brian Quinn is Social Sciences Librarian, Texas Tech University Libraries, Lubbock, TX 79409 (E-mail: libaq@lib.ttu.edu).

[Haworth co-indexing entry note]: "How Psychotherapists Handle Difficult Clients: Lessons for Librarians." Quinn, Brian. Co-published simultaneously in *The Reference Librarian* (The Haworth Information Press, an imprint of The Haworth Press, Inc.) No. 75/76, 2002, pp. 181-196; and: *Helping the Difficult Library Patron: New Approaches to Examining and Resolving a Long-Standing and Ongoing Problem* (ed: Kwasi Sarkodie-Mensah) The Haworth Information Press, an imprint of The Haworth Press, Inc., 2002, pp. 181-196. Single or multiple copies of this article are available for a fee from The Haworth Document Delivery Service [1-800-HAWORTH, 9:00 a.m. - 5:00 p.m. (EST). E-mail address: getinfo@haworthpressinc.com].

© 2002 by The Haworth Press, Inc. All rights reserved.

and treat difficult patients. It explains the psychology of difficult clients, techniques psychologists use in working with them, and how these might be utilized by librarians. The importance of seeing difficult clients as a means of personal growth is also emphasized. *[Article copies available for a fee from The Haworth Document Delivery Service: 1-800-HAWORTH. E-mail address: <getinfo@haworthpressinc.com> Website: <http://www.HaworthPress. com> © 2002 by The Haworth Press, Inc. All rights reserved.]*

KEYWORDS. Difficult patrons, psychology, coping, definition, techniques, personal growth

It is not uncommon for librarians to encounter what they might regard as a "difficult" patron at one time or another in their career. Fortunately, in most cases these encounters have been limited to an occasional interaction with a difficult person or two. Rarely is it the case that a librarian must contend with difficult patrons on a frequent and extended basis.

The same cannot be said for psychotherapists. As a profession, psychotherapists are much more likely to have what might be termed "difficult" persons as clients. Some of these individuals may be drawn to therapy in order to seek treatment for their difficulties, and many more are likely to be forced to seek therapy because they have been characterized by others as being difficult. Teachers, police, judges, employers, and physicians are occupational groups that are likely to refer those whom they regard as "difficult" to psychotherapists.

The interesting question for librarians then becomes, if psychotherapists are likely to work with difficult clients on a regular basis, how do they manage? How is it that they manage these individuals on a routine basis, and how are they themselves able to cope? Psychotherapists are able to listen to and work with a steady stream of belligerent, complaining, obnoxious individuals and still take considerable satisfaction in their work. How is this possible?

It is the purpose of this study to investigate why it is that psychotherapists are so capable of dealing with some of society's most troubled persons. Is it something about the personality of the psychotherapist that makes this possible? Or is it because of techniques that a psychotherapist uses? The results have obvious implications for the field of librarianship, because it would seem that librarians could use some of these same techniques in their encounters with difficult patrons. If librarians are better able to understand how it is that psychologists successfully treat difficult patients, they might use that knowledge to improve their relations with their own difficult patrons (Schwenk, Marquez, Lefever, and Cohen 1989).

THE DIFFICULTY OF DEFINING "DIFFICULT"

Although psychologists have written many articles about treating difficult patients, they acknowledge that it can sometimes be difficult to define what they mean by "difficult." Perhaps the reason for this is that there are many different ways people can be difficult. To try to simplify the definition by focusing on one particular way in which people are difficult does not do justice to the complexity of the difficult person or the problem in general. Instead, it might be better to acknowledge that there is no single authoritative definition of a difficult patient, but a range of them.

Among the ways psychotherapists have defined "difficult" include a person who seeks help but then fails to listen to advice or rejects it (Yalom 1985). The famous psychiatrist Eric Berne suggested that even though difficult people ask for help they do not really want it. They are actually playing a game in which the real reason they ask for advice is so that they can reject it (Berne 1964). Many psychotherapists have noted that difficult people complain to achieve various forms of psychological gratification, not to actually get help or solve a problem (Berger and Rosenbaum 1967). One therapist has suggested that "difficulty" is to some degree in the eye of the beholder, and that the needs, expectations, and tolerance level of the psychotherapist all contribute to who is defined as "difficult" (Noonan 1998).

Other therapists have pointed out that the definition of "difficult" is not so much subjective as it is social. A difficult person is one who is perceived by others to be abrasive, irritating, aggressive, or annoying (Wepman and Donovan 1984). In other words, one sure means of determining objectively whether a person is "difficult" is the degree to which others feel uneasy when the person is around. Another indicator of "difficult" would be the extent to which people will engage in avoidance behaviors in order to not be around the person (Litvak 1994). So it appears that "difficult" is not merely a subjective label but has an objective social dimension to it. This social definition of "difficult" would seem to be the most compelling. The author has worked in several libraries, each of which had certain patrons that were known to the public services librarians as being "difficult." In each case, there was a high degree of social consensus and no instances in which librarians could not agree on whether the person in question was really "difficult" or not. In other words "difficult" was not a subjective judgment.

THE PSYCHOLOGY OF DIFFICULT PERSONS

What makes difficult patrons behave the way they do? Psychologists attribute difficult behavior to several possible causes. Some therapists believe that difficult persons may themselves have been abused by difficult people in their early years. The difficult person later grows up to be deeply ambivalent: the difficult person wants help, but also fears it. Psychologically, their abrasiveness is a defense against closeness, the fear of being injured by the person they are seeking help from (Stern 1984).

Many therapists feel that the difficult person tries to unconsciously re-create in the present the early abusive relationship they experienced with an early caretaker. That is, a difficult patron will at times try to make the librarian behave in the same abusive manner that the early caretaker did. At other times, the difficult person will try to make the librarian feel like the abused, victimized recipient of the caretaker's mistreatment by acting in an aggressive and abrasive manner. Psychotherapists hypothesize that the reason difficult patients attempt to recreate the early difficult relationships they experienced in their relations with others is because of their inability to articulate these traumatic experiences (Book 1997).

In a psychological sense, difficult persons are deeply contradictory. It is not that they dislike other people, it is others that dislike them. They often act like victims, but actually act to aggressively destroy relationships. Help is rejected in order to avoid being rejected by their helpers. Helpers are viewed as antagonists, and difficult patrons are likely to be hypersensitive to the slightest indication of dislike on the part of those who try to help them (Davis 1984).

The difficult person will frequently alternate between being victim and abuser in the manner he relates to others. Many therapists have noted that the difficult person will at times exhibit behavior that resembles that of a demanding, needy child. Difficult people want a great deal, but are unwilling to extend themselves. Many difficult persons think that they somehow deserve and must be given special treatment. Difficult persons can be so demanding that it seems inevitable that they will never get everything they want (Messer 1999). Once they realize this, they slip into a victimized complaining mentality that serves to further alienate them from those who attempt to help them.

Clearly, the difficult person syndrome is extremely complex psychologically. In attempting to help difficult persons, the psychotherapist–and the librarian–have their hands full. Difficult patients, as the above explanation makes clear, are among the most challenging clients therapists face. If they represent a challenge to therapists, who have such extensive training in psychology, imagine how much more difficult they appear to librarians. With this in mind it may be helpful to examine closely how psychotherapists contend with these challenging patients. Psychotherapists have much to teach librarians about what to do the next time they encounter a difficult patron at the reference desk.

HANDLING THE DIFFICULT PATRON

Psychotherapists have researched extensively the question of how to successfully treat difficult patients. The results of some of the studies seem to be what one might expect. One study, for example, found that the greater the degree to which therapists relied on optimistic perseverance, the better they saw themselves as coping with stressful clients (Medeiros and Prochaska 1988). This might be said of many activities however, and does not seem especially insightful. Another study was conducted of how therapists are able to overcome difficult, resistant, uncooperative patients. It found that therapists that dressed and talked informally and that made frequent references to their own experience were more effective in reducing resistance among difficult clients. Therapists who behaved in a more formal, reserved "expert" role were less successful (Miller and Wells 1990). It also seems likely though, that any client, difficult or not, would find someone who treated them less formally and in a more self-disclosing manner attractive.

Other studies of working with difficult clients are more interesting. They go beyond the obvious and examine the psychology of handling these kinds of people in more depth. Many of these studies are written from a psychoanalytic perspective, because it was Freud who originally defined the difficult patient. According to Freud, a difficult client was one who could not form a positive transference with the therapist. Before going any further, it may help to take a look at what a few of these technical psychoanalytic terms mean.

TRANSFERENCE AND COUNTERTRANSFERENCE

In a general sense, transference is a psychological process that occurs when a patient relates emotionally to a therapist in a manner similar to the way he or she related to early important figures in the patient's life. The patient, for example, may regard the therapist as hateful because the therapist somehow reminds him of an uncle whom he never liked as a child. Earlier, it was suggested that difficult people tend to relate to others as a result of the way they have been treated earlier in life. When a difficult patron treats a librarian as an abuser or as a victim, these are forms of transference. The difficult person attempts to recreate the abusive relationship that the person experienced from early caretakers, and alternates, at times taking on the role of the abuser and at times the role of the victim (Ivey 1995).

Even more interesting is the flip side of this emotional coin. Not only does the patient react emotionally to the therapist to create a transference of feelings, but the therapist also reacts emotionally to the patient. This emotional reaction on the part of the therapist is referred to in psychotherapy as countertransference. Particularly in the course of treating difficult patients, psychotherapists are likely to experience strong countertransference feelings. These are engendered as a result of the especially difficult behaviors and ways of relating that such patients exhibit. Although therapists strive to be objective and scientifically neutral in an emotional sense, they are also human and vulnerable. As a result, they must at times struggle to control their emotions in working with the difficult client (Marshall and Marshall 1988).

These emotional struggles are understandably difficult for the therapist. Much like a librarian, a therapist confronted by an abrasive, complaining, obnoxious, manipulative, or aggressive client may find this emotionally wrenching. This may seem surprising, since many people regard psychotherapists as having a degree of self-awareness and emotional control, or at least more than the average person. The psychological literature suggests that this is not always the case.

Countertransference feelings are particularly difficult for those in the helping professions. Psychotherapists and librarians have both been trained to help people, and both are members of occupational groups that have a strong ethos of helping associated with them. When an encounter with a difficult person causes librarians to feel anger, disgust, contempt or disdain toward the person, it is especially upsetting because of the occupational and professional values they have been socialized into and have internalized. A librarian is likely to feel guilty for regarding the patron in such a negative manner. It is natural for librarians to feel that their feelings have been manipulated. Difficult patrons are skilled at "pushing people's buttons," and at causing emotional upset in others (Hinshelwood 1999). This can cause unprepared professionals to rapidly lose self-esteem and self-confidence and can cause them to place their professional identity in question.

COPING WITH COUNTERTRANSFERENCE REACTIONS

Given the strong professional emphasis on helping, the librarian may well try to deny his or her feelings of anger, aversion or helplessness. Psychotherapists suggest doing the opposite. Instead of becoming overwhelmed by one's emotional reaction and immediately trying to deny it, psychotherapists recommend that the helper fully acknowledge his or her negative feelings toward the difficult client (Staley 1991). While it is admirable to try to be as objective and impartial toward the client as possible, when negative emotions do arise psychotherapists try to acknowledge and accept those feelings and impulses as part of being human. To try to deny or suppress them creates psychic turmoil and increases a helper's stress level. It is important to recognize that they are human and have needs like everyone else, including a desire to feel needed and respected. It is also important for the librarian to realize that the emotions being experienced are not particular to him or her. Anyone confronted with the same difficult individual would experience similar feelings.

Often the librarian will feel as if he or she is being put into a role by the difficult patron. In fact, this is often the case. Psychologically, the difficult patron has a tendency to unconsciously recreate early divisive relationships. The difficult patron will cast the librarian in the role of the abusive person by acting abrasively in order to test him or her and see if he or she will react negatively. The intention of the difficult person is to see whether the librarian will in turn become abusive or mistreat him. Difficult persons are unable to articulate or explain their psychological problem, so instead they act it out because it is the only way they know how to communicate their early traumatic experience with caretakers (Book 1997). Unleashing their emotions can also serve as a form of catharsis for them.

The natural reaction of the psychotherapist or the librarian, when confronted by the difficult person is that most basic and primitive of stress reactions: fight or flight. Yet neither of these reactions will help the situation. A withdrawal response on the part of the librarian will encourage the difficult person to become more abusive, because the librarian's victim-like reaction triggers memories of the role the difficult patron was forced into by early caretakers. If the librarian initiates a fight response and becomes angry or retaliatory, the difficult person will react by assuming the role of victim, and complain of mistreatment or lack of respect on the librarian's part. When faced with this difficult double-bind situation, what can a librarian do?

UTILIZING THE CONTAINMENT FUNCTION

The way that psychotherapists handle this kind of situation is to serve, in a psychological sense, as a container. What this means is that instead of reacting to the difficult patient's behavior with aggression or withdrawal, the therapist simply allows the patient to act out, or actually re-enact the troubled way of relating to others that is so characteristic of the difficult patient's past. The difficult patron is testing the helper to see how much the person is willing to put up with (Siegel 1990). By not reacting as most people have in the past, the therapist or the librarian serves to defuse the situation emotionally. By remaining as calm and objective as possible, the librarian is actually educating the difficult patron. Adopting a non-flight response shows the difficult patient that there is another way to relate to people that is outside the aggressor-victim dichotomy that the difficult patron typically gets stuck in. On the other hand, if the librarian reacts with anger or anxiety, the difficult patron is likely to unconsciously relate to the librarian as either aggressor or victim.

Instead, what is called for is that, utilizing the containment function, the librarian does not allow his own emotions to overwhelm him to the point that they interfere with his helping role. As challenging as it may be, the librarian must try to utilize his or her cognitive understanding of the psychology of the difficult patient to realize that he or she is there simply to "be with" the patron rather than become aroused, provoked or otherwise phased by the difficult person's behavior (Fiore 1988). Not allowing the behavior of the difficult person to trigger an emotional reaction frees the librarian to focus or whether there is a real need for library help that is obscured by the difficult person's obnoxious behavior. By understanding that the difficult person's behavior is not a personal attack on them, but simply how that person relates to everyone, librarians can regard these tortured individuals empathetically rather than hatefully or with fear.

Many psychotherapists have mentioned the importance of acceptance in working with the difficult patient (Otani 1989). In order to treat difficult behavior, it is first necessary to accept it rather than avoid it or condemn it. Trying to control the behavior will only aggravate or escalate it. The librarian who accepts the difficult patron and lets him or her know this stands a much better chance of getting that person to cooperate, judging from the results of controlled studies of psychology outcomes (Orlinsky and Howard 1986). In other words, the best strategy to manage difficult behavior is to accept it. Arguing with the patron only serves to reinforce resistance. Some therapists have even used paradoxical techniques that involve agreeing with the patient rather than trying to refute him. If an angry patron comes to the reference desk complaining that the online catalog is too slow, it might be better to say "I know, I hate it too when I'm doing research and it begins to just hang there," than to say, "It probably has something to so with our Internet connections, which is something we have no control over." The librarian, by exhibiting a degree of empathy, sets the groundwork for forming an alliance with the patron. This kind of paradoxical approach can be effective in disarming the patron who approaches the desk looking for a confrontation (Carberry 1983).

MODELING AND KINESICS

Irritable and abusive clients are among the most challenging and difficult problems that psychotherapists face in their work. The same holds true for librarians. When an angry patron is acting or speaking abusively, it does little good to try to face the person down. Engaging in a contest to see who has more power is a futile exercise. It is also pointless to attempt to tell them to calm down. It is necessary to try to help them regain their composure, but the best way to do it is to model it. If the librarian uses kinesics, or "body language" as it is commonly known, and deliberately speaks and moves in a slow, calm, deliberate manner, the patron will get an indirect message that the situation is deescalating and that there is no reason to act hysterically or irrationally (Davenport 1999).

INVOLVING OTHER STAFF

Some difficult patrons may be unable to obtain the satisfaction they seek from one librarian, and may then try obtaining it from other librarians. They may try various tactics to obtain what they want, like playing one librarian off another. Many librarians have experienced a situation in which a patron approaches them at the desk and asks a question. When an answer is offered, the patron then says "But the other librarian told me something else." The author has even experienced situations in which a dissatisfied patron will walk over to the other librarian sharing the desk and ask them the same question.

When faced with a difficult client, psychotherapists will often consult with colleagues about the person. Librarians might consider doing the same. There are several benefits to doing this. To begin with, other colleagues are alerted to the possibility that they may encounter this person. Second, the librarian can get advice and suggestions for how to handle the individual. Some colleagues may already know the person in question, and may be able to offer the benefit of their experience (Kottler 1992). Others may have encountered a similar patron at some point in their careers.

Turning to colleagues for advice and support can be very helpful, but there are also some caveats to be aware of. It is important to act professionally and avoid contests to see who can complain the most about a patron, or who has encountered the most awful patron. It is important to try to maintain some sense of empathy and compassion for even the most abrasive and obnoxious patrons. It is easy to label a client as "difficult" and thereby reduce them to the status of deviant, rather than regard them as the complex, suffering individuals that they are (Norton and McGauley 1998). Labeling a patron as "difficult" can be a way of stigmatizing them so that they are easier to dismiss as beyond help. Once this occurs, there can be little possibility of making any real progress with the patron, since they have been relegated to a class of patrons that are often merely tolerated rather than genuinely cared for.

VICARIOUS TRAUMATIZATION AND SELF CARE

Working with difficult clients is extremely demanding for both psychotherapists and for librarians. As mentioned earlier, difficult clients tend to re-enact their traumatic interactions with those they encounter. This can create a kind of vicarious traumatization in professional helpers that can sap one's ability to be empathic and to believe in one's self-efficacy. The therapist is alternately cast in the role of abuser and victim, and indirectly exposed to the often intense emotions and mood swings that can be characteristic of the difficult client.

Psychotherapists realize that working with difficult clients can be stressful and are proactive about being self protective. They have developed strategies for balancing and countering the negativity they are exposed to in the course of their work. Among the strategies that they can use to stay healthy and maintain perspective is to seek out various kinds of rejuvenating experiences and relationships. Spending quality time with friends and family or taking time out to attend artistic or cultural events can be ways to restore the helper's perspective.

Psychotherapists also make use of various relaxation strategies to promote self care. These include deep breathing to relieve stress, progressive relaxation, and the use of guided imagery to enhance relaxation. Some therapists engage in meditation to alleviate tension. Others keep a journal of their experiences and emotions, which can be not only cathartic but also a way of gaining insight into one's thought processes. Psychotherapists use various combinations of these techniques to maintain maximum effectiveness with clients (Brems 2000).

Experienced therapists understand that it is important to engage in both physical and psychological compartmentalization. Boundaries need to be drawn physically between work and home, and boundaries need to be established mentally as well. An encounter with a difficult patron can sometimes result in intrusive thoughts, flashbacks, and dreams. The librarian may find that even after work he or she may mentally reenact the encounter numerous times and think about how it might have been handled differently or better. This kind of reflection is problematic if it becomes obsessive. Therapists are able to counteract it by recalling successes–even small ones–with clients, and librarians can do the same (Ryan 1999).

In fields like psychotherapy and librarianship that have traditionally maintained a strong service orientation, the idea of self care may strike some as sounding self-indulgent or even narcissistic. Should we not be spending all our time trying to do everything we can for patrons, and worry about ourselves second? Psychotherapists say no. They argue that not engaging in various forms of self care can be irresponsible and potentially damaging to one's self and eventually to one's clients. They believe that focusing exclusively on the care and well being of clients leads to distress and ineffectiveness among practitioners. Adequate self care is necessary to prevent burnout and promote optimal functioning. Working long hours without a break, failing to take adequate vacations, and harboring unrealistic expectations about how much can be accomplished with difficult clients can all take their toll on the librarian emotionally and physically. Ultimately it is the patron who loses because the stressed, impaired librarian cannot deliver an adequate level of service (Carroll, Gilroy, and Murra 1999).

At least in theory, many psychotherapists have the professional training and sensitivity to be aware that they may be stressed and not capable of functioning well. Many have been in therapy themselves and are aware of how their mind works and of what their emotional weaknesses and limitations may be. They should therefore be capable of recognizing when it is necessary to engage in various forms of self care needed to restore themselves. The same cannot be said for librarians, who are likely to have less self awareness and be less attuned to their own needs for restorative measures. Librarians are likely to engage in more self denying, masochistic behaviors that if left unchecked could not only compromise the efficacy of the librarian with patrons, but result in physical, emotional and social problems for the librarian. Self care awareness and training programs need to be better integrated into library training and supervision. The stigma associated with self care, that it is selfish and indulgent, needs to be removed. Librarians need to realize what psychotherapists are increasingly coming to terms with: that they are human and vulnerable and in need of self care as a preventative measure.

DIFFICULT PATRONS AS A MEANS OF GROWTH

Librarians typically regard difficult patrons the same way most other people regard them. They are seen as an annoyance, and interacting with them is something to be avoided as much as possible and when unavoidable, something to be endured. But some psychologists take a different view, and regard difficult clients as a potential means of growth. From this perspective, difficult clients provide helpers with a means by which they can hone their professional skills and also become better people in the process.

How is it that this is possible? One reason has to do with the fact that most patrons do not offer much of a challenge in terms of their interactive style. They behave in fairly predictable ways and cause us as librarians to respond in fairly predictable ways. The lack of variation can be a source of comfort, but also limiting in some regards. We become so accustomed to treating patrons in a standardized fashion that we lose the ability to respond well to people and situations that are out of the ordinary (May 1983).

The difficult person challenges us to break out of our secure, routine ways of interacting and take risks. Psychologists have an approach to therapy called "stress inoculation." By exposing patients to low levels of stress in controlled situations, the therapist gradually works toward building up a tolerance or resistance to stress in the patient. Working with difficult patrons may have a similar effect, in that the librarian learns to cope with the patron. This makes handling other difficult patrons easier, not to mention ordinary patrons (Meichenbaum 1985).

The librarian is able to learn much about the behavior of the difficult person, but also about his or her behavior in regard to that person. By observing his or her own assumptions and reactions, the librarian may be able to enhance his or her self understanding. Difficult people force us to stretch ourselves to tap resources we seldom utilize in our work with ordinary patrons. Librarians who work with difficult patrons learn to think under pressure. They are required to extend themselves by exhibiting exceptional levels of tolerance, patience, empathy, and courage. Difficult patrons also require a large amount of self control on the part of librarians. The librarian's personality may be enhanced by these demands (Tennen and Affleck 1998).

Not surprisingly, librarians who have worked with difficult patrons are likely to feel more adaptable and resourceful in the face of stress and uncertainty. Suspending customary habits and meeting the challenge posed by difficult patrons can lead to a sense of mastery (Wethington, Casper, and Holmes 1997). It instills a feeling of self confidence and self reliance, that one can handle anything. Difficult patrons force the librarian to think on his or her feet, to be more spontaneous and creative than situations normally call for. Librarians ordinarily do not receive much training in how to relate to patrons as part of their professional education, so they must rely on their intuition and judgment. Difficult patrons help librarians develop their own personal style of relating to patrons, since this is an aspect of librarianship not taught in books. It must be learned through experience, much as the psychotherapist learns how to handle difficult patrons through internships and practicums rather than in the classroom (Wolgien and Cody 1997).

CONCLUSION

Psychotherapists appear to have much more formal and strategic ways of handling difficult clients than librarians. They have studied the difficult patron carefully and have a more sophisticated understanding of why difficult patrons behave the way they do. One reason psychologists are able to manage difficult clients is that they understand that difficult people behave the way they do as a result of a difficult upbringing. This upbringing has damaged them psychologically, which helps therapists feel empathy toward them rather than anger or anxiety. Librarians must learn to feel a similar regard for these individuals with a tortured past.

Understanding the dynamics of the transference and countertransference processes is another way that therapists are able to maintain self control. By expecting to be provoked and not reacting to the difficult patient's provocation, they are able to remain calm and focused enough to be of real assistance to the difficult patient. Once librarians understand how transference and countertransference work, they too can muster the composure necessary to be of genuine help to their difficult patrons, rather than get caught up in the emotional turmoil of the immediate encounter. By stepping back, taking a deep breath, and acknowledging to themselves that the negative emotion that the difficult person generates is not directed toward them personally, but is projected on almost everyone the difficult person interacts with, librarians can concentrate on the patron's research problem rather than the overwhelming feeling that the patron *is* the problem. Letting one's emotions overwhelm one's cognitive reasoning processes can only serve to impede the transaction.

The challenge then for both psychotherapist and librarian is not only to realize that there will be uncomfortable feelings generated in them by the difficult person, it is also to be able to acknowledge these strong feelings of aversion and fear. Then, instead of denying them or suppressing them, one can utilize them constructively so that the difficult patron receives help. By being keenly aware of one's own reactions to the difficult patron and, to the extent possible, anticipating them, the librarian can approach a degree of self control. For the difficult patron, who is used to provoking emotional reactions in others, the presence of a relatively un-reactive person who does not reflect back negative affect will not only be novel, but hopefully also disarming, comforting, and possibly even therapeutic.

REFERENCES

Berger, M. and M. Rosenbaum. 1967. Notes on help-rejecting complainers. *International Journal of Group Psychotherapy* 17: 357-370.

Berne, E. 1964. *Games People Play*. New York: Ballantine Books.

Book, Howard E. 1977. Countertransference and the difficult personality-disordered patient. p. 173-203 in *Treating Difficult Personality Disorders*, edited by Michael Rosenbluth, San Franscisco: Jossey-Bass, Inc.

Brems, Christiane. 2000. *Dealing with Challenges in Psychotherapy and Counseling.* Belmont, CA: Brooks/Cole/Thomson Learning.

Carberry, Hugh. 1983. Psychological methods for helping the angry, resistant, and negative patient. *Cognitive Rehabilitation* 1 (4): 4-5.

Carroll Lynne, Paula J. Gilroy and Jennifer Murra. 1999. The moral imperative: self-care for women psychotherapists. *Women and Therapy* 22 (2) 133-143.

Davenport, Gloria M. 1999. *Working with Toxic Older Adults: A Guide to Coping with Difficult Elders.* New York, NY: Springer Publishing Company.

Davis, Haddy. 1984. Impossible clients. *Journal of Social Work Practice* May: 28-48.

Fiore, Robert J. 1988. Toward engaging the difficult patient. *Journal of Contemporary Psychotherapy* 18 (2): 87-104.

Hinshelwood, R.D. 1999. The difficult patient: the role of scientific psychiatry in understanding patients with chronic schizophrenia or severe personality disorder. *British Journal of Psychiatry* 174: 187-190.

Ivey, Gavin. 1995. Interactional obstacles to empathic relating in the psychotherapy of narcissistic disorders. *American Journal of Psychotherapy* 49 (Summer): 330-370.

Kottler, Jeffrey A. 1992. *Compassionate Therapy: Working with Difficult Clients.* San Francisco: Jossey-Bass, Inc.

Litvak, Stuart B. 1994. Abrasive personality disorder: definition and diagnosis. *Journal of Contemporary Psychotherapy* 24 (1): 7-14.

Marshall, Robert J. and Simone V. Marshall. 1988. *The Transference-Countertransference Matrix.* New York: Columbia University Press.

May, Rollo. 1983. *The Discovery of Being: Writings in Existential Psychology.* New York: Norton.

Medeiros, Mary E. and James O. Prochaska. 1988. Coping strategies that psychotherapists use in working with stressful clients. *Professional Psychology: Research and Practice* 19 (1): 112-114.

Meichenbaum, D. 1985. *Stress Inoculation Training.* New York: Pergamon.

Messer, Stanley B. 1999. Coping with the angry patient. *Journal of Psychotherapy Integration* 9 (2): 151-156.

Miller, Mark J. and Don Wells. 1990. On being "attractive" with resistant clients. *Journal of Humanistic Education and Development* 29 (December): 86-92.

Noonan, Maryellen. 1998. Understanding the difficult patient from a dual person perspective. *Clinical Social Work Journal* 26 (2):129-141.

Norton, Kingsley and Gill McGauley. 1998. *Counselling Difficult Clients.* London: Sage Publications.

Orlinsky, David E. and Kenneth I. Howard. 1986. Process and outcome in psychotherapy. p. 311-381 in *Handbook of Psychotherapy and Behavior Change*, 3rd ed., edited by Sol L. Garfield and Allen E. Bergin, New York: Wiley.

Otani, Akira. 1989. Resistance management techniques of Milton H. Erickson, M.D.: an application to nonhypnotic mental health counseling. *Journal of Mental Health Counseling* 11 (4): 325-334.

Ryan, Katherine. 1999. Self help for the helpers: preventing vicarious traumatization. p. 471-491 in *Play Therapy with Children in Crisis: Individual, Group, and Family Treatment*, 2nd ed., edited by Nancy Boyd Webb, New York: Guilford.

Schwenk, Thomas L., John T. Marquez, Dale Lefever, and Marion Cohen. 1989. Physician and patient determinants of difficult physician-patient relationships. *The Journal of Family Practice* 28 (1): 59-63.

Siegel, Howard B. 1990. Working with abrasive patients *Issues in Ego Psychology* 13 (1): 48-53.

Staley, Judith C. 1991. Physicians and the difficult patient. *Social Work* 36 (1): 74-79.

Tennen, Howard and Glenn Affleck. 1998. Personality and transformation in the face of adversity. p. 65-98 in *Posttraumatic Growth: Positive Changes in the Aftermath of Crisis*, edited by Richard G. Tedeschi, Crystal L. Park, and Lawrence G. Calhoun, Mahwah, NJ: Lawrence Erlbaum.

Wepman, Barry J. and Molly W. Donovan. 1984. Abrasiveness: descriptive and dynamic issues. p. 11-19 in *Psychotherapy and the Abusive Patient*, edited by E. Mark Stern, New York: The Haworth Press, Inc.

Wethington, Elaine, Hope Cooper, and Carolyn S. Holmes. 1997. Turning points in midlife. p. 215-231 in *Stress and Adversity Over the Life Course*, edited by Ian Gotlib and Blair Wheaton, Cambridge University Press, Inc.

Wolgien, Cyril S. and Nick F. Coady. 1997. Good therapists' beliefs about the development of their helping ability: the wounded healer paradigm revisited. *The Clinical Supervisor* 15 (2): 19-35.

Yalom, I. D. 1985. *The Theory and Practice of Group Psychotherapy*. New York: Basic Books.

The Common Sense of Customer Service:
Employing Advice
from the Trade and Popular Literature
of Business to Interactions
with Irate Patrons in Libraries

Glenn S. McGuigan

SUMMARY. The trade and popular literature of business provides a rich source of commentary upon interactions with difficult people. Examining information from the literature concerning this topic and applying it to the library setting, the reference librarian or public services staff member may acquire techniques for use in confronting a patron who, for one reason or another, is angry or hostile. The activities suggested here–clarifying a misunderstanding, insulating oneself from negativity, showing empathy, and listening–are common sense elements of successful customer service and coping techniques. *[Article copies available for a fee from The Haworth Document Delivery Service: 1-800-HAWORTH. E-mail address: <getinfo@haworthpressinc.com> Website: <http://www.HaworthPress. com> © 2002 by The Haworth Press, Inc. All rights reserved.]*

KEYWORDS. Problem patrons, library service, public relations

Glenn S. McGuigan is Business Reference Librarian at Penn State Harrisburg–The Capital College, 351 Olmsted Drive, Middletown, PA 17057-4850 (E-mail: gxm22@ psu.edu).

[Haworth co-indexing entry note]: "The Common Sense of Customer Service: Employing Advice from the Trade and Popular Literature of Business to Interactions with Irate Patrons in Libraries." McGuigan, Glenn S. Co-published simultaneously in *The Reference Librarian* (The Haworth Information Press, an imprint of The Haworth Press, Inc.) No. 75/76, 2002, pp. 197-204; and: *Helping the Difficult Library Patron: New Approaches to Examining and Resolving a Long-Standing and Ongoing Problem* (ed: Kwasi Sarkodie-Mensah) The Haworth Information Press, an imprint of The Haworth Press, Inc., 2002, pp. 197-204. Single or multiple copies of this article are available for a fee from The Haworth Document Delivery Service [1-800-HAWORTH, 9:00 a.m. - 5:00 p.m. (EST). E-mail address: getinfo@haworthpressinc.com].

© 2002 by The Haworth Press, Inc. All rights reserved.

INTRODUCTION

The trade and popular literature of business provides a rich source of commentary upon interactions with difficult people, delivering practical advice relating to various types of professional situations or business settings, whether dealing with a difficult colleague or manager, a customer or client. Examining information from the literature concerning this topic and applying it to the library setting, the reference librarian or public services staff member may acquire techniques for use in confronting a patron who, for one reason or another, is angry or enraged. Addressing this issue illuminates the similarities of our experiences within public services in the library with those of customer service representatives, salespeople, executives, and agents of all different types within the business world. Considering that much of the literature cited in this article relates to the basic "people skills" associated with good customer service, we may use these techniques, relevant to any public services or customer services setting, in identifying and handling difficult patrons in our libraries.

RATIONALE

Whether a public or academic library, a high tech consulting company or an office cleaning service, positive customer/patron relations may determine the survival of the organization. In a recent survey of business owners asking for reasons that customers had given for leaving and taking their business to a competitor, the largest percentage, 68%, replied that it was due to "an attitude of indifference on the part of a company employee" (Hartley, 1998, p. 290). As opposed to dissatisfaction with a particular product or service, the overwhelming majority of consumers who decided not to return to a business did so based upon a negative interaction with an employee. Just as businesses are challenged by the changes in technology that may lead to their redundancy because of consumers' new choices available by way of the Internet and other media, libraries, just like businesses, need to stay relevant and offer reasons for patrons to continue to visit us and desire our services. Interacting with a difficult customer/patron in an appropriate manner through fostering positive behaviors and coping techniques is critical. It is just as important for librarians and library staff to learn strategies in dealing with difficult people in the professional environment as it is for agents and salespeople in the business setting. If patrons/customers are not handled with tactful care, the consequences to the organization can be dire.

As we all know there are numerous types of "difficult," "problem," or "negative" behaviors that people exhibit and these can be categorized and classified in a variety of ways. I am sure that every librarian or public services staff member has more than one tale to tell about shocking experiences in dealing with a "difficult" patron. Acknowledging that human beings are extremely complex and cannot simply be labeled and classified into one dimensional personality types, we can at least construct broad generalizations to create an understanding of the person's behavior in order to approach the situation in an appropriate manner. It is important for us to identify patterns of behavior of our clientele, because "finding and labeling these patterns helps set the stage for taking effective action" (Bramson, 1981, p. 5).

Within the popular business and trade literature, there exist a myriad of characterizations of difficult people both as colleagues and as customers that are similar to those depictions from library literature. For example, Carter-Scott, in her book *The Corporate Negaholic*, depicts the "negaholic" office characters of "the rebellious rabble-rouser" and "the chronic cynic" (1991). In the popular journal *Inc.*, Caggiano (1999) identifies various problem customer types to beware of in the sales setting, such as "the serial pain," "the emergency victim," and the "the impolite lout" (p. 9). Similarly, in the esteemed library reference work, the *Whole Library Handbook*, of the many types identified by Cirino (1995) in his article on difficult people, "aggressors" and "bombs" stand out as two hostile types to be prepared to confront in the library setting (p. 433). Gothberg (1988) in the *Reference Librarian* declares the "hostile-aggressives" as "among the most difficult patrons for librarians or others to work with in providing reference service" (p. 276). For the purpose of this article, I shall focus on the experience of encountering a hostile or aggressive patron and offer strategies in dealing with this type of individual. Gleaning methods from various business and trade articles, we can learn much from those in the business world dealing with customer service. In examining the encounter with hostile/aggressive patrons, we may look to business and trade literature to determine the possible reasons for their behavior and the potential responses to that behavior that we may provide.

BRIDGE THE GAP OF MISUNDERSTANDING

In many circumstances, the person we think of as the "angry patron" or the "irate customer" may actually be someone who is simply in a state of confusion or misunderstanding about a certain policy or service. In the *Sales Channels* column of *Wireless Review*, editor Chaffee (1999) notes that in the cellular phone industry, the customer "may have trouble explaining what he needs without someone more knowledgeable guiding him to the right choice" (p. 47). She explains that there often exists a disconnection between the expectations of both the sales representative and the customer in dealing with a particular issue or problem. Don Mills (1996) in *Canadian Underwriter* comments, in describing how to resolve a problem with an angry customer involved in an insurance sale, that "when you open them up, most problems stem from a basic misunderstanding or lack of knowledge" (p. 22). Explaining clearly the issues involved with the sale or the transaction clarifies the situation and builds trust. People become frustrated when they do not understand something or find something confusing, which gives rise to conflict or negative behavior. This is as true in the business world, when someone is dealing with a customer not understanding the nuances of insurance coverage, as with a patron confused with locating a certain piece of statistical data.

As the world becomes more technologically sophisticated in all aspects of life, most library public services professionals will deal with exasperated patrons experiencing computer difficulties. The revolution in computing technology and information access has so dramatically transformed the library experience that many patrons, especially those unfamiliar with computer use, feel paralyzed and unable to overcome the technology barrier. The constantly changing formats of information, the various types of information tools, the classification systems, the nuances of computer use, and even rules concerning borrowing, all lead to a certain level of confusion and consequent hostility on the part of certain patrons.

The challenge for librarians is to acknowledge that libraries can be confusing and intimidating places for many of our users. A simple explanation about the availability or use of a database can do much to relieve potential anxiety and subsequent hostility. The use of non-technical vocabulary concerning many of the various issues relating to librarianship or technology may assist in defusing a confused patron or an irritated customer. Examples of this may be to refer to the "Web address" rather than the "URL," or to use the term "catalog" rather than "OPAC." It is important that we be tactful and not pedantic in this endeavor by educating the patron without insulting them or speaking down to them. Sarcastic or pedantic responses will only infuriate the angered person further.

INSULATE YOURSELF FROM THE NEGATIVITY

Many individuals who are verbally attacked react with anger or condescension towards the irate person initiating the confrontation. In dealing with the angry customer/patron, this may be the worst reaction in order to diffuse the situation. One must strike a balance by maintaining a professional detachment but also not appearing unconcerned or blasé about the situation. By insulating yourself from the negativity and not exploding, you do not respond to the hostility with more ire, which just increases the tension within the encounter. In maintaining self-control, "you will be able to slow your thought process and give yourself time to analyze why he/she is upset" (Evenson, 1998, p. 27).

In the management trade journal *Supervision,* Bielous (1996) relates that while dealing with a difficult person, "you must keep emotionally distant through the entire conversation. Remember that you want to be as professional as possible at all times" (p. 114). This point is critical for us to acknowledge when being on the receiving end of an irate patron's wrath. Being cool and in control reflects and enhances our professionalism. By remaining emotionally detached, one will not take the anger personally and can focus instead upon finding a solution to the problem. This reinforces our enactment of the first principle of the *Code of Ethics of the American Library Association*, which states, in part, "we provide the highest level of service to all library users" through "accurate, unbiased, and courteous responses to all requests" (American Library Association, 1995). Retaining the emotional response to the patron's negativity, the librarian will more effectively solve the problem at hand by exhibiting cool headedness and professionalism.

SHOW EMPATHY

Attempting to emotionally insulate oneself from the anger of the patron does not mean that one should not attempt to empathize with the feelings of the patron. To the contrary, exhibiting empathy, as opposed to sympathy, will more clearly help one to understand the problem being experienced by the patron. Empathy may be seen as the "capability of mentally putting yourself in the shoes of the other–being able to see things from their viewpoint and to share in their feelings" (Peterson, 1999, p. 28). This action of empathizing does not correlate to absorbing or agreeing with the sentiments of the patron. As Greenberg and Amabile (1996) explain in their article "Empathy: The First Element of Success" in *Agency Sales Magazine*, the key difference in the sales setting between empathy and sympathy is the loss of objectivity on the part of the agent (p. 25). The authors state: "if you identify with and feel the emotions of another, you cannot view them in a dispassionate, objective and helpful manner" (p. 25). The effective professional will empathize with the frustrated or angry patron/client in order to understand and even vicariously experience the sentiments, but still remain focused on solving the problem that initiated the reaction through objectively analyzing the situation without becoming emotionally entangled within it.

Empathizing with the angry patron will assist in cooling off the situation by focusing upon the thoughts or feelings of the patron and showing them that we care. We have to remember that generally the patron is angry with a certain situation, such as a missing volume from a set of encyclopedias, rather than with the librarian. In *The American Salesman*, Peterson (1999) discusses how the provision of empathy to the client leads to solving the customer's problem and simultaneously instills trust (p. 28). He states, in referring to interaction with the "prospect" or client, that without empathy, "we cannot be creative problem solvers. It is difficult for us to envision what products and services the prospect really needs. It is hard to give them an impression that we are really being sincere" (Peterson, 1999, p. 29). By empathizing with the irate patron, we may attempt to look through their eyes and creatively solve the problem as if it were our own.

Technology contributes much to the hostility that we receive and it is critical that we try to put ourselves in the shoes of the angry patron who is fed up with a computer problem. In *Computerworld*, Melymuka (1999) contends that for help desk analysts dealing with constant "user rage," the most important job requirement is empathy (p. 62). She states that it changes the interaction from a confrontation, of you versus them, to a situation in which you are trying to resolve the problem together. It should not be difficult for us to be empathetic towards a patron frustrated with a computer or application since we all know the feeling all too well. In fact many of us probably experience similar annoyance on a regular basis. By transforming the scenario as Melymuka suggests, from one of confrontation to one of cooperation, we destroy adversarial tension and resentment by forming a bond with the patron as mutual problem solvers.

LISTEN

Again and again, the trade literature within business refers to the most obvious and common sense piece of advice in dealing with an angry customer: listen to them. By listening, we can truly understand the problem or issue and thus solve it. Listening, McCann (1998) argues in the article "Talk 'Em Down" in *Credit Management*, not only lets you find out what exactly needs to be done to resolve the problem, but also allows the customer to just vent the anger that she/he is experiencing (p. 36). This will then allow the hostility to dissipate so that a productive encounter may take place. The author of "Calming Upset Customers" in *Sales and Marketing Management* relates the advice of following up with relevant questions and offering responses that show that you're listening (1994, p. 55). A follow-up question that reveals you have listened to the grievance will relieve tension and proclaims that you are sincere in your commitment to solve the problem. Listening carefully to the complaint and responding appropriately allows the patron/client to vent the hostility that they are experiencing and makes them aware of our resolve to deal with the problem.

In listening to the complaint of the irate customer/patron, we may separate the tone from the content of the message in order to clearly understand what is being asked or communicated. It assists us in stepping back from the situation to analyze what is being said as opposed to how it is being said. Listening tells the customer or the patron that they are important.

CONCLUSION

The activities suggested here, clarifying a misunderstanding, insulating oneself from negativity, showing empathy, and listening, are common sense elements of successful customer service and coping techniques. An unfortunate reality concerning interactions with certain patrons or customers exhibiting anger is that it may not be humanly possible to satisfy them or alter their behavior. Rather, the reference librarian or public services staff member must develop ways to change his/her behavior, or that of other colleagues, in dealing with that individual. While there is no panacea for dealing with difficult or angry patrons/customers, coping methods provide the opportunity to interfere with the successful functioning of the negative behavior in order to establish the most positive outcome possible.

The topic of the reference librarian or public services staff member engaging with a difficult or hostile patron is a vital, important and necessary subject. In considering our reactions to this situation, it is appropriate for those working in the library setting to look to business and trade literature in order to find techniques for dealing with angry customers. Enhancing our perspective on public services, we may benefit by examining how other professions discuss similar situations that we encounter. Obviously, there are no simple answers. However through the use of certain techniques, such as some of the practical methods discussed here, we may attempt to make the best out of the difficult situation of interacting with an irate patron.

REFERENCES

American Library Association. 1995. *Code of Ethics of the American Library Association*. ALA Office of Intellectual Freedom. Retrieved February 7, 2001 from the World Wide Web. <http://www.ala.org/alaorg/oif/ethics.html>.

Bielous, G. (1996). Five Ways to Cope with Difficult People. *Supervision*. 57, 14-16.

Bramson, R. (1981). *Coping with Difficult People*. Garden City, NY: Anchor/Doubleday.

Caggiano, C. (1999, May). Seller, Beware! *Inc.* 21, 99-100.

Calming Upset Customers. (1994). *Sales and Marketing Management*. 146, 4.

Carter-Scott, C. (1991). *The Corporate Negaholic: How to Deal Successfully with Negative Colleagues, Managers and Corporations*. New York: Villard Books.

Chaffee, M. (1999, July 15). Tough Customers. *Wireless Review*. 16, 46-47.

Cirino, P. (1995). Difficult People. In G. Eberhart (Ed.), *Whole Library Handbook*. Chicago and London: American Library Association.

Evenson, R. (1998, July). How to Deal with a Difficult Customer: A Positive Solution to a Negative Situation. *The American Salesman*. 43, 26-30.

Gothberg, H. (1988). Managing Difficult People: Patrons (and Others). *The Reference Librarian*. 19, 269-283.

Greenberg, H.M., & Amabile, D.T. (1996, October). Empathy: The First Element of Success. *Agency Sales Magazine*. 26, 25-26.

Hartley, J. (1998). Cooling the Customer with HEAT. In R. Zemke & J.A. Woods (Eds.), *Best Practices in Customer Service*. Amherst: HRD Press.

Melymuka, K. (1999, April). Raging Users. *Computerworld*. 33, 62.

McCann, D. (1998, July). Talk 'Em Down. *Credit Management*. 36-37.

Mills, D. (1996, September). The Peripatetic Rep: Handling the Problem Customer. *Canadian Underwriter*. 63, 22-23.

Peterson, R. (1999, September). Empathy: What Is It and How Do I Learn It? *The American Salesman*. 40, 28-30.

The Customer Is Always Right:
What the Business World Can Teach Us
About Problem Patrons

Rebecca Jackson

SUMMARY. Dealing with difficult patrons can be stressful. However, if we look at business literature and practice, we can learn much about how to deal with these difficulties. This paper focuses specifically on customer complaints. The business world regards complaints as valuable opportunities to improve customer service and satisfaction. Libraries should provide channels for their patrons to make complaints, follow up on those complaints, and train staff to deal with user dissatisfaction. Otherwise, our users may decide the library is not valuable to them, and we could lose valuable support. *[Article copies available for a fee from The Haworth Document Delivery Service: 1-800-HAWORTH. E-mail address: <getinfo@haworthpressinc.com> Website: <http://www.HaworthPress.com> © 2002 by The Haworth Press, Inc. All rights reserved.]*

KEYWORDS. Complaints, user satisfaction, customer service

Dealing with problem patrons, specifically patrons making complaints, is never fun. On a personal level, confrontations with difficult

Rebecca Jackson is Head, Social Sciences and Humanities Department, and Associate Professor, Iowa State University Library, 152 Parks Library, Ames, IA 50011 (E-mail: rjackson@iastate.edu).

[Haworth co-indexing entry note]: "The Customer Is Always Right: What the Business World Can Teach Us About Problem Patrons." Jackson, Rebecca. Co-published simultaneously in *The Reference Librarian* (The Haworth Information Press, an imprint of The Haworth Press, Inc.) No. 75/76, 2002, pp. 205-216; and: *Helping the Difficult Library Patron: New Approaches to Examining and Resolving a Long-Standing and Ongoing Problem* (ed: Kwasi Sarkodie-Mensah) The Haworth Information Press, an imprint of The Haworth Press, Inc., 2002, pp. 205-216. Single or multiple copies of this article are available for a fee from The Haworth Document Delivery Service [1-800-HAWORTH, 9:00 a.m. - 5:00 p.m. (EST). E-mail address: getinfo@haworthpressinc.com].

© 2002 by The Haworth Press, Inc. All rights reserved.

205

people can be stressful, resulting in frustration and anxiety, and often a major headache. On an organizational level, complaints signal dissatisfaction–with our services, collections, facilities, or with specific individuals. Other articles in this issue discuss skills to help deal with difficult patrons, on a one-on-one basis. Others consider dealing with difficult patrons in specific library contexts. In this article we will examine what we can learn from business about dealing with customer complaints to improve our customer service and, ultimately, our patrons' loyalty.

WHAT WE LEARN FROM THE BUSINESS WORLD ABOUT COMPLAINING CUSTOMERS

In recent years, management tools, such as Total Quality Management and Continuous Quality Improvement, have focused on customer satisfaction and loyalty. Businesses and business researchers have studied customer behavior and attitudes with the aim of increasing their markets and their sales. They have switched from being product-driven to customer-driven in an effort to retain customers–retaining loyal customers is more cost effective than establishing new customers. As a part of the shift to the customer-driven philosophy, customer complaint patterns have also been studied.

It may seem that everyone has complaints, especially on bad days. But the fact is that most people do not complain when they have a problem with a product or service. A study by the Technical Assistance Research Program found that 96% of the customers who do have problems with a business do not complain.[1] "This means that for every complaint the average business receives, there are 24 silent unhappy customers."[2] And what happens to those silent customers? "Complaining customers do not simply go away. They go away, stay away, and, worse yet, take every opportunity to tell anyone who will listen about the rotten treatment they had to endure at the hands of your company. Call it the 'grapevine effect.'"[3] Estimates vary, but studies have shown that a dissatisfied customer will tell from ten to twelve other people about a bad experience with a business; a person who has had a satisfying encounter with a company will only tell from three to five people about it. Thus, those complainers are the spokespeople for many others, all of whom take great pleasure in telling all their friends about the bad service they received, adding up to a considerable quantity of negative publicity for a business.

The upside of complaint management is that customers who do complain will continue their business with a company if they feel their complaint was dealt with quickly and satisfactorily.[4] Even customers who complain and get no response may retain their loyalty with a business in many cases.[5] Thus, businesses have learned that it is to their advantage to systematically track complaints and have policies and practices set in place for speedy resolution of customer complaints. Some businesses have quite sophisticated complaint management systems that "track complaints carefully, breaking them down into specific categories which can be used to discern both volume and category trends over time. This allows them to reduce the number of complaints category by category and to respond quickly if a sudden spike in one complaint category becomes apparent."[6] Careful complaint management can also help to fix a mistake early, before too much damage is done.

Complaint management involves the whole organization. "Top level commitment to effective complaint management establishes the motive and incentives for all personnel to strive for consumer satisfaction."[7] This means that everyone in the organization must be focused on customer service, and that top-level administrators must reward efforts by all employees to satisfy customer problems. It also means that administration must invest in training employees in the skills necessary for dealing with complaints. If there is a pattern of complaints in a particular area, customer-driven businesses not only work to "make it right" with an individual customer, but they also commit to "tackle the underlying problem that created the negative experience in the first place."[8] In addition, because they are well-trained, frontline employees have the power to solve many individual problems on the spot, leading to a quick resolution of the problem, and better customer satisfaction. "Customers do not want to be passed all around the [company]; neither do they want the 'it's not my fault–you'll have to speak to the manager who isn't around at the moment.' "[9]

Actually, a customer-focused organization benefits both the customers and the employees. It is not satisfying to deal with customer complaints; it is even less satisfying if the employee cannot resolve the problem, but must send the customer elsewhere to get a resolution. Employees who are empowered to solve problems on their own feel more of a sense of ownership of the organization and greater satisfaction with their positions.

Leaders who hope to motivate their employees to create value for their customers must also generate a spirit of excitement, pride, and *esprit de corps*. Companies with a strong, positive corporate culture have an almost tangible spirit of excitement. In these enterprises, employees know how to work together as a team toward the common aim of serving customers, and their pride comes from setting and meeting challenging goals.[10]

Thus, learning to handle customer complaints effectively can lead to greater satisfaction among employees.

What we learn from business, therefore, is that complaints "are a valuable way to stay in touch with the needs and expectations of your customers and an investment in customer goodwill that will strengthen your business position for the future."[11] True customer-driven businesses regard complaints as valuable opportunities to learn from customers what is not working and to correct problems. Complaints also provide powerful occasions to strengthen customer loyalty. We learn that handling complaints is a critical part of business, and should be planned for at the highest levels of the organization; this requires policies and processes that allow resolution of complaints wherever and whenever they occur. Frontline staff should be carefully trained to deal with complaints to both resolve them on the spot and to document them for further examination by the organization. Finally, follow-up is crucial to the success of complaint management. Did the problem get fixed to the customer's satisfaction? How does the customer feel about the business now? Will the customer continue to do business with the organization?

HOW DOES THIS APPLY TO LIBRARIES?

Many librarians argue that libraries are not businesses and therefore should not be compared to businesses. McCandless says "Libraries . . . are not businesses that offer products for sale at a profit. Libraries, by their very nature, cannot be cost-effective because they do not sell services. Therefore, applying business management techniques to libraries is questionable in light of the disparate missions of the two types of organizations."[12] While it is true that libraries–public, academic, and school–do not sell their services, Weingand has a different perspective, which she explains:

[An] older paradigm portrays the library as a "public good," with as high ranking on the "goodness" scale as the national flag, parenthood, and apple pie. As a public good, the library "should" receive public support. However, today's library is in increasingly tight competition for declining resources, and unless it adopts and masters the language and techniques of its competitors, it faces a future of declining support and significance.[13]

According to Weingand, libraries that do not focus on customer service may face outcomes of "poor public image and publicity" and "unsatisfied customers."[14] All libraries are dependent on the good will of their patrons if they want to continue to get necessary funding.

Businesses ultimately lose customers if they do not seek to satisfy them–those customers will simply go elsewhere. But in the case of libraries, this has not been possible–there is no other service that does what the library does. Is that true today? Weingand says that "libraries are but one group of players in competition with increasing numbers of others, such as vendors, publishers, media and multi-media producers, mass media, online services, the Internet, and the World Wide Web."[15] Libraries require a lot of money to operate. Public libraries must compete with schools, fire, police, and recreation departments, and other local services; academic libraries must share funding with academic departments and other campus services, all of whom have needs that they consider the most important. "Unless libraries . . . recognize and respond to customer needs, customers will vote with their feet–and find information elsewhere."[16]

Librarianship is a service profession; we serve our communities' needs for information. In many cases, and for many of our patrons, there really is no alternative to the library. Without a real commitment to customer service, Senge explains that service businesses focus on what is tangible–numbers of customers served, costs of the service, and revenues. He continues: "But focusing on what's easily measured leads to 'looking good without being good'–to having measurable performance indicators that are acceptable, yet not providing quality service. Work gets done but at a steadily poorer standard of quality. . . ."[17] Is this what we want to happen to libraries? Will our publics continue to fund a service which does not answer their needs? Without a focus on customer satisfaction, libraries may become simply warehouses of information and stored knowledge.

CUSTOMER COMPLAINTS IN LIBRARIES

Considering the numbers of patrons who walk through the doors of our libraries on a daily basis, we can assume that the statistics concerning the numbers of complaints at our libraries are consistent with those of businesses. Libraries, however, have their own complexities. For instance, Stalker points out that "many library users are reluctant to reveal problems with reference service: in some cases, they do not know that they have problems, and in other cases, they are unaware that their problems can be solved."[18] Often patrons have no idea what services are available to them, nor do they understand what tools they can use to solve their information problems. In a survey done at this author's library, users requested several services that were already available to them, such as online forms for interlibrary loan requests and specific online catalog search options. Further, how many of us have worked with patrons who had no idea that indexes were available to help them access periodical articles on a particular subject? Stoan refers to academic libraries when he says that "Faculty complaints . . . derive in no small measure from the (faculty) perception that, not understanding research, librarians end up organizing the library, its services, and its resources in terms of their own logic, not that of researchers."[19] Faculty members are probably not the only patrons who feel that the library's organizational scheme does not serve their needs.

When patrons do complain, their problems can be categorized into several consistent types. Weingand lists the typical patron complaints:

1. Customer is unable to locate materials or information
2. Telephone is not answered promptly when customer calls
3. Length of time until a reserve material is available seems too long
4. Library staff is not friendly or helpful
5. Library staff appears to be busy or unapproachable
6. Parking is not available nearby
7. Line at check-out is too long
8. Librarian is not available to assist in locating material or information
9. Customers are notified at inappropriate times that requested items have arrived
10. Library staff interpret policies literally and display a lack of flexibility
11. Library hours are not convenient
12. Customers must wait at the service desk while staff answers the phone.[20]

In addition, the introduction of computers and electronic resources have added their own set of inconveniences: the printer is out of paper or ink; the computer is frozen; the patron cannot get into a particular database, usually from home; or the patron simply cannot find the information she needs. The survey done in this author's library also indicated problems with the library's facilities, such as the lighting in some of the stacks areas and the temperature of the building. All of these things can lead to the patron becoming disgruntled, not wanting to use the library, and spreading bad publicity about the library.

Christopher says that "customer service is essentially about *perceptions*."[21] Weingand includes a wonderful table in her book *Customer Service Excellence* that demonstrates how a library's employees' perceptions may differ from a library patron's perceptions. Here are just a few of her examples:

How a staff member sees it:	*How a patron sees it:*
I really would rather not work weekends and evenings.	If the library is not open when I can use it, I'll find my information elsewhere.
I have so much work to do, and there never seems to be enough time in the day.	I rarely ask questions of the library staff because they always seem so busy.
It's budget time and the city council should give the library more money; after all, the library is a good thing.	I don't want my taxes to go up. The library isn't important in my life, so why should I have to pay more taxes?
Why should we have a display of third grade drawings? That's not what the library is for.	If my child's drawing is displayed in the library, I'll stop in to see it. Otherwise, I visit the library rarely.[22]

Whether or not patrons' perceptions are correct, it is those perceptions that determine whether or not a person will become or remain a loyal library user.

> Long-term nurturing of the library-customer relationship has an outcome far beyond the obvious increase in customer satisfaction: the development of both internal and external stakeholders. . . .

Stakeholders do more than simply use the library: they *care* about its success, they promote its activities, and they are active *lobbyists* in its behalf.[23]

Those are the kinds of patrons we need if the library is to remain a vital part of the community.

COMPLAINT MANAGEMENT IN THE LIBRARY

So how can we "turn every customer contact [even difficult ones] into an opportunity to solidify the relationship"[24] with our patrons? One suggestion from a management researcher is

> by making the environment knowable and predictable; by creating a customer-friendly environment in which people feel smart, competent and important, and comfortable; and by offering them choices.... [Though] providing customers with too many choices may overwhelm them and result in compromised feelings of competency and control.[25]

Specific ways to ensure this type of environment come from the business world:

1. *Offer opportunities to complain:* Consider again the statistics concerning how many people actually complain when they are dissatisfied. Part of the reason for lack of complaints is that people may not know where to go to complain. Make sure they have plenty of opportunities. Place suggestion boxes in different areas in the building, with large signs indicating their purpose. Conduct user surveys on a regular basis. Keep complaint forms at all the service desks. Make sure your websites have prominent suggestion links on each page. Encourage patrons, in one-on-one interactions, to let you know of problems they encounter. Let your patrons know that their opinions are important.

2. *Prepare library staff:* Our service desks *are* our frontlines. Often staff at these locations provide the only human contact the patron has with the library. Frequently, these desks are staffed by students or non-librarian permanent employees. These people need to know from day one what it means to be customer driven. They need to be thoroughly oriented to the building and the services, so they know where and when to make referrals. Continuous customer service training must be provided to all employees, including students. They need to under-

stand how what they do contributes to the perceptions our patrons have of our libraries, and how important those perceptions are. They need to know how far they can go to resolve a patron's complaint. They should be allowed the satisfaction that comes from making a patron happy. And they need to be rewarded for good service.

Knowledge about resources is equally important. The business librarian at the Iowa State University Library was confronted by a new faculty member who questioned why the library did not subscribe to a database he had used at another institution. The librarian prepared a presentation for that faculty member, demonstrating that another database the library did subscribe to not only provided a good alternative to the faculty's preferred database, but also offered options the first did not. The delighted faculty member went back to his department and told his colleagues about the wonderful resources in the library and the knowledgeable staff; the librarian felt good about making the library look good. Training, knowledge, and a customer-driven culture are critical to a library's success.

3. *Plan for complaint management:* "Management's responsibility begins with the preparation of written policies and procedures for speedy and fair complaint resolution."[26] Libraries collect data on all kinds of transactions; keeping track of complaints should be part of that data collection. Suggestions in suggestion boxes or from library websites provide written documentation that can then be logged and categorized. Trends can be tracked and underlying problems can be resolved. Surveys provide means by which a collection of patrons, as well as non-patrons, can voice their opinions about particular services and products. At service desks, there should be policies for documenting the types of complaints patrons bring to the staff; this could be done fairly simply with forms, either at the desk or online.

Policies for resolving complaints also need to be documented. Under what circumstances should a fine be waived? When can a faculty member take a periodical out of the library, and for how long? With the proper training, frontline staff should be able to resolve all but the most complex problems.

4. *Respond to complaints:* Sometimes a thank-you is enough. Sometimes just having a listening ear helps dissipate the frustration. By tracking complaints, libraries can often make policy decisions that will result in higher patron satisfaction, without having a major impact on the library. For instance, if you have a steady stream of patrons complaining that coming into the library to renew books is terribly inconvenient, then make it possible for them to renew books over the phone or by

e-mail. Some complaints are not so easy to resolve. Constant complaints that students cannot find books on the shelves that should be there could be the result of different underlying problems. One could be that students do not know how to read call numbers correctly; in that case, education is definitely in order. Another reason could be that the books are not shelved correctly. The library will have to explore all of these possible causes, and often the solution may be complicated. However, a solution is required if we want to maintain our users' satisfaction.

If your library has suggestion boxes, it is a good idea to publicly exhibit, either in a prominent place in the library or online, representative suggestions and responses to them. Of course, not all suggestions or complaints will be of interest to all library users. But if a number of people tell you the building is too warm, it will make them feel better to know you have heard them, and that you are taking steps to make the building more comfortable. If one patron suggests renewals by phone, then probably many more would like that option; if it is already available, a public posting of the suggestion and the means for renewing by phone will help your patrons and your library's image.

5. *Follow up on complaints:* If a patron bothers to complain rather than just leave the library, it is in your best interest to acknowledge the contribution that person has made to your operations. If possible, send a letter or an e-mail to that person, thanking them for the interest in your library, and explaining how you are working to resolve their problem. If a person comes to a service desk with a problem, check with that person later on to make sure your response was satisfactory; that can be as simple as approaching that patron at a workstation and asking if they are finding what they need or if that particular database worked for them. If a problem will take some time to resolve, stay in contact with the customer, letting them know where you are in the process, and when you hope to have results for them. Even if you cannot give all patrons exactly what they want, it makes them happier to know that you care and are interested in seeing that they are satisfied with what you *can* do.

CONCLUSION

No doubt about it—dealing with difficult patrons can be challenging. In our busy, often stressful world, a complaining library customer just seems to complicate matters. "Today's library faces a series of continuing challenges brought about by evolving technologies, consumer desires, and shrinking funds. If excellence in customer service is to be a primary library goal, then problem solving must be viewed as a vital management and personnel skill."[27] We can, with training, policies, and a customer-driven culture, turn those disgruntled library users into happy, loyal customers by adopting the principle that complaints are opportunities to strengthen our organizations.

REFERENCES

1. *Consumer Complaint Handling in America: An Update Study*, by the Technical Assistance Research Program's Institute for the Consumer Affairs Council, United States Office of Consumer Affairs, September 30, 1985.

2. Rebecca L. Morgan, *Calming Upset Customers* (Menlo Park, CA: Crisp Publications, 1989): 7.

3. Ron Zemke, *Knock Your Socks Off Service Recovery* (New York: AMACOM, 2000) [Online]. Available: NetLibrary [October 10, 2000].

4. "Customer Services and Satisfaction," Mississippi State Extension Service Home-Based and Micro *Business Briefs*, December 15, 1998. Available: http://ext.msstate.edu/newsletters/hb-mbb/19981215.htm [October 11, 2000].

5. "Effective Management of Customer Complaints," *International Journal of Retail and Distribution Management* 25, 6-7 (June-July, 1997): 237-239.

6. William A. Band, *Creating Value for Customers: Designing and Implementing a Total corporate Strategy* (New York: John Wiley & Sons, Inc, 1991): 261.

7. U.S. Department of Commerce, Office of Consumer Affairs, *Managing Consumer Complaints* (Washington, DC: U.S. Government Printing Office, 1992): 3.

8. Oren Harari, "Thank Heavens for Complainers," *Management Review* 86 (March 1997): 25-29.

9. Rhymer Rigby, "The Alchemy of Complaint Management," *Management Today* (April 1998): 90-92.

10. Band, 180.

11. Band, 263.

12. Patricia A. McCandless, "Service-Oriented Personnel," in *People Come First: User-Centered Academic Library Service*. ACRL Publications in Librarianship no. 53. (Chicago: Association of College and Research Libraries, 1999): 142-156.

13. Darlene Weingand, *Customer Service Excellence: A Concise Guide for Librarians* (Chicago: American Library Association, 1997): 3.

14. Weingand, 5-6.

15. Weingand, 32.

16. Weingand, 28.

17. Peter M. Senge, *The Fifth Discipline: The Art and Practice of the Learning Organization* (New York: Doubleday, 1990): 333.

18. John C. Stalker, "Reference: Putting Users First," in *People Come First: User-Centered Academic Library Service*. ACRL Publications in Librarianship no. 53. (Chicago: Association of College and Research Libraries, 1999): 79-92.

19. Stephen K. Stoan, "Research and Library Skills: An Analysis and Interpretation," *College and Research Libraries* 45 (March 1984): 99.

20. Weingand, 73.

21. Martin Christopher, "Creating Effective Policies for Customer Service," *International Journal of Physical Distribution and Materials Management* 13, 2 (1983): 3-24.

22. Weingand, 115.

23. Weingand, 58.

24. Weld F. Royal, "Cashing in on Complaints," *Sales and Marketing Management* 147 (May 1995): 86-92.

25. Benjamin Schneider and David E. Bowen, "Understanding Customer Delight and Outrage," *Sloan Management Review* 41 (Fall 1999): 35-45.

26. U.S. Department of Commerce, 3.

27. Weingand, 62.

Zen and the Art
of Dealing with the Difficult Patron

Louisa Toot

SUMMARY. Half the battle of dealing with a difficult patron is changing one's own perspective. This paper uses core Zen Buddhist ideas and viewpoints to discuss ways of dealing with difficult patrons. The basics of Zen Buddhism are explained and Zen concepts such as Openness, Mindfulness, Compassion and Beginner's Mind are applied to problem solving within the context of library public service. The paper also explores the difference between "difficult" and "problem" patrons in order to help readers determine when a Zen perspective is useful. *[Article copies available for a fee from The Haworth Document Delivery Service: 1-800-HAWORTH. E-mail address: <getinfo@haworthpressinc.com> Website: <http://www.HaworthPress.com> © 2002 by The Haworth Press, Inc. All rights reserved.]*

KEYWORDS. Zen, Buddhism, difficult patrons, problem patrons, conflict, problem solving, library public service

Louisa Toot is Technical Reference Librarian, Sherman Fairchild Library, California Institute of Technology, Pasadena, CA 91125 (E-mail: louisa@library.caltech.edu).

The author wishes to thank Kimberly Douglas and Daniel Taylor for their suggestions and comments; Shahla Shahsavari for her lunchtime discussion about difficult patrons; and Jay Williams, Professor of Religious Studies at Hamilton College for his inspirational teachings on Buddhism.

[Haworth co-indexing entry note]: "Zen and the Art of Dealing with the Difficult Patron." Toot, Louisa. Co-published simultaneously in *The Reference Librarian* (The Haworth Information Press, an imprint of The Haworth Press, Inc.) No. 75/76, 2002, pp. 217-233; and: *Helping the Difficult Library Patron: New Approaches to Examining and Resolving a Long-Standing and Ongoing Problem* (ed: Kwasi Sarkodie-Mensah) The Haworth Information Press, an imprint of The Haworth Press, Inc., 2002, pp. 217-233. Single or multiple copies of this article are available for a fee from The Haworth Document Delivery Service [1-800-HAWORTH, 9:00 a.m. - 5:00 p.m. (EST). E-mail address: getinfo@haworthpressinc.com].

© 2002 by The Haworth Press, Inc. All rights reserved.   *217*

INTRODUCTION

The idea for this paper came about over a year and a half ago as I was sitting in a three-day workshop on collection development. My mind, sparked by something a presenter said, started thinking about how well my undergraduate studies in Asian Religions had prepared me for reference librarianship. I began to list some basic Zen Buddhist concepts I had studied, ones that specifically applied to reference work:

> one mind
> beginner's mind
> humbleness
> always changing
> flexibility
> observation
> giving up of self
> letting go
> non-duality
> meditation
> mountain in environment of change
> reference = 'Zen koans'
> compassion
> not one right path

This was written on a blank piece of paper the conference organizers included for note taking inside the workshop binder. The workshop finished and I found a place for the binder on my office bookshelf forgetting a while about the list inside.

When the call went out for contributions to this special issue of *The Reference Librarian,* my immediate reaction was, "Thank goodness we don't have any difficult patrons here!" Then a little voice on my other shoulder said, "Or do we?" I started to kick around the question of what exactly is a problem patron? I thought back to each time I had encountered what could have been perceived as a difficult patron and realized that the concepts I had learned by studying Zen Buddhism had actually changed my perception of patrons, minimizing the tendency to categorize patrons as good or bad. It was not that a difficult patron was such a rare occasion, it was just that I usually did not distinguished between "difficult" and "non-difficult" patrons. This was non-dualism! This was Buddhist philosophy! Inspired, I returned to my list and decided the topic of my paper would be: *Zen and the Art of Dealing with the Difficult Patron.*

THE RESEARCH COMMUNITY: A SHAMBHALA

Working as a librarian at a small, private university whose students and faculty mainly focus on research in science and engineering *is* a Shambhala of sorts. Researchers are highly motivated, intelligent and well educated. They would not have made it to our institution without possessing certain traits: perseverance, initiative, diligence and ingenuity. These same characteristics might also be used to describe the perfect library patron. An article by Jack Alan Hicks is the only one I have come across that actually analyzes "the successful client." He states, the successful client,

1. Assumes a personal relationship with the librarian.
2. Assumes ownership for the transaction.
3. Is always prepared to accept the information provided and then evaluate the data.
4. Comes as prepared as possible–tries never to pose a question in a vacuum.
5. Is persistent, stopping the query only when he or she has all the information needed (Hicks 1992, 59).

Needless to say, difficult patrons exist at any institution; however, since a small research environment does not tend to have the same sort of difficult or problem patrons as a public library or even a large academic library, I think it is necessary to make a distinction between what I will define as a *difficult* patron versus a *problem* patron. This paper will focus on dealing with the category of patron I have defined as "difficult." It is with occurrences of this category that Zen philosophies work best at lessening conflict and keeping the library staff's well-being, self-esteem and confidence intact during and after a difficult encounter.

PROBLEM PATRON OR DIFFICULT PATRON: SOME DEFINITIONS

In a search on the subject of "difficult or problem patron" in Library Literature, I came across papers that talked about "problem patrons," papers discussing "difficult patrons" and also papers on "patrons with problems." All of these seemed to be more or less lumped together under the subject heading "Problem patrons." I saw a muddling of two fairly distinct sets of users and realized that further refining of definitions was needed in order to better address the issue of "problem patrons." I make a distinction between a "problem patron" and a "difficult patron" not only because I feel that they connote different types of patrons but also because I think it will help the reader to better distinguish when the Zen attitudes put forth in this paper are useful.

The phrase "problem patron" implies that the problem has a solution and that once the solution is found then either the problem or the patron will no longer exist. Problem patrons at the extreme end are the mentally ill, belligerent or perverted patrons, and those using the library as their primary shelter. On a less extreme scale, problem patrons can be those that bring food and drink into the library, those that conduct their library business loudly, book thieves and vandals, to name a few. I classify all of these as problem patrons because when a solution is found to rid the library of either the patron *or* the patron's activity then the problem patron does not exist any longer. The problem is inherent to the patron or to the patron's activity–an activity that the particular library restricts or that should not occur in a library altogether.

The "difficult patron," in contrast, cannot be solved because the difficulty may or may not be inherent either to the patron or the patron's activity. In short, the difficult patron is one whose expectations have not been met and has decided it would be advantageous to be difficult. The patron who decides to be difficult one day, may not normally be a difficult person. The difficult patron is one who must be *managed* rather than *solved* because getting rid of a difficult patron is not a solution; although sometimes we wish it were and like to treat it so by using coping mechanisms such as ignoring, withdrawing or avoiding. Examples of difficult patrons would be the angry patron, the knows-it-all or expert patron, the impatient patron, the patron who demands services or supplies not available, the chronically complaining patron, or the patron who, because of cultural differences or otherwise, has misperceptions of the library. On any given day the same patron who could fall into one of these types may be the perfect patron. Sometimes difficult patrons arise out of the patron's mood or the librarian's mood or both. At other times, difficult patrons are created due to excessively restrictive attitudes or policies or because the patrons' expectations of what the library's policies and services should be do not match what they actually are.

There is no cut-and-dried boundary between "problem patrons" and "difficult patrons." A difficult patron could possibly become a "problem patron" over time. The distinction I am trying to make is that with the "problem patron" there is no leeway–either the patron or the patron's activity will not be tolerated in the library's environment according to the library policies. The problem patron, as I define it, should be dealt with according to the library's predefined procedures. Much of the literature discusses the importance of having procedures for "problem patrons" and how to go about creating and implementing those procedures. With the "difficult patron," on the other hand, neither the patron nor the activity is necessarily banned from the library. The difficult patron may not always get what they want in the way they want it, but the library should do its best to provide options for the difficult patron to get what they need.

WHAT IS ZEN?

Zen is a particular sect of Buddhism which advocates finding one's true self, by oneself, through meditation and everyday living. This definition, as all definitions of Zen, does not aptly describe what Zen is. However, it will give you some idea of what is meant by Zen when referred to in this paper. I want to emphasize that Zen is not a religion and, in fact, most of what I will be writing in this paper is perhaps not new to you at all, not so much because you have studied Zen, but rather from your own life experiences.

Bernard Phillips, in the Introduction to D. T. Suzuki's *The Essentials of Zen Buddhism*, has this to say about Zen, "Zen Buddhism is not so much a religion as it is a pointing to the religious life itself. It is not concerned to defend a point of view or to propagate a set of beliefs *about* the absolute basis of life, but rather to lay hold on that absolute life itself" (Suzuki 1962, xviii). The point is that Zen philosophy is not a finite activity but a continual process, which does not end when you close a book on it or finish reading this article. In short, Zen is a way of being.

HOW CAN ZEN PHILOSOPHY BE USED
TO HELP DEAL WITH DIFFICULT PATRONS?

Zen and other Buddhists base their practices on the philosophy that everyone is already enlightened and that there is no need to seek enlightenment. However, the perfect Buddha Mind, which we already possess, has been clouded by our desires. All desire leads to suffering. Only by overcoming the ego that causes one to desire can one then alleviate one's own suffering. As Tibetan Buddhist Tulku Thondup explains,

> Buddhism is centered on the principle of two truths, the absolute truth and the relative truth. The absolute is that the true nature of our minds and of the universe is enlightened, peaceful and perfect. The relative . . . truth is that . . . the world is experienced as a place of suffering, ceaseless change, and delusion, for the face of the true nature has been obscured by our mental habits and emotional afflictions, rooted in our grasping at 'self.' . . . Buddhism . . . understands 'self' as any phenomenon or object . . . that we might grasp at as if it were a truly existing entity. It could be *the self of another person*, the self of a table, the self of money, or *the self of an idea*. [italics mine] (Thondup 1996, 18)

How does this fit into helping us deal with difficult patrons? A difficult patron situation arises out of some level of conflict occurring between the library staff and the patron. Conflict results as one person desires not to be influenced by another. Two opposing opinions, wants or beliefs come together and conflict arises out of the attempt of one person to impose his or her opinion, want or belief on another. The desire not to be influenced (which Buddhists would call "grasping at ego") causes us pain. If we do not care about being influenced or if we do not desire to influence another there is no conflict. It is this suffering, caused out of a desire not to be influenced (i.e., our ego) that is the basic condition which Zen and all Buddhism seeks to overcome. In summary, the difficult patron situation arises out of the conflict of two parties desiring not to be influenced, and the desire not to be influenced is the source of all suffering. Recognizing the true source of our own suffering is the basis of Buddhism.

Many of the articles I read focused on what library staff should do, what their actions should be in order to not escalate situations and to "calm the patron." Most of these articles neglected to also address the flipside of the coin, the library staff. What about the library staff's emotional and psychological well being before, during and after an encounter? I believe that taking a Zen philosophical approach to problem-solving not only helps conflict between patrons and library staff, but also results in greater emotional and psychological well-being for library staff during and after the occurrence of what I am labeling "conflict."

Practicing the Zen concepts I am writing about in this paper demands introspection and self-awareness and encourages the search for understanding as a process of life. This sort of approach results in win-win outcomes. It diminishes, if not eliminates, conflict because there are no opposing positions. Nobody loses. Perhaps, best of all, when you are mindful and remember to practice Zen during an encounter with a difficult patron, it works!

FOUR BASIC ZEN TENETS

Previously we talked about the two truths of Buddhism: that of Buddha Mind and that of suffering born of desire. Zen philosophy alters one's perception of a situation, or rather, ourselves in a situation, and helps us to realize "Buddha Mind." Four important tenets of Zen, which lead us back to our own Buddha nature while dealing with patrons, are: Openness, Mindfulness, Compassion, and Beginner's Mind. Rather than try to define what each of these mean with relation to Zen, let me explain how each tenet can work for us in the case of dealing with difficult patrons.

OPENNESS

Openness is the mindset that whatever comes our way we are open to experiencing it without labeling it good or bad, easy or difficult. Librarians sometimes refer patrons to another library for their information needs; it is a natural tendency to let the receiving librarian know if the patron has been giving us some difficulty. This forewarning immediately changes our idea of the patron coming to us for help and our minds may become closed to the idea that this patron will be anything other than difficult. This is also true of those patrons you might have experienced difficulty with in the past. With openness we become less fearful of the difficult patron when we see him or her coming. Normally the tendency is to withdraw or avoid a difficult person, especially when we are aware beforehand that he or she will be coming to the reference desk. With no prior judging we can deal with a situation more effectively because our mental energies are focused on the matter at hand and not on judging it. When we judge a situation we are internally (if not externally) saying to ourselves, "This is so difficult," "This person is rude," "I shouldn't have to deal with this," "I am a nice person. Why is this happening to me?" On and on our mind goes until we somehow escape the unpleasantness. Openness helps us to accept the fact that not everyone will act in a pleasant manner at all times and we can experience the situation without letting it affect us psychologically and emotionally.

MINDFULNESS

Mindfulness is something that as reference librarians we have trained ourselves to do when we are searching, organizing, collecting, preserving or disseminating information. As a librarian you cannot accomplish these activities successfully without being mindful or fully aware of the information itself. Mindfulness with information, though, is an inward mindfulness. Helping patrons mindfully means that not only are we open to any patron that comes to us, we are focused completely on him or her. Our mind is fully concentrated on the patron and nothing except the patron, as if the patron has become our whole world for the time being. Shunryu Suzuki writes,

> Mindfulness is, at the same time, wisdom. By wisdom we do not mean some particular faculty or philosophy. It is the readiness of the mind that is wisdom. . . . Wisdom is not something to learn. Wisdom is something that will come out of your mindfulness. So the point is to be ready for observing things, and to be ready for thinking. (Suzuki 1970, 111)

It is often difficult to be truly "ready for thinking" when one is at a busy reference desk or working with a difficult patron. At these times our mind can become tense and distracted, but practicing mindfulness will relax and ease the mind, allowing us to be alert and know what to do without hesitation. When we focus on the patron we know exactly what to do because that is what we have been trained for as librarians. However, when we are only half focused on the patron and the other half of our mind is focused on ourselves, we cannot think clearly and we are confused about what to do. At these times we make things more difficult than they really are. Jean Engler writes,

Switch the focus away from yourself . . . and the situation becomes less threatening. In other words, concentrate on what you're giving instead of what you are getting. The person who is comfortable . . . dealing with difficult patrons, is one whose energy is directed wholeheartedly toward accomplishing the goal. (Engler 1992, 15)

Mindfulness subtly says to the patron that he or she is important enough to be listened to and helped. Being mindful means not just listening actively but includes observation of the person. An article from Pivotal Point Training & Consulting, Inc. explains it perfectly,

Don't just wait for your turn to talk. What is this person saying? Take notes if necessary. Listen with your eyes as well. What is their body language revealing about their state? How can you address their concerns, which they may be indirectly revealing to you? Seek first to understand others and then be understood. (Pivotal Point 2000b)

COMPASSION

We have all experienced or heard that those that are the strictest with themselves are also strict on those around them, or, how about the idea that you cannot truly love someone else until you love yourself first. In Buddhism too, you cannot have compassion for another without self-love. Shundo Aoyama writes, "When we achieve ultimate self-love, then, for the first time, the boundary between self and others naturally disappears, and others' joys and sorrows truly become one's own" (Aoyama 1990, 136). In a similar vein, Tulku Thondup writes, "Taking care of our true needs and those of others is the way to find peace . . ." (Thondup 1996, 27). This can also help us deal with the difficult patron. If we dig deep enough, each of us can remember a time when we were a difficult patron too, perhaps not in a library but as a customer elsewhere. A time when we were having a bad day, stressed out, in a hurry, or otherwise became annoyed, angry, spiteful, or downright nasty. Sometimes people were compassionate to us and other times they let us have it, as we probably deserved! If you have never had the experience of becoming angry, impatient or frustrated with someone then it might be difficult for you to show compassion to the difficult patron. This is not to say that you should go out and start yelling at people! Try to think of a time when you were suffering and transfer that experience onto what the difficult patron must be feeling. Having had the experience will help you deal with those who come to the library and find themselves annoyed, impatient, or angry and decide to take it out on you. It is not you that they really wish to hurt, after all they probably do not even know you. Just remember, they are in pain and it has nothing to do with you.

Compassion is a key component when working with the difficult patron. As we said earlier, we cannot have compassion towards another without first having it for ourselves. If we do not recognize that we might be having a bad day and give ourselves a little bit of compassion first, then we cannot sympathize with someone else when the moment comes. In "Tactics to Tame Tough People," Pivotal Point Consulting writes, "Personal awareness and understanding is 95% of the cure" (Pivotal Point 2000a). On days when I am aware of being tired or stressed, I make a point of recognizing my internal state and giving myself the necessary attention I need before I go out on the reference desk. I notice that on the days that I do this I want to be more helpful to patrons coming up to the desk because I do not want them to have to suffer the same as I am suffering. It also helps take my mind off of whatever it is that is causing me hardship! By giving yourself the attention you need, you will feel more generous when the demands of others greet you.

Openness, mindfulness and compassion help us cope with difficult patrons because they get us ready to receive and work with them. If you look back to instances where you were able to handle a difficult patron very well it was probably because you were, in one way or another, ready for the situation, paying attention and felt for the other person's predicament.

While openness prepares you to receive any patron that comes to you, mindfulness will aid you in knowing when the patron is ready to end the interaction. Many times it is difficult for us as librarians to just "let it go." We need an answer and we will sometimes strive for one even when we are not the appropriate person for the job. This can put our relation with the patron in jeopardy without intending to.

Being open and mindful does not mean expecting that every patron might potentially be or turn into a difficult patron; it means transcending the labeling of good or bad in the first place, paying close attention to the person and making sure that you are really the best person to help.

BEGINNER'S MIND

The Zen concept of "beginner's mind" is strongly related to reference work. Shunryu Suzuki states, ". . . in the beginner's mind there are many possibilities, but in the expert's there are few" (Suzuki 1970, 17). How can we apply this to conflict and the idea of the difficult patron? Beginner's mind can help us deal with the difficult library patron because it frees us to think of unique resolutions to conflict. The beginner's mind sees things differently because it is not cluttered with experience. Because the beginner's mind is not restricted to those solutions that have worked (or failed to work) in the past, many more options are open. If we have experienced a particular type of difficult patron before, we are apt to draw on that experience the next time we recognize a reoccurrence. Each time we encounter a particular type of difficult patron the tendency is to become more and more restricted in thinking of creative solutions. Before we can even discern what the problem may be, we have already labeled it (correctly or incorrectly) as a "such-and-such" type of problem and move on to the solution that worked in the past. When we label a problem according to past experiences without fully listening to the problem then we become less attentive to whether or not the solution really worked for the person involved and less creative in finding alternative solutions. Furthermore, if we have jumped to a hasty solution based on past experience without fully understanding the problem for this particular person, then we might inadvertently exacerbate the conflict or otherwise harm relations with the patron. It is important to look at each patron with a beginner's mind so that all possible solutions are open to us.

Beginner's mind stops us from giving an automatic response such as "that's impossible" or "it's against library policy." Even if the request is impossible or against library policy, chances are the patron has already been told this previously by you or by another staff member. The last thing a patron wants to hear is what he or she cannot do. Focus on what *is* possible then present options and let the patron be the expert and choose which route he or she would like to take.

A CASE STUDY

To illustrate how openness, mindfulness, compassion and beginner's mind help avoid conflict, consider the following scenario.

Scene: Marion the Librarian has just returned from a weeklong conference and finds a note on her desk: *"Mrs. Patron would like to donate books to the library, please return her call."* Marion, facing 222 emails in her inbox and several other projects on her desk, distractedly gives Mrs. Patron a call to get it done with as soon as possible. As she dials the number Marion thinks, "Another one of those hopelessly outdated donations that someone cannot bear to throw out and just wants to get off their hands."

Marion: Hello, is Mrs. Patron in please? (Marion asks to the pleasant voice on the other end of the line.)

Mrs. Patron: Yes, this is she.

Marion: Hello, It's Marion from XYZ Library. I'm returning your call about a book donation.

Mrs. Patron: Donation? No, I do not want to donate the books; I want to sell them. Some of these books are classics in the field and *very* valuable. Besides they are all in the area of ABC, a *very* specialized collection, and I also have an invention in that area, soon to be patented, I might add, that I've called XYZ Faculty about. I've left a message with his secretary but I have not yet heard back–

Marion: (Not letting Mrs. Patron finish her sentence.) Sell? We do not usually buy used book collections, but your donation can be used for tax deduction purposes.

Mrs. Patron: Tax purposes? Well, I don't think so. Like I said, some of these books are *very* valuable. These are classics in the field. One title is over $300 on Amazon, I looked it up!

Marion: Okay, well, let me see if we have a copy. What is the author and title? (The woman gives Marion the title and Marion looks it up.) We do have two copies of that title already, but like I said, if you want to donate the books just to get rid of them–

Mrs. Patron: No, I do not want to just *get rid of them!* (Mrs. Patron's voice is getting increasingly irritated over the phone.) But what do you mean for tax purposes, how does that work? Do you tell me how much each book is worth?

Marion: No, you would need to appraise them yourself–

Mrs. Patron: Appraise them myself! Well, how am I supposed to do that? I can't go through *all* of these books!

Marion: Well, I'm sorry, (Marion replies, a little annoyed that the conversation is taking longer than expected) but we do not appraise books, we will send you a letter of acknow-

Mrs. Patron: (Not letting Marion finish.) I don't have time to appraise them! I live in LMN City and have been flying back and forth trying to get this estate in order–

Marion: Well, I am just telling you that we do not provide estimates, if you need that done because you want to use the donation for tax reporting purposes you will need to either do it yourself or get someone else to do it for you. (Marion is frustrated that the woman is not listening to her, but the slight pause in the conversation encourages Marion to continue.) We reserve the right to put any books not added to our collections into our book sale.

Mrs. Patron: Book sale? I don't want them just put into a book sale! I am trying to sell them myself!

Marion: Well, perhaps a used book dealer would want to purchase them from you, I could look up the names of a few local–

Mrs. Patron: (Cutting her off again.) I don't want them going to just *anybody!* Besides, as I said before I need to get through to XYZ Faculty whom I think would be *very* interested in this invention in his area of ABC. Would you please tell me his direct phone line?

Marion: What is the invention? I would be happy to email the faculty about it and give him your contact information to get back to you if he is interested.

Mrs. Patron: I'm *not* going to explain it to a layperson! What is his phone number?!

Marion: We do not give out faculty phone numbers.

Mrs. Patron: You will not give me his number?

Marion: No.

Mrs. Patron: Fine then, GOOD DAY!!!! (Mrs. Patron slams down the phone ending the conversation.)

Technically, Marion did not do anything wrong in this conversation, but the resulting interaction was not a satisfactory one for either her or the patron. The patron did not start out being difficult. What happened, and how might this conversation have avoided the level of conflict that occurred?

1. Self-Compassion: Marion did not take stock of her internal state. She was distracted and anxious to get on with work after having been away for a week, yet she gives the patron a call in order to "get it out of the way." She has not given herself the attention she needs and therefore finds it difficult to have a compassionate attitude towards the book donor.
2. Openness: Marion is taken off guard by the fact that the woman wants to sell her books rather than donate. Marion continues to relay information about donating even though the woman does not want to donate the books.
3. Mindfulness: Marion did not pay attention to the hints that should have told her the book collection was important to the woman (the fact that she wanted to sell it and that she kept mentioning its value). She also ignores the mention of the invention the first time around which subtly indicates to the woman that she is not being listened to.
4. Compassion: If Marion had been more mindful she would have been able to exhibit greater compassion towards the patron, showing an interest in the collection and working with the patron to find a resolution.
5. Beginner's Mind: Beginner's mind would have enabled Marion to think of alternative options for the patron. Because Marion is at first not open to the patron's wish to sell the books, she comes up with a solution (to find a local book dealer) too late in the conversation. Prejudging the collection as outdated before calling the patron also hinders Marion from showing more of an interest in the collection.

Let's take another look at how the conversation might have gone.

Scene: Marion gets the note but decides that she needs to finish some higher priority tasks before returning the call. She waits until that afternoon when things are less hectic to make the call.

Marion: Hello, is Mrs. Patron in please? (Marion asks to the pleasant voice on the other end of the line.)

Mrs. Patron: Yes, this is she.

Marion: Hello, It's Marion from XYZ Library. I'm returning your call about a book donation.

Mrs. Patron: Donation? No, I do not want to donate the books; I want to sell them. Some of these books are classics in the field and *very* valuable. Besides they are all in the area of ABC, a *very* specialized collection, and I also have an invention in that area, soon to be patented, I might add, that I've called XYZ Faculty about. I've left a message with his secretary but I have not yet heard back from him yet.

Marion: I see. XYZ Faculty is a good person to talk with about your invention, I'm sure he will get back to you if he's interested. Unfortunately, the library does not buy used book collections, but I could help you look for a local used book dealer who might want to buy it. (Alternatively, Marion might ask more questions about the collection to get more information about it and decide if maybe the library could make an exception and purchase a few needed titles. Still the focus is on the patron and what she is saying.)

What are some differences between the start of this conversation and the last one?

1. Marion has called the patron at a time when she is less busy and has completed some of her most pressing projects. She is ready to take the time to help the patron.
2. Marion does not make a prejudgment about the collection or why the patron is calling.
3. Marion is mindful of the patron's need to have her invention recognized and shows compassion by assuring her that the Faculty will get back to her if he is interested.
4. Marion is open to the patron's wish to sell the books rather than donate them.
5. Marion informs the patron directly that the library does not buy used book collections and then creatively comes up with the option of helping her to find a local book dealer.

The conversation at this point still has many possible directions it could go. It might develop into Marion referring the patron to possible buyers or end with the patron deciding not to have Marion help her at all. Maybe the patron would rethink donating the books and ask for more information. The patron might still become difficult and insist that the librarian buy the books. At that point Marion need only repeat that the library does not buy used book collections instead of trying to persuade the patron to do what the library will do, accept a donation. Even if the conversation ends with the patron upset that she was not able to persuade the library to buy the books, the conversation will be a much shorter one if Marion is not trying to counter-persuade the patron to donate the books.

CONCLUSION

Difficult patrons exist at every institution, public or private, large or small. Half the battle of dealing with a difficult patron is changing one's own perspective. Using the Zen tenets of Openness, Mindfulness, Compassion and Beginner's Mind when interacting with a difficult patron helps one to shift the focus from one's own involvement to the patron and the patron's difficulty. Openness allows us to receive the difficult patron without judgment or prior expectation. Mindfulness shifts focus from oneself and places it wholeheartedly on the patron. Compassion allows one to feel for another's predicament as if it were your own. We exhibit compassion best when we have been attentive to our own needs. Compassion is a means of recognizing another's suffering without necessarily alleviating it. Many times having an attitude of compassion alone will diminish a conflict. Beginner's mind is also an important concept in reference work whether or not you are dealing with a difficult patron. Many times we jump to false conclusions because of what we have experienced in the past. Beginner's mind also unblocks our minds so that we are free to create alternative solutions. Instead of automatically stating that what a patron wants is impossible, beginner's mind helps us to focus on the positive, what can be done, and present options to the user.

The case scenario presented is an example of how using more of the Zen tenets discussed might have resulted in a more satisfying outcome. Because Zen is all about personal experience and growth, it is important to recall your own stories in order to learn what your role has been in encounters with difficult patrons. In using these techniques as a means for defusing conflict, one cannot be certain of whether or not conflict would have occurred without using them. You cannot go back and do it a second time to see if a patron might become difficult if you are less open or show less compassion toward them. The point of these techniques is not so much to be able to control the difficult patron but to make one aware of how both parties contribute to conflict. On occasions where a patron continues being difficult, Zen techniques will help you remain poised and focused and avoid aggravating a conflict. In closing, I encourage you to continue learning new ways to cope with difficult library patrons for they are, after all, those who need us the most.

REFERENCES

Aoyama, Shundo. *Zen Seeds: Reflections of a Female Priest.* (Tokyo: Kosei Publishing Co., 1990).

Engler, Jean. "A Matter of Focus," Library Mosaics 3 (July/August 1992): 15.

Hicks, Jack A. "Mediation in Reference Service to Extend Patron Success," The Reference Librarian 37 (1992): 49-64.

Pivotal Point Training & Consulting, Inc. "Tactics to Tame Tough People" 2000a. Available from <http://www.pivpoint.com/article2.htm>.

Pivotal Point Training & Consulting, Inc. "10 Steps for Winning Every Argument" 2000b. Available from <http://www.pivpoint.com/article.htm>.

Suzuki, Daisetz T. The Essentials of Zen Buddhism, selected from the writings of Daisetz T. Suzuki. Bernard Phillips, editor. (New York: Dutton, 1962).

Suzuki, Shunryu. Zen Mind, Beginner's Mind. Trudy Dixon, editor. (New York: Walker/Weatherhill, 1970).

Thondup, Tulku. The Healing Power of Mind. (Boston: Shambhala Publications, Inc., 1996).

OTHER RECOMMENDED READINGS

Gothberg, Helen M. "Managing Difficult People: Patrons (and Others)," The Reference Librarian 19 (1987): 269-83.

Nichol, James W. "Zen and the Art of User Friendly Service: 1–Organizational Culture," State Librarian 35 (November 1987) 35-37, 39.

Nichol, James W. "Zen and the Art of User Friendly Service: 2–Communication Skills," State Librarian 36 (July 1988) 19-21, 24.

Rubin, Rhea J. "Anger in the Library: Defusing Angry Patrons at the Reference Desk (and Elsewhere)," The Reference Librarian 31 (1991): 39-51.

Healing After the Unpleasant Outburst: Recovering from Incidents with Angry Library Users

Kathy Fescemyer

SUMMARY. Library personnel encounter angry library users regularly at various service points. Unpleasant incidents are detrimental to library staff attitudes and morale, and may have a lasting effect on the library staff member. This article describes techniques to lessen the impact of an emotional outburst of a library user and decrease the library staff member's recovery time from the incident. *[Article copies available for a fee from The Haworth Document Delivery Service: 1-800-HAWORTH. E-mail address: <getinfo@haworthpressinc.com> Website: <http://www.HaworthPress. com> © 2002 by The Haworth Press, Inc. All rights reserved.]*

KEYWORDS. Anger, recovery, coping

INTRODUCTION

Imagine this scene: it is December 1st, right after the Thanksgiving break. The students are back and it is just a few weeks before finals.

Kathy Fescemyer is Life Sciences Librarian, Life Sciences Library, The Pennsylvania State University, 408 Paterno Library, University Park, PA 16802-1811 (E-mail: kaf12@psu.edu).

The author would like to thank Justina Osa and Nancy Slaybaugh for taking the time to review and make recommendations on this article prior to publication.

[Haworth co-indexing entry note]: "Healing After the Unpleasant Outburst: Recovering from Incidents with Angry Library Users." Fescemyer, Kathy. Co-published simultaneously in *The Reference Librarian* (The Haworth Information Press, an imprint of The Haworth Press, Inc.) No. 75/76, 2002, pp. 235-244; and: *Helping the Difficult Library Patron: New Approaches to Examining and Resolving a Long-Standing and On-going Problem* (ed: Kwasi Sarkodie-Mensah) The Haworth Information Press, an imprint of The Haworth Press, Inc., 2002, pp. 235-244. Single or multiple copies of this article are available for a fee from The Haworth Document Delivery Service [1-800-HAWORTH, 9:00 a.m. - 5:00 p.m. (EST). E-mail address: getinfo@haworthpressinc.com].

© 2002 by The Haworth Press, Inc. All rights reserved.

Term papers, projects, take-home exams and other work are all due in just a few days, and people are at their worst. One student is talking to a reference librarian and is beginning to rant and rave. It might start like this "What do you mean all the books on interpersonal skills and human communication are checked out! And why isn't that most wonderful computer database system in the world not working? My family spends gazillions of dollars a year to send me to this University. Why can't I get anything to write my term paper? It's due in 3 days! I need articles now!"

Everyone working in public service at a library has been through this kind of outburst. Unpleasant, unhappy and pressured people show up at our service points on a regular basis. The majority of library users are polite, nice and understanding, but there is a small group of library users who are volcanic time bombs ready to explode at you or your colleagues. Sometimes we can stop or lessen the explosion. Other times, it just happens, and if you are on the receiving end of an outburst, it hurts. Finding ways to recover from it quickly can improve your attitude and health.

In the days of road rage, grocery store checkout line rage, and other bouts of temper, angry people increasingly confront public service personnel in libraries. This article was initiated by two events. The first event was listening to a new graduate student describing several incidents with angry people from her weekend shifts on the reference desk. The conversation occurred 3 or 4 days after the incidents, but the events still bothered her and she was still hurt and upset about what had happened.

The second event occurred during a seminar on coping with difficult people. The leader of the seminar asked what we hoped to take away from the seminar. I requested that I would like to learn how to recover from unpleasant incidents with difficult people. Unfortunately, the leader of the seminar did not take my question seriously. Her response was "get on with it, let it go, move on." Her response was the easy thing to say, but did not answer my question. Public service personnel may not let the incident go from their minds easily. Sometimes the incident and the bad feelings remain for hours and even days. When this happens, we need to reflect on why the incidents happened and learn about techniques to help decrease the negative feelings and recover from these scenes.

And that is the purpose of this paper. Better answers and methods are available to help staff members recover from unpleasant incidents. This article emphasizes the library staff member's reactions after the angry user has left the scene and describes many different ideas to help library personnel recover from incidents with angry library users.

LITERATURE REVIEW

Public service personnel in many professions encounter angry customers on a regular basis. Unfortunately, measuring these occurrences is difficult, and surveys are often the only recorded measurements. The Library Crime Research Project conducted in the early 1980s surveyed nearly 3,000 public libraries in all 50 states and provided much of the available data on library safety and security. One of the survey questions was on verbal abuse of the staff, and 45% of the libraries surveyed checked that staff had been verbally abused at least one or more times in the past year.[1] Medical personnel, especially nurses, report large amounts of verbal abuse. A 1994 California study of nurses found that 89% reported verbal abuse in their practice, and 47% reported verbal abuse during a one-month period.[2] In 1998, another study of 151 nurses was conducted, and 85% of the nurses surveyed reported that they had experienced verbal abuse. In the past 15 working days 45% had been verbally abused.[3] Statistics on verbal abuse of teachers show that 7.5% of teachers surveyed in 1990-1991, and 11.1 % in 1993-1994 considered verbal abuse a serious problem in their school.[4] A survey of network managers reported that 83% of the managers had angry, frustrated users who had destroyed parts of their computers.[5] A recent report of surveys conducted by the United States Postal Service (USPS) comparing 3,000 postal workers to 3,000 workers in the national workforce showed that 36% of postal service workers and 33% of members of the national workforce reported verbal abuse at work in the past year.[6] The USPS survey showed that 1 in 3 workers reported verbal abuse at work in the last year. This research reveals a high incidence of demanding encounters for public service personnel and shows that verbal abuse in the workplace is common and therefore may be a significant source of stress.

Many books and articles have been published about library security, crime in the library, library safety and problem patrons. Shuman[7] and Switzer[8] provide full literature reviews on these topics. The majority of the articles discuss working with the angry library user in the immediate circumstances and what can be done to satisfy the library user. Few articles discuss the effects of the library user's anger on the library personnel. Active listening techniques, as defined by Smith and Adams, recognize the patron's feelings and allow the patron to solve his own problems.[9] Rubin discusses working with the angry patron during the confrontation and several coping mechanisms for the library staff.[10,11] Different techniques to improve communication skills between library users and library workers are recommended by Turner.[12] Changes in society may be part of the reason for increased incidents with problem patrons and Curry discusses the rights of library users and library staff, tips to avoid confrontations, telephone skills and techniques to use with specific groups of patrons.[13] Arterburn describes techniques which may prevent an unpleasant situation from becoming a crisis.[14] In *Library Security and Safety Handbook: Prevention, Policies and Procedures*, Shuman describes problem behaviors in libraries and how to treat and prevent these behaviors.[15] Willis describes how to deal with many types of difficult people in the library and how to prevent unpleasant scenes.[16]

RECOMMENDATIONS

During or Immediately After the Incident

It is late afternoon at a library service point. The last person you tried to help just walked away in a huff. It really does not matter what the person's question or problem was–you are still feeling that departing person's anger. You are feeling some emotions, and many of them are not pleasant. And you must remain at the service point and help other library users. What can you do to decrease these unpleasant feelings now? What can you do after you leave the service point, so that these feelings are reduced and your time away will be enjoyable and you will not dread returning?

Begin by admitting that working with an angry individual is not fun and hurts. Then as the upset person is talking, take a moment and quietly get a deep breath.[17] Breathing helps in many ways to control feelings by diluting the fight-or-flight mechanism and providing an instant to assess the situation. The fight-or-flight mechanism prepares one for action during a threatening circumstance. Angry people are threatening, so it is a natural reaction to want to flee from the situation, even if you must remain at the service desk. At this point, you may tense your muscles and instinctively hold your breath. By taking a deep breath, oxygen is supplied to your body, which helps relax the fight-or-flight response, and helps you to begin controlling the situation. A deep breath may also provide a moment to devise a solution to the problem. Deep breathing is easy. Exhale slowly and quietly through your mouth, and inhale through your nose.

Next, step back physically and mentally from the emotions of the situation. Take a tiny step away from the angry person. The action will help disconnect your emotions from the scene. Listen quietly as the user speaks for a possible clue to a solution that will satisfy the user. Ask if there is something that could be done to help. Sometimes the user provides hints as to why he or she is angry or pressured, and often these hints include the fact that someone else has been angry with him or her recently. Listen carefully, even if the message comes across in a loud obnoxious manner, and you might get a clue as to how to solve the dilemma. The person is probably not yelling at you personally, but at the situation that caused the problem. Unfortunately, you are caught in the middle, having to communicate information that the user does not want to hear. If possible, try to understand and empathize with the user. For example, if the book he or she wants cannot be located, it might be fine to say to the person "I wish you could have the book too." Just be sure not to interrupt, because interrupting may anger the library user more.

Try to phrase your responses using a gentle answering technique that does not increase the emotions of the situation. Try to stay away from negative phrasing, which may increase the user's ire. For example, instead of saying "Reference books are never loaned," you might say, "Reference books are used regularly and need to remain inside the library." Use a gentle but assertive tone.

Begin rationalizing. Probably fancier psychology terms such as reframing may describe this concept, but it is all the same idea, that is, to change your perception of the event.[18] Excuse or understand the library user's poor behavior by offering a different explanation of the incident. A health reason such as a painful ingrown toenail, a migraine, backache or a toothache might cause someone to be irritable. The user might be worried or fatigued by a sick child or other relative. He may have had a misunderstanding or an argument with a family member, coworker, or friend. He could have a pressure due to a deadline for a project. He could also be just plain ornery. Whatever the reason, try to understand the person or give him an excuse to be upset. By trying to be understanding of the person's behavior, your frustration could be decreased.

After the Person Has Departed and the Incident Is Over

If you can leave the service point without disrupting service, take a short break. If leaving is not an alternative, take a 15-30 second timeout before talking to the next person, even looking at the reference books or the computer. Take 15-60 seconds to relax, and quietly breathe, and have a short transition time before beginning to help the next library user.

After the Time at the Service Point Is Completed

After your time at the service point is finished or during a break or lunch, take time to escape and relax. If you have a few moments and the weather is cooperative, go outdoors for a short walk. Fresh air, natural light, different scenery and a little exercise can provide a new perspective on the situation. Take some big breaths to release tension and bring energizing and calming oxygen into your body. If there is a fountain or a wooded area nearby, walk to it and focus on the beauty and quiet of the scene.

If you cannot get outside, take a mental vacation to a favorite place from your desk.[19] A small picture of a favorite place is a good way to start a short imaginary trip. Several pictures of coastal scenes and wildflowers are on my bulletin board. With them I can easily picture myself at the shore or in the woods. Some ideas for pictures are the seashore and blue sky, forests and waterfalls, the mall, or your favorite sports arena. Imagine another scene, and change your thoughts to more pleasurable ones.

Another way to take a mental break is to put an imaginary balloon over your head and fill it with grumpy thoughts or insults which you may not say aloud. Some of my favorite balloon fillings are jerk, yoyo, dingbat, or dodobrain. Keep it around as long as necessary, and then imagine it floating away into the sky. However, be careful about filling your balloons with violent imagery, which may backfire and increase your emotional turbulence.

Talking to a sympathetic friend who is trustworthy may provide feedback and relief. Sometimes another person's view may help in understanding the situation. Being able to talk to someone else will help you release the problem. A talk with a friend may help you put the incident in perspective as a small part of the day and not allow you to take it too seriously.

If the incident is serious, fill out an incident report. Compose it while the circumstances are fresh. If needed, write the first draft in totally venomous terminology, and be prepared to destroy this copy quickly. Then start anew and write an official copy with much less emotion. Describe the episode honestly with as few negative terms as possible. Record threatening or offensive language or cursing that occurred. Submit the report promptly, and keep a copy for your files.

Reflect. Ask yourself after a conflict, did you do your best to help that library user? If so, do not feel guilty. If you could have done better, then resolve to learn better techniques to aid other users. Or if you need to know more about the systems, services and guidelines of the library in which you are employed, then resolve to find ways to gain that knowledge.

As you reflect, remember that responsibility for the project or work belongs to the library user. If the project is left until the last moment, then it is the user's responsibility to complete it. Library workers help users to locate the best information available, but that may be difficult when the time frame is too short and sometimes it is not possible to fulfill a request.

After the Workday Is Over

If the incident is still troubling when you leave the library, then it is time to try to get a change of view. It is time to find something to enjoy that evening, to change your thoughts and help you relax. Each of us has our own unique set of likes and dislikes.

Begin by appreciating your set of living circumstances. Enjoy your personal circumstances whether you live alone or with others. If you live alone, enjoy the quiet, a condition that some of us with families rarely experience. Take time to enjoy your pets, plants, artwork, music, books, pictures, needlework or any other hobbies. If you live with others, enjoy your time with them. If you can spend time with children, do so. Children and their activities will not let you think about the earlier incidents: they are too busy making you play with them and creating their own imaginary worlds. Coloring, reading, playing with trucks or stuffed animals, sidewalk chalking, taking a walk, playing ball or many other activities will keep your mind away from the tensions of the day.

Physical exercise can also alleviate stress.[20] A long brisk walk, cleaning house, swimming, a workout, biking or a sports activity can send the tension away. Additionally with housekeeping, you get the added bonus of a neat and tidy home. Exercise releases the tension from muscles and forces you to concentrate on the activity. Currently, I am on the Penn State exercise program, which means that my car is parked a half mile from the library. Before and after work, I get a 10-15 minute walk and time to make the transition from work to home.

Another trick to rid yourself from the feelings of a confrontation is to soak in a nice long shower or bath right after getting home. While bathing, imagine that the ugliness of the incident is washed off and down the drain and far away. Afterwards I feel cleaner, more relaxed and have mentally washed the incident away.

Please be cautious about using alcohol or drugs or too many calories, especially chocolate, to decrease the stress of an incident. In the short term, they might ease a problem, but in the long term they may cause much larger problems. Use in moderation.

Get enough rest and healthy food. A nutritious meal and a good night's sleep is an obvious approach to feeling better. Who would not feel better after a delicious, healthy meal with proteins and vitamins, and then 8 hours of refreshing sleep?

If doing other things throughout the evening has not decreased the thoughts of the incident, try some relaxing routines. If the incident keeps you awake, then try relaxation breathing or muscle relaxing routines.[21] Another idea is to write the incident down with the thought of releasing it from your mind. If you write anything really malicious, be sure to destroy the writings. I have ripped up such writings and burned them in my charcoal grill.

Several Days Later or Over Time, Preventative Actions

If dealing with difficult people is causing health problems or if difficult scenes happen more often to you than to others, then it is time to reflect and determine if changes can be made to prevent future incidents.

Find the time to read some of the literature about dealing with difficult people.[22] Afterwards, take time to reflect techniques you can learn to prevent difficult situations from occurring. If there is a specific group of library users that cause difficult encounters, such as teenagers or senior citizens, learn additional ways to communicate with them effectively. If e-mail is an option for communicating with library users, use it with difficult users that you work with on a regular basis. E-mails take the emotions away from communicating with unpleasant users and make the job easier by decreasing the time spent with them.

Using gentle language reduces the likelihood of an outburst. Lower the number of the negative phrases in your answers to the library users. Rephrase the wording of negative statements to the best available options. For example, you might say "We don't have change at this desk, but the change machine is available one floor below." Or, "this book is not available currently, but it can be recalled, and you will be the next person who will be able check it out." Or "reference books must stay in the library, but you may make copies from them."

Increase your knowledge of the library. The more knowledge staff members have about the library, the easier it is to provide the best answers for user's questions. Take classes, ask questions, or request cross training in other departments to increase your knowledge about the library. One of the most enjoyable parts of being a librarian is learning something new every day. Increasing your knowledge of the library will increase your confidence in working with library users and will help prevent angry encounters.

If you find yourself becoming too angry or too unhappy about work, do not be afraid to try to discover the reasons by attending a class or seeking counseling. If you have the time, energy and funds, consider taking a stress management course, or an anger management course. If any of the above is limited, then find the time to explore stress management sites on the Web, and then reflect on methods to decrease the stress in your life.

CONCLUSION

Working with angry people is one of the most difficult aspects of public service work. Fortunately, for the majority of library personnel it occupies only a small portion of the day. The majority of library users are pleasant, polite, and appreciative of the service and knowledge shared by library personnel. Remembering the good manners and behavior of the typical library user may help when tolerating the outbursts of the angry users. Also keeping perspective on working with the unhappy library user will help decrease the time and energy it takes for reducing the unpleasant feelings. This paper has provided suggestions on reducing the effects of angry encounters with the library users. Learning to reduce the stressful aftermath can improve the quality of life and relationships with other library users, coworkers, family and friends.

REFERENCES

1. Lincoln, A. J. (1984). *Crime in the Library: A Study of Patterns, Impact and Security.* New York: R. R. Bowker.

2. Hilton, P. E., J. Kottke, & D. Pfahler. (1994). Verbal Abuse in Nursing: How Serious is It? *Nursing Management, 25,* 90.

3. Cameron, L. (1998). Verbal Abuse: A Proactive Approach. *Nursing Management, 29*, 34-36.

4. U.S. Department of Education. (1999). Table 27. Teachers' Perceptions about Serious Problems in Their Schools, by Type and Control of School: 1990-91 and 1993-94. *Digest of Educational Statistics, 1999*. Retrieved September 25, 2000 from the World Wide Web: <http://nces.ed.gov/pubs2000/digest99/d99t027.html>.

5. Melymuka, K. (1999). Raging users. *Computerworld*. Retrieved Oct 13, 2000 from the World Wide Web: <http://www.computerworld.com/cwi/story/0,1199,NAV47_STO35364,00. html>.

6. United States Postal Service Commission on a Safe and Secure Workplace. (2000). Report of the United States Postal Service Commission on a Safe and Secure Workplace. Retrieved October 13, 2000 from the World Wide Web: <http://www. casacolumbia.org/usr_doc/33994.pdf>.

7. Shuman, B. A. (1989). Problem Patrons in Libraries: A Review Article. *Library and Archival Security 9*, 3-19.

8. Switzer, T. R. (1999). *Safe at Work? Library Security and Safety Issues*. Lanham, MD: Scarecrow Press.

9. Smith, N. M. & I. Adams. (1991). Using Active Listening to Deal with Patron Problems. *Public Libraries 30*, 236-239.

10. Rubin, R. J. (1991). Anger in the Library: Defusing Angry Patrons at the Reference Desk (and Elsewhere). *Reference Librarian 31*, 39-51.

11. Rubin, R. J. (2000). *Defusing the Angry Patron: A How to Do it Manual for Librarians and Paraprofessionals*. New York: Neal-Shuman Publishers, 2000.

12. Turner, A. M. (1993). Dealing with Angry People. In A. M. Turner (Ed.), *It Comes with the Territory: Handling Problem Situations in the Library* (pp. 45-54). Jefferson, NC: McFarland.

13. Curry, A. (1996). Managing the Problem Patron. *Public Libraries 35*, 181-188.

14. Arterburn, T. R. (1996). Librarians: Caretakers or Crimefighters? *American Libraries 27*, 32-34.

15. Shuman, B. A. (1999). *Library Security and Safety Handbook. Prevention, Policies and Procedures*. Chicago: American Library Association.

16. Willis, M. R. (1999). *Dealing with Difficult People in the Library*. Chicago: American Library Association.

17. Rubin, 2000, 77-78.

18. Posen, D. B. Stress Management for Patient and Physician. (1995, April). *Canadian Journal of Continuing Medical Education*. Retrieved February 19, 2001, from the World Wide Web: <http://www.mentalhealth.com/mag1/p51-str.html>.

19. Stress Management for Parents. Retrieved February 23, 2001, from the World Wide Web: <http://childdevelopmentinfo.com/parenting/stress.shtml>.

20. Caputto, J. S. (1991). *Stress and Burnout in Library Service*. Phoenix AZ: Oryx Press, 128.

21. Capputto, 111-116.

22. See references 10-13 and 16.

Gypsies, Tramps and Rage:
Coping with Difficult Patrons

Sharon W. Bullard

SUMMARY. This paper proposes that encounters with problem patrons and reader rage will continue to increase. In order for the library and its staff to survive they must adhere to some basic ideas including acknowledging that a problem exists, creating a code of conduct, hiring and training staff for the task, and providing them ways to deal with the problems and the stress. *[Article copies available for a fee from The Haworth Document Delivery Service: 1-800-HAWORTH. E-mail address: <getinfo@haworthpressinc. com> Website: <http://www.HaworthPress.com> © 2002 by The Haworth Press, Inc. All rights reserved.]*

KEYWORDS. Difficult, problem patrons, clientele conduct, staff communication, empowerment, flexibility, authorities

INTRODUCTION

Today's libraries no longer resemble the quiet solitudes of yesteryear. They are filled with the interaction of users and the noise of copy machines, printers and computers. Patrons use cellular phones, pagers and computers with little regard to others. Even the sound of personalized lis-

---

Sharon W. Bullard is Administrative Services/Personnel Librarian, Walter Clinton Jackson Library, University of North Carolina, UNCG, PO Box 26175, Greensboro, NC 27402-6175 (E-mail: sharon_bullard@uncg.edu).

[Haworth co-indexing entry note]: "Gypsies, Tramps and Rage: Coping with Difficult Patrons." Bullard, Sharon W. Co-published simultaneously in *The Reference Librarian* (The Haworth Information Press, an imprint of The Haworth Press, Inc.) No. 75/76, 2002, pp. 245-252; and: *Helping the Difficult Library Patron: New Approaches to Examining and Resolving a Long-Standing and Ongoing Problem* (ed: Kwasi Sarkodie-Mensah) The Haworth Information Press, an imprint of The Haworth Press, Inc., 2002, pp. 245-252. Single or multiple copies of this article are available for a fee from The Haworth Document Delivery Service [1-800-HAWORTH, 9:00 a.m. - 5:00 p.m. (EST). E-mail address: getinfo@haworthpressinc.com].

© 2002 by The Haworth Press, Inc. All rights reserved.

tening devices can often be heard. And today's libraries have become a haven for the homeless, the young, the substance abuser, the sexual deviant, the elderly, the criminal-minded and the mentally disturbed.

With the change in clientele and their increased use of libraries, behavior of library patrons has become the subject of many books, articles and workshops today, leading one to believe problem behavior is a new phenomenon for libraries. In fact, the problem behavior of patrons dates back to the early beginnings of libraries. Otherwise, why were books chained to the desks in medieval times; why are curses found against those who "stealth a book"; and, why were there library rules published in the 1700s barring snoring?

The growing emphasis on the problem patron today is due to the increased number of incidences of undesirable behavior and the intensity of reader's rage. People seeking shelter from the streets often create complaints ranging from their body odor to their talking to no visible party. Latch key children produce a special problem for libraries as the safety of the child and the library's responsibility for providing that safety become an issue. Teens gathering after school often intimidate other users due to their robust activity. Patrons are content to wait in long lines for lunch knowing if they do not have a credit card, they must pay cash. However when they come to the library they demand instant gratification at the reference desk and special treatment when they have no valid identification.

Angry patrons still create the greatest problems for staff and these encounters are growing in number. In short, the social ills of America's society have moved into the library, and the staff, especially those in frontline positions, are subjected to the disruptive and problem behaviors on a daily basis.

Library staffs operate on the basic assumption that they are to provide service to those seeking assistance, information or knowledge. There is also the idea that "no one has the right to interfere with anyone else's right to use the library."[1] Add the American concepts of "the customer is always right" and "everyone is innocent until proven guilty" and one begins to see how the changes in patron behavior patterns in today's libraries are having a negative and draining effect on the library staff.

SURVIVAL

In order for library staff to survive and overcome the conflicts abounding in the libraries of today, some very basic ideas must be recognized and adhered to, which will enable employees to dance with the problems rather than fight with them.

Acknowledgement

First, there must be an acknowledgement that there is a problem, not just problem patrons. The acknowledgement has to be accepted not only by the staff at the front desks but by all library employees, especially library administrations and their governing bodies. Too often the behavior of a patron is singled out and efforts are made to modify the behavior of that particular patron or patron group, rather than addressing the problem and its cause. Use the recurring problems to review and evaluate the problems caused, whether it is anger over policies or the library having become a refuge for undesirables. Looking at user complaints offers an opportunity to evaluate operations from another perspective and offers a chance to solicit input from the complainer on how to resolve the problem. In evaluating a policy and possible solutions, keep the administration informed and involved. Be cautioned that a number of complaints received about a particular policy or procedure does not preclude that the problem lies with the practice. Resolving the situation may be as simple as making sure the patrons are aware of a policy or procedure or that they understand the reason for a practice.

Code of Conduct

The library should have a formal written code of conduct, which defines and identifies those behaviors that are unacceptable in the library. The code should be well written and well publicized. Post the library code of conduct on the library's web site as well as in highly visible locations throughout the building. Any handouts given during orientation or registration for a library card should include the code of conduct. Handouts, which include the code, should be available for users to pick up as they browse through other handouts provided by the library. Personnel providing library security should be able to supply a copy of the code to misbehaving persons, as they are being reprimanded or escorted out of the building. Staff should be provided with recommended sanctions and recommended guidelines for enforcement. The code of conduct should be applied fairly and equitably to all patrons.

Staffing

Staff that work directly with the public must have a combination of skills and talents that should be sought during the recruitment process.

Included in these abilities are the need for excellent interpersonal and communication skills, the proficiency to make quick and accurate judgments, the willingness to assume authority and, most important, the possession of common sense. During the interview process questions should be asked, including hypothetical situations that probe an interviewee's abilities, skills and talents.

Training

Staff training is an ongoing process, beginning on the new employees' first day and ending as they leave on their final day. Staff should be trained to enable them to respond to questions, to handle situations and to cope with negative feelings. Training exercises are not only done in formal workshops, but in informal settings. Utilize a mentoring program by pairing newer employees with more experienced staff members. If at all possible, provide a place for staff to share ideas and situations informally as well as allow time during regularly scheduled staff meetings for problem situations to be reviewed and discussed.

Communication

The importance of good communication skills cannot be over emphasized. A person is not listening if he or she is formulating a response to be given as soon as the other person quits talking. Staff should be trained in active listening, which acknowledges that the other person owns the problem and reflects back to the person what one thinks they are hearing. There are several techniques of active listening. Paraphrasing is one of them. When talking with a person, use his or her name. Nothing is more beautiful to someone than hearing one's own name spoken by another. Use phrases, such as "I understand your feelings," or, "I can appreciate your being upset," but use them with sincerity.

When handling problem situations, staff should be aware of body language. "It has been suggested that only 10 percent of what is heard is actually what is being said and 30 percent of what is heard are formed by impressions composed from body language and tone of voice."[2] Folded arms, hand on hips, pointing fingers or speaking faster and louder indicate hostility.

In some instances, it becomes clear that additional dialog will not resolve the issue being discussed. In these cases, acknowledge that under the circumstances, resolution is not possible. Make such a statement to the patron, or be prepared to refer the patron to someone else, such as a co-worker or a supervisor. When two different people make the same statement using different words, the concept may become clearer. It is also known that when a person hears the same response from two difference sources, he/she is more willing to accept the validity of the response. Some people do not respond to being told what to do by a female, members of certain ethnic groups or someone they perceive as not being in charge. If one is able to make that determination while working with the upset patron, make a shift to a staff member who fits the perceived "person in charge."

Post Trauma

The biggest problem with handling angry patrons is the psychological effect they have on the staff members' emotions. In spite of staff being trained not to internalize verbal abuse, it is often humanly impossible not to do so. "Consumer research shows that 90 percent of discontented customers never return and tell 9 friends about their unhappiness. They also remember the problem 23.5 months later, whereas the satisfied customer remembers for 18 months."[3] These figures may also be reversed and applied to the staff who remember encounters with angry and/or abusive patrons for almost two years. Immediately after an encounter with an angry patron a staff member requires a minimum of one hour to adequately recover emotionally and be able to continue his or her job effectively. Staff must have time to recover from emotional encounters.

One way for supervisors to help is to require a written report detailing each incident. These reports may be kept as computer files within the department and may serve as a log. Providing an index by name, date, time and type of incident, will enable easy access and may be used to show behavior patterns, the times problems most often occur and what types of situations the library is experiencing. By writing about an incident the staff member is able to vent his/her feelings as well as provide written documentation in the event the patron's behavior becomes so inappropriate as to require referral to authorities. Another method is for the supervisor and employee to discuss the situation behind the scenes. It is also helpful to have a "venting center" where staff can blow off steam as well as have a sympathetic ear from fellow employees.

Common Sense

Just as policy and procedure manuals are not enough to guide staff through problem situations, time spent in staff training cannot overcome the lack of common sense. The most important asset for library staff is common sense and the ability to apply it in any situation. The use of common sense can defuse a situation before it becomes hostile or embarrassing.

Empowerment

Library staff empowerment is vital to allow staff to handle situations as they arise. "Empowerment is an employee who can do whatever he has to do on the spot to take care of a customer to that customer's satisfaction, not to the company's satisfaction."[4] Managers must learn to trust their employees to do the right thing in any situation. In the beginning, hire good personnel by asking questions that explore a candidate's communication skills and their ability to make quick and accurate judgments during the recruitment process. Proceed to train employees to do their best in difficult situations and finally, trust them to make the right decision. Employees who are trusted respond to that trust. They are more committed to their work and are happier employees with higher morale.

Administration

Do not refer everyday problems to the administration, but do seek their support. Too often when a single patron complains to an administrator, solutions are formulated without first seeking input from the staff and the results decrease staff morale. Impress on the administration that they must support staff who are serving on the front lines.

Administration must be flexible as well as allow staff flexibility in dealing with situations. There is an unwritten rule that when dealing with the disgruntled the more options available, the better the chance of turning an incident into a win-win situation. Procedures should provide flexibility at all levels.

Self-Help

Wherever possible, allow patrons to do the work themselves. When showing them how to search, let them use the computer and move the mouse. Provide self-tutorials for heavily used databases and self-guided tours of the building and its collections. Allow patrons to place their own interlibrary loan requests, check out and renew their own materials, and see their own accounts. Businesses such as service stations, banks, supermarkets and even airlines have been empowering users for years. Just as staff feels more comfortable with self-empowerment, users may also wish to have control and be able to do things for themselves.

Outside Resources

In libraries of yesterday, each institution worked alone and resolved its own problems the best way possible. Today there is an incredible wealth of knowledge available by contacting colleagues through list-servs or e-mail. Utilizing sources such as LIBREF-L, CIRCPLUS and SAFETY-L will provide access to hundreds of years of experience as well as offering one assurances that incidents involving difficult patrons are wide spread and are not unique to any one library.

Local Authorities

When a difficult patron's behavior goes beyond that which can be handled or abided by the staff, it is time to seek additional professional help. Intervention by outside authorities may include the library security, the office overseeing student conduct or local school authorities or the police department. Develop a positive working relationship with these offices. When notifying them of problems, have the facts outlined and available. Be reasonable when asking for their help and know what kind of help they will be able to provide. Contact offices of student conduct and request access to their policies and regulations governing student behavior. When working with these agencies be able to offer suggestions as to what regulations have been abused. Know what the police consider a "criminal action" and refrain from calling them into situations they cannot assist in resolving.

CONCLUSION

Given the history of the disruptive patron and the increasing number of encounters with enraged users, dealing with problem patrons will continue to require more and more staff time. In order for library staff to do their job, which is to deliver services in the area of information to all people, they must be equipped to cope with resolving problems. Well trained staff with common sense, good communication skills, the power to take care of a user's problems and the support of the administration are destined to produce better results and cause staff to feel good about themselves, their job and their accomplishments. Complaints should be used as an invitation to review policies and procedures in an effort to improve service and minimize encounters with enraged readers. It will take time and effort, but eventually the staff will be enabled to dance with the problem patrons.

REFERENCES

1. Turner, Ann M. *It Comes with the Territory: Handling Problem Situations in Libraries.* Jefferson, North Carolina and London: McFarland & Co., Inc. 1993, 4.

2. Ibid. 48.

3. Rhea, Joyce Rubin. "Anger in the Library: Defusing Angry Patrons at the Reference Desk (and Elsewhere)." *The Reference Librarian* 31 1990, 49.

4. Tschohl, John. "Empowerment: the key to customer service." *Nation's Restaurant News.* 31:31, 40. In Sarkodie-Mensah, Kwasi. "The Difficult Patron Situation: A Window of Opportunity to Improve Library Service." *Catholic Library World.* March 2000, 159-167.

BIBLIOGRAPHY

Bangs, Patricia. "When Bad Things Happen in Good Libraries: Staff Tools for the '90s and Beyond. *Public Libraries* 37:3, My/Je 1998, 196-199.

Canal, Bruce A. "Libraries Attract More than Readers: Investing in Library Safety. *Indiana Libraries* 7:1, 1998, 15-17.

McNeil, Beth and Denise J. Johnson. *Patron Behavior in Libraries: A Handbook of Positive Approaches to Negative Situations.* Chicago: American Library Association, 1996.

Rhea, Joyce Rubin. "Anger in the Library: Defusing Angry Patrons at the Reference Desk (and Elsewhere)." *The Reference Librarian* 31, 1990.

Rhea, Joyce, Rubin. "Defusing the Angry Patron" *Library Mosaics* 11:3, My/Je 2000, 14-15.

Sarkodie-Mensah, Kwasi. "The Difficult Patron Situation: A Window of Opportunity to Improve Library Service." *Catholic Library World.* March 2000, 159-167.

Shuman, Bruce. *Library Security and Safety Handbook: Prevention, Policies and Procedures.* Chicago: American Library Association, 1999.

Turner, Anne M. *It Comes with the Territory: Handling Problem Situations in Libraries.* Jefferson, North Carolina and London: McFarland & Co., Inc.1993.

Help Yourself:
Front-Line Defense in an Academic Library

Diane J. Turner

Marilyn Grotzky

SUMMARY. One of the biggest challenges in libraries today is how to empower front-line employees to be able to deal with the unique problems and people that society unloads on us daily. Some of these problems, like staff morale, are with us all the time. Others, such as developing workable policies and procedures and dealing with problem patrons, are like housework, done for the moment but never complete. A third category consists of the rare event that threatens the lives or wellbeing of library employees and users–issues of personal safety in the workplace.

This article will discuss, from the perspective of two veteran staff of the Auraria Library, the need for clear communication, up to date policies and procedures, and effective training. Although every problem cannot be solved or every situation diffused, it is best to empower employees to know what to do for all the "what ifs" that may arise. *[Article copies available for a fee from The Haworth Document Delivery Service: 1-800-HAWORTH. E-mail address: <getinfo@haworthpressinc.com> Website: <http://www. HaworthPress.com> © 2002 by The Haworth Press, Inc. All rights reserved.]*

KEYWORDS. Libraries, common problems, policies and procedures, training, communication, empowerment

Diane J. Turner is Senior Instructor/Reference Librarian (E-mail: dturner@carbon. cudenver.edu) and Marilyn Grotzky is Library Technician III (E-mail: Mgrotzky@ carbon.cudenver.edu), both at Auraria Library, 1100 Lawrence Street, Denver, CO 80204-2095.

[Haworth co-indexing entry note]: "Help Yourself: Front-Line Defense in an Academic Library." Turner, Diane J., and Marilyn Grotzky. Co-published simultaneously in *The Reference Librarian* (The Haworth Information Press, an imprint of The Haworth Press, Inc.) No. 75/76, 2002, pp. 253-262; and: *Helping the Difficult Library Patron: New Approaches to Examining and Resolving a Long-Standing and Ongoing Problem* (ed: Kwasi Sarkodie-Mensah) The Haworth Information Press, an imprint of The Haworth Press, Inc., 2002, pp. 253-262. Single or multiple copies of this article are available for a fee from The Haworth Document Delivery Service [1-800-HAWORTH, 9:00 a.m. - 5:00 p.m. (EST). E-mail address: getinfo@haworthpressinc. com].

© 2002 by The Haworth Press, Inc. All rights reserved.

253

AURARIA LIBRARY BACKGROUND

If there is such a thing as an ordinary academic library, Auraria Library is not it. The Auraria campus was planned to be non-traditional, a place where, in theory, a student could enter, even without a high school diploma, at Community College of Denver (CCD), complete his or her bachelor's degree at Metropolitan State College of Denver (MSCD), and continue through a doctorate at the University of Colorado at Denver (CU-Denver), if the student desired to do so. Thirty years later, that's still true. For the convenience of the commuter students, classes are offered throughout the day and evening as well as on weekends and held on campus, at off campus sites, and online. The options and possibilities are almost limitless.

All of this affects the Library. We serve a population that may truly be unique: CCD sends us everything from basic readers to graduating vocational and business students. MSCD is the largest baccalaureate-only college in the nation with degrees in aviation, criminal justice, and various business specialties as well as the traditional arts and sciences. CU-Denver supplies both graduate and undergraduate students in architecture, public administration, international business, and many other fields. The faculty of all three schools is involved in research, as are many administrators. Since all three institutions are taxpayer supported, the library assists every sort of public patron, and because it is downtown, many business people use the library. All three schools have sizable English-as-a-second-language populations of both immigrants and international students. Auraria is the largest campus in Colorado, with an enrollment of approximately 33,000 students.

Like most library personnel, the Auraria Library staff tends to be service-oriented, and there is a lot of opportunity to provide service here, but there can also be a lot of frustration. Our expectations of ourselves are high: though the library is only medium sized and fairly new, we want to provide appropriate materials, excellent service, and inspirational instruction to this extraordinarily varied user group. Like many library users, their expectations are both lower and higher than ours–lower because in this age of the Internet many students (and some administrators) believe that libraries are hopelessly outdated, and higher because they expect all material to be instantly available and free. One librarian said, "They seem to feel that I should just reach under the desk and pull out exactly what they want, a speech by Jimmy Carter, a mathematical formula, an annual report. They do not even want me to think about what they want, they just want me to hand it over, in exactly the format they want." Another said, "What they really want is a website called EverythingIWant.com." Someone else replied, "That should be 'dot org.' They don't want to pay for it."

This sort of frustration comes with working with library users or students at a service desk or in library instruction. Front-line workers expect it. We improve what we can, we laugh when we can, and we treasure the thanks we get, which often comes unexpectedly. The frustration that is harder to deal with comes from within the library.

MORALE

Some years ago, a tactless administrator told a group of staff members that they should be grateful for their jobs. One staff member responded that if the economy had been different, many of us would not be here–administration ought to be grateful for their staff. That may be the root of many morale problems–both administration and staff see the other as unappreciative. Staff at least may feel powerless, with little input into decision making but a great deal of responsibility for carrying decisions out because of their frontline positions. When staff members have remained with the library for many years, they may feel trapped by the retirement plans that they are also grateful for. People who have made library work their life's work and who feel powerless, trapped, and underpaid probably have a morale problem, and who can blame them? When staff members hold themselves responsible for a high level of service and have established a high level of expectation in library users, is it surprising that they should feel discouraged when they feel unappreciated?

Beginning psychology students are sometimes told of an experiment in a factory. When the level of light was raised, production went up. Researchers thought that when light was decreased, the work level would go down. Instead it went up again. After interviewing a number of workers, they discovered that the workers interpreted change as an attempt to make their conditions better, and they responded accordingly.[1]

There is a fair chance that a series of attempts to make the library a better place to work will change the morale level, and therefore make the library a better place to work. If some things are beyond the control of staff, administration, or the two working together, other things are not. Why not begin to make the changes we can?

POLICIES AND PROCEDURES

Having current policies and procedures in place will empower the frontline staff to deal with day to day operations. A senior staff member explained many years ago that the purpose of the frontline staff was to expedite research and study, not to throw roadblocks in the way. That is probably as good a general guideline to policy making as any, though it is useful to remember that it is our job to expedite research and study for all the library's users, not just the one standing in front of us now, and to keep in mind that situations change.

Debra Wilcox Johnson, in her teleconference, "The Public and Policies: Interpreting and Applying Library Service Policies," 17 November 2000, brought up some very valuable points about policies: policies should exhibit trust of staff and their judgment; policies should remove barriers to service, not create barriers; policies are not open and shut cases; and policies are situation dependent.[2] The success of a policy depends on the frontline staff. Frontline staff members are the ambassadors of the library and need the support of management.

STAFF INVOLVEMENT

In every organization there is a vital need for up to date policies and procedures which reflect what actually should occur and who should do what. Wilbur Cross defines *empowerment* as "a personnel theory that holds that individual motivation is increased and improved when employees are given opportunities to become more involved in their work and the decisions and goals that pertain."[3] Empowerment means that the staff must have a voice in developing the policies and procedures they must carry out. Out of date and irrelevant policies and procedures are not only ineffective but they could lead to lawsuits from angry patrons and even disillusioned employees who find themselves in threatening situations caused by trying to enforce an outdated policy. More likely than a lawsuit is a further breakdown of morale if efforts toward staff involvement are seen as insincere. "The problem is, 'employee involvement' programs often consist of frantic management teams trying to placate frustrated employees with a litany of gimmicks. Those programs are often met with employee cynicism because they lack any real mechanism for involving team members in the decision making process and because management has little or no intention of following up on employee ideas," say Hawk and Garrett J. Sheridan in *Management*

Review.[4] Involvement must be meaningful. When policies are created, they must be current, enforceable, have both staff and management backing, and serve library users.

PROBLEM TO SOLUTION TO NEW PROBLEM

Consider, for example, our problem of e-mail in the library. When we first obtained terminals that accessed both our library catalog and research databases and the Internet, we hoped to make the terminals completely free access with no restrictions. In only a short time we discovered that terminals were being used for chat rooms, e-mail, casual surfing, and other non-research purposes, while students desperate to do research stood in line shifting from one foot to the other in frustration. Our policy had to change. We added signs to each station asking students to refrain from these things and notified them that if they were using a terminal for those purposes, we would ask them to surrender the workstation to a student who needed it for research. This allowed the more courageous of the students and library staff to identify non-researchers and ask them to give up their workstations. Many of us were not satisfied with the policy because we did not like the policing role.

We identified e-mail as the major problem and set up two terminals in the back of the library for e-mail. They were inconveniently located for us to offer assistance and the subject of complaint by students. In response, we dedicated four easily located terminals for e-mail, established a 10 minute time limit when there are people waiting, and gave the terminals no printers. Students who do need printers can go to computer labs. We keep handouts on computer lab locations at the Reference desk. The current policy regarding the use of library terminals for e-mail works now, but increasing numbers of teachers are establishing web sites to use for instruction (homework assignments, supplementary reading, etc.). This is going to create a demand for printers. Thanks to our director, the library is fortunate to have acquired a grant for an in-house computer lab and since our grand opening, students have been very pleased. The new lab has solved a few problems and created a few new opportunities of policy making.

COMMUNICATION

This looks like a success story, but it is more than that. Each of our policies eventually created a new roadblock. To deconstruct the roadblocks, two things are important–flexibility and communication. When students and staff communicated their frustration, we had to be flexible enough to begin working for a new solution. When we communicate our willingness to listen and work for solutions, their frustration level diminishes.

In today's libraries, we are going to have to recognize that some of the policies we labor over are going to need changing soon and often. Effective enforcement of policy is going to require effective communication. Everyone who will be involved in dissemination and enforcement needs to know the policy and the reasons behind it.

Sometimes a policy is necessary but unpopular or difficult to explain. Scripting an explanation is often a good idea. If everyone explaining the policy puts it in the same way, it is easier to enforce, while if everyone explaining gives a different reason for the policy, those who object are given more grounds for argument. It is important that staff members are able to adjust the script to their own style and vary the words–otherwise we sound like robots and are completely unconvincing. Rehearsal is also important. It often takes more than one try to produce a clear, competent, courteous but non-apologetic reading of a script, as two of us noticed recently. One of the librarians was overheard explaining that if a user could not be civil, she could not continue to help him. As we tried to duplicate her words for our own use, we noticed how changing intonation of a single word changed the intention of the statement. It was amazingly easy to be condescending or insulting, using exactly the same words that our courteous co-worker had used.

Some policies are best clearly made public to all who enter the building. Some libraries post acceptable standards of behavior near the entrance of the library and keep copies at the service desks. It is very hard to argue with a staff member who says, "Excuse me, sir. We have a policy that says . . . It's posted near the front door and I have a copy here." If library employees wanted to be authority figures, they would have attended police academies; most prefer to spend our time assisting patrons, not confronting them.

As with spoken language, written language must be carefully composed. One person's polite notice is someone else's insult. Committee work is often appropriate here, and even then the language should be reviewed by others for clarity and tact. Having a part in choosing the language of a policy gives those who composed it more interest in it, makes it more likely that they will help enforce it, and makes them more likely to notice the success or failure of the policy and its phrasing.

EMPLOYEE BUY IN

Any policy not backed by both staff and management needs to be reconsidered. It is nearly impossible to force staff members to follow a rule they consider unreasonable, especially when many staff members work relatively unsupervised in the evenings or on weekends. Very few things cause as much resentment and confusion as policies that are enforced only at some times and only in some departments or by some people. Almost nothing does as much to create problem patrons.

Employee feedback is of paramount importance when developing policies and procedures that they will be expected to carry out. Since frontline employees set the tone in libraries, it is important that they believe in and can enforce the policies and procedures that make the library function. Staff needs to be confident that their managers will be supportive of their decisions. In our various jobs in libraries, the military, teaching, and retail establishments, we have noticed that one of the big management mistakes made is that policies and procedures are developed at the top with little feedback from the people that must carry them out.

UPDATING POLICIES AND PROCEDURES

Both policies and procedures need to be kept up-to-date, but it is the nature of such manuals to be out of date. Technology to the rescue! Software programs such as Office Wizard, created by the McKee Co. in Littleton, CO, provide templates for employees to fill out which explain what they do, how they do it, and where to find the equipment needed for it. Policies can be put on library intranets for easy access for everyone. Certain staff members can be assigned to check each policy periodically. Just as many listservs post their policies monthly, an administrative assistant can post a pre-determined e-mail message each month (or other suitable time period) reminding staff to check the policies they are responsible for to see if they need updating. Reviewing policies and procedures regularly means knowing the policy or procedure rather than dimly being aware that there might be a policy or procedure. Problems and discussions can be posted through a library or departmental list. Procedures and policies that are current can aid frontline staff members when someone calls in sick, when there is an emergency, or when there is doubt about what to do. Knowing what to do and how to do it can alleviate unnecessary staff and customer confusion and the possibility of negative confrontations.

As Rhea Joyce Rubin points out in her book *Defusing the Angry Patron*, "More often than not, the library's policies and procedures inadvertently trigger a patron's unexpected anger."[5]

PROBLEM PATRONS

As Teresa and Mahmoud Omidsalar state in "Customer Service: A View from the Trenches," "Library personnel no longer cater only to a reading public in search of edification. Because of the general decline in the level of public civility, we often have to deal with disruptive patrons who don't know how to conduct themselves in libraries or other public places."[6] Personnel in the Auraria Library had to deal with an individual who harassed and intimidated people at the reference desk and although incidents were documented, the problem was not solved until the man spent months harassing the Denver police chief.[7] The individual is now spending a well-earned rest in jail. Unfortunately, library workers seldom see such as satisfactory solution to harassment. Harassment is uncomfortable; other levels of violence are much more threatening. A suspected library bomber was recently arrested in Denver after pipe bombs were found in book drops at two branches of the public library.[8] And of course, the mass murder at nearby Columbine High School ended in the school library. Incidents like these indicate that the issue of safety in our workplace is growing more important. The situations that library staff must deal with are becoming more and more complex, and it is in the best interest of every library to communicate at every level to provide safety in the workplace.

To begin with, we should "learn to discriminate between the customers from hell and customers who have gone through hell. The distinction is crucial." So says Oren Harari in *Management Review*.[9] We meet library users who have gone through hell every day–a student whose teacher has given him the wrong spelling of an author's name; someone who hates the computer and has proof the feeling is mutual; a patron who has been sent from one desk to another one time too many. A little extraordinary customer service will usually defuse the situation.

And then there are the other kind. We had one user who apparently came in periodically for some "soggy potato chip therapy." The idea here is that a soggy potato chip is better than none, or even negative attention is better than no attention. Once when he began to throw his usual temper tantrum, a patron who knew him called him by name and said, "You know, and I know, that that is inappropriate behavior." He stopped screaming immediately. Sometimes what is needed is training.

TRAINING

There are three things about training: everybody needs it, everybody wants it, and nobody has time for it. Training must be mandatory because often it is the people who need the training most that do not attend training sessions. Make attending training sessions a part of the yearly performance appraisal process and follow up on training with refresher courses. Managers should lead by example and be at the training sessions to stress the importance. What kind of training would help library staff deal with patrons with problems? There is no shortage of ideas in library and human resource management journals. In her article "Workplace Violence in Libraries,"[10] Barbara Pease looks at the library-related value of public service and the need for security and suggests, among other things, assertiveness training. In the spring 1997 issue of *Colorado Libraries*,[11] Patricia Wellinger outlines crisis prevention tips from the National Crisis Prevention Institute. These include (1) be empathetic, (2) permit verbal venting where possible, and (3) avoid overreacting. In the summer 2000 issue of the same journal,[12] Nicole Steffen offers an amalgamation of theories and practical suggestions, including using active listening skills, finding alternatives, and verifying that the patron understands both the alternatives and the consequences. In an interesting article in *Workforce*[13] Gillian Flynn takes on harassment from within the workplace, stating that "tolerance is the biggest factor that allows managers to abuse or misuse their authority."

Last but certainly not least in the training department, everyone in the library should know evacuation routes for fire and bomb threats, the safest retreats in case of hurricanes or tornadoes, and what to do in case of flood. Empowerment can save lives.

CONCLUSION

The article "The Difficult Patron Situation: A Window of Opportunity to Improve Library Service"[14] highlights many of the problems all libraries deal with and offers some of the same solutions found in this article. There are also some new books out such as *Library Security and*

Safety Handbook: Prevention, Policies, and Procedures by Bruce A. Shuman, and *Dealing with Difficult People in the Library* by Mark R. Willis. What all of us who work in libraries must realize is that being prepared is becoming more and more necessary in this fast-paced, stressed out world, and difficult and unexpected situations will constantly present themselves. Making sure that frontline staff has the proper tools to deal with these situations is of monumental importance and cannot be put aside. There is no time like the present and the present is now!

REFERENCES

1. Roethlisberger, F.J. and William J. Dickson. Management and the Worker. (Cambridge, Massachusetts: Harvard University Press, 1939) see also; Rieger, Bradley J., "Lessons in Productivity and People." Training & Development, October 1995, v. 49, n. 10, pp. 56-58.

2. Johnson, Debra Wilcox. "The Public and Policies: Interpreting and Applying Library Service Policies." 17 November 2000. Soaring to Excellence Teleconference. <http://www.cod.edu/teleconf/Soaring/>. The Public and Policies: Interpreting and Applying Library Service Policies.

3. Cross, Wilbur. Encyclopedic Dictionary of Business Terms. (Englewood Cliffs, New Jersey: Prentice Hall, 1995).

4. Sheridan, Hawk and Garrett J. Sheridan. "The Right Staff." Management Review, June 1999, v. 88, n. 6, pp. 43-48.

5. Rubin, Rhea Joyce. Defusing the Angry Patron: A How-To-Do-It Manual for Librarians and Paraprofessionals. (New York: Neal-Schuman Publishers, Inc., 2000).

6. Omidsalar, Teresa Portilla and Mahmoud Omidsalar. "Customer Service: A View from the Trenches." American Libraries, February 1999, v. 30 n. 2, pp. 24-25.

7. Pankratz, Howard. "Man Held in Harassment of Police Chief." Denver Post, September 21, 2000, p. B03.

8. Fong, Tillie. "Women Arrested Over Bombs at Libraries, Denverite 42, Being Held Without Bail." Denver Rocky Mountain News, October 3, 2000, p. 10A.

9. Harari, Oren. "To Hell and Back." Management Review, July 1996, v. 85, n. 7, pp. 55-58.

10. Pease, Barbara. "Workplace Violence in Libraries." Library Management, v. 16, n. 7, 1995, pp. 30-39.

11. Wellinger, Patricia. "Workplace Violence: Is Your Library At Risk?" Colorado Libraries, Spring 1997, v. 23, n. 1, pp. 16-17.

12. Steffen, Nicolle. "Rising to the Occasion:Working with Angry People at the Reference Desk." Colorado Libraries, Summer 2000, v. 26, n. 2, pp. 11-13.

13. Flynn, Gillian. "Stop Toxic Managers Before They Stop You." Workforce, August 1999, v. 78, n. 8, pp. 40-44.

14. Sarkodie-Mensah, Kwasi. "The Difficult Patron Situation: A Window of Opportunity to Improve Service." Catholic Library World, March 2000, v. 70 n. 3, pp. 1559-1567.

The Difficult Patron Situation: Competency-Based Training to Empower Frontline Staff

Justina O. Osa

SUMMARY. Problem/difficult patron incidents that occur in libraries are on the rise. Library administrators and library employees have attempted to decrease the number of incidents by providing staff training and formulating policies and rules to control the situation. The purpose of this article is to share the proactive steps that the Education and Behavioral Sciences Library, Penn State University Libraries, took to prevent or decrease the incidences of difficult patrons as the library prepares to relocate. The focus was on assisting the frontline staff members, who work on the reference desk, to acquire the competencies they need to provide consistent quality reference services to patrons, and to reduce incidences of unsatisfied, difficult, and problem patrons. *[Article copies available for a fee from The Haworth Document Delivery Service: 1-800-HAWORTH. E-mail address: <getinfo@haworthpressinc.com> Website: <http://www. HaworthPress.com> © 2002 by The Haworth Press, Inc. All rights reserved.]*

KEYWORDS. Problem patrons, competencies, empowering frontline staff, training

Justina O. Osa is Education and Behavioral Sciences Librarian, The Pennsylvania State University, University Libraries, Education & Behavioral Sciences Library, E-502C Paterno, University Park, PA 16802 (E-mail: joo2@psu.edu).

[Haworth co-indexing entry note]: "The Difficult Patron Situation: Competency-Based Training to Empower Frontline Staff." Osa, Justina O. Co-published simultaneously in *The Reference Librarian* (The Haworth Information Press, an imprint of The Haworth Press, Inc.) No. 75/76, 2002, pp. 263-276; and: *Helping the Difficult Library Patron: New Approaches to Examining and Resolving a Long-Standing and Ongoing Problem* (ed: Kwasi Sarkodie-Mensah) The Haworth Information Press, an imprint of The Haworth Press, Inc., 2002, pp. 263-276. Single or multiple copies of this article are available for a fee from The Haworth Document Delivery Service [1-800-HAWORTH, 9:00 a.m. - 5:00 p.m. (EST). E-mail address: getinfo@haworthpressinc.com].

© 2002 by The Haworth Press, Inc. All rights reserved.

263

INTRODUCTION

Librarianship is a service profession and the sacred activity at the reference desk is service. Reference librarians have perhaps the toughest job in the library.[1] They staff the information and question desk. Reference services involve working daily with patrons with diverse characteristics and helping them find the information they need on a countless number of subjects, and on a wide range of questions on a varying level of complexity–from trivial to challenging. The library employees who staff the reference desk are the frontline staff and they may be the most precious asset the library has. Patrons come to the library with certain expectations. When these expectations are met by the services provided by the staff a win-win situation is created. Patrons leave the library happy and satisfied, and the library staff feels happy, competent and fulfilled.

Patrons have the power to make the job of library workers a joy or/and a living hell. Since patrons wield so much influence on our job, anything that focuses on making our interaction with patrons more pleasant is important to us. "Research on stress among library staff found that patrons were the major source of stress; however, patrons were also the most commonly cited source of satisfaction to library workers."[2] It is somewhat ironical when one hears library workers say, "This would be a great job, except for the patrons." But we need the patrons. They are the raison d'être of all we do. Without them there would be no need to acquire resources, manage them, or open the library door. It would be realistic to expect that library employees who provide public service will run into difficult and problem patrons from time to time because problem or difficult patrons go with the territory when working in public services or the reference desk. The issue of problem or difficult patrons is perennial and chronic. Some of the reasons it is receiving increasing attention in all types of libraries include the fact that there is an increased demand for customer satisfaction and customer service. Meeting their information needs and having them leave the library happy is our raison d'être.

Who are difficult or problem patrons and what behaviors do they exhibit? Defining difficult or problem patrons is complex. Justice Potter Stewart speaking of obscenity said, "I am disinclined to define (it), I doubt that I could ever successfully manage to do so. But I know it when I see it."[3] And Bruce A. Shuman commented, "Much the same definition applies to problem patrons . . . but you know problem behavior when you see it."[4] Problem patrons are generally individuals who display disruptive, uncooperative, aggressive, aberrant, or criminal behaviors within the library.

Several factors that contribute to produce a difficult patron could be external or internal to the library. Encounters with difficult patrons constitute one of the job hazards of librarians, especially the frontline staff members. We need to have an intelligent and informed insight into the issue of difficult patrons before we can begin to address it.

BACKGROUND

In 1999, the plan was well under way to move the Education and Behavioral Sciences Library of Penn State University from Rackley Building to the 5th floor of the newly renovated state-of-the-art Paterno Library. For the first time, the Education and Behavioral Sciences Library will have all its collections in one location. We anticipated increase in patron traffic in our new location, and we also anticipated that frontline staff would be called upon to provide answers and information on more complex reference questions than they were doing in Rackley. It is our dream that we will consistently provide quality services to all our patrons, and have them leave the library happy and satisfied even when we relocate.

The author is of the opinion that it would be better for the Education and Behavioral Sciences Library to be proactive rather than reactive in dealing with issues that have the potential to produce problem or difficult patrons. We cannot afford the luxury of waiting until problems occur before we think of solving them. It will be really wise and insightful to:

1. Anticipate and identify the types of patrons and the nature of reference questions and situations that may arise;
2. Know the level of competence and preparedness of the frontline staff to perform adequately; and
3. Design and implement a plan that has the possibility of equipping the frontline staff with the knowledge, skills, and competences they need to provide quality services.

As Rubin affirmed, most patrons enter library transactions in a calm and civilized manner. If they become angry, or difficult to serve, it is because one or more expectations were not met. Other patrons arrive at the library in a frustrated or irate mood–one look at their faces and you can tell that you have a ready-made angry patron.[5] The important issue becomes being prepared to be in control and having adequate competencies in our repertoire that will enable us keep the cordial patron cordial and avoid driving a frustrated patron into fury.

For budgetary reasons, libraries have been forced to use library assistants and sometimes student workers to man the reference desk. The patrons of the 21st century cannot be easily fooled. They know when the person on the reference desk is competent and is providing quality reference and fast. Therefore it would be reasonable to put knowledgeable staff on the reference desk, thereby eliminating or at least reducing the incidences of problem patrons. The purpose of this study was to: (1) identify the type of problem patrons the frontline staff encounter while on the reference desk and (2) assist our frontline staff in developing competencies to provide quality services and consequently reduce incidences of unsatisfied and unpleasant patrons.

REVIEW OF THE LITERATURE

In her book, *Defusing the Angry Patron*, Rubin affirms that angry patrons are the most often-encountered problem patrons in the library and that incidents of uncontrolled anger are on the rise in public places throughout America.[6] Sociologists, psychologists, and psychiatrists all put forward reasons for the display of anger, rudeness, violence and dissatisfaction. The leading causes of customer frustration and anger enumerated by Ensman include the inability to provide needed answers or information. He affirms that an encounter with an angry patron is the most threatening battle a frontline staff has to cope with.[7] When patrons come to the reference desk, they expect the library employee, irrespective of his/her job title or classification–be he/she a professional librarian, paraprofessional, or student worker–to answer the question he/she has and to successfully locate the information he/she needs. When the library employee fails to provide the needed answers or information (Ensman)[8] and when one or more expectations are not met (Rubin)[9] patrons become disappointed, frustrated, angry, and unpleasant. In most cases, library employees find patrons whose expectations are not met difficult and unpleasant to serve. The patron who comes to the reference desk already unhappy and in a foul mood will become even more moody and unhappy if he/she fails to get the information or receive the services he/she was expecting to get. Patron frustration often comes from getting the wrong information.[10] Bunge believes that competence is the most crucial obligation we owe our patrons.[11] He is convinced that we can begin to expect our patrons to leave the library satisfied and happy when we are able to provide skillful and accurate responses to their questions. A review of relevant literature on the issue of difficult or problem patrons in the library reveals that the issue could be addressed from different perspectives, and that there is no one solution that is a panacea for the problem. Some authors treat it from the interpersonal perspective, others treat it from the conflict management viewpoint. There is literature written on how librarians are to react when patrons elicit undesirable behaviors, but not much has been written on assisting staff to acquire the competencies they need to prevent the situation in the first place. "Many libraries do not place a high priority on training staff to deal with this problem despite its severity, and this leaves front-line clerks and paraprofessionals frustrated and defeated."[12] This article focuses on coping with the issue of difficult patrons from the domain of competency, and specifically on the professional growth and development of the frontline staff as a strategy to prevent the situations where patrons and library employees get angry, frustrated, and experience unpleasant encounters as a result of lack of adequate knowledge and skills.

WHAT COMPETENCIES DO WE NEED ON THE REFERENCE DESK?

Every job requires specific tools, expertise, knowledge and skills. After a series of observations and interviews with the frontline staff, this author arrived at the conclusion that there are baseline competencies which individuals who staff the reference desk of the Education and Behavioral Sciences Library need to adequately meet the expectations of our patrons, especially when we move into our new location. Baseline competencies are defined as a body of knowledge every person staffing the reference desk should master in order to provide a consistent level of service.[13] Reference librarians like Johannah Sherrer, have commented that "we need to look for people who excel beyond basic competencies and we need people who will challenge existing ones."[14] The frontline staff need training to maintain professional competence and currency. In libraries, especially academic libraries, it is expected that students and faculty would find the information they need for assignment completion, research, or instructional activities. It is crucial and imperative that the frontline staff members meet these expectations.

METHODOLOGY

The frontline staff who provide public services and have direct personal contacts and interactions with the patrons are in a position to provide the needed information. Therefore the samples for the study are drawn from the reference desk staff. The study focused on seeking information on:

1. Who the frontline staff perceive as the difficult or problem patrons and what they do to make serving them difficult
2. How difficult or problem patrons make reference desk staff feel–how this feeling affects their work
3. What positive outcomes result from encounters with difficult patrons
4. What reference desk staff can do to prevent users from becoming difficult patrons
5. What the library can do to help the frontline staff reduce the frequency of difficult patron situations.

PROCEDURE

The author of this study conducted oral interviews and administered a questionnaire to investigate the issue of difficult library patrons, and to gather information that would enable us to develop a staff training program to enhance the competences of our reference services. During a staff meeting the reference staff members of the Education and Behavioral Sciences Library were reminded that for the first time all our collections would be in a single location. Therefore it would be reasonable to expect more patron traffic, a change in the types of reference questions patrons will be asking, more complex reference transactions and requests for information on a broader range of subjects and topics, and a higher demand for successful negotiation of reference questions. The staff was told that if we are to provide consistent quality reference services and make our patrons happy we needed to collect information on reference desk transactions. The items on the questionnaire were explained to staff members and they were instructed to provide honest responses. They were not required to write their names on the questionnaire. Care was taken to establish a non-threatening, non-judgmental, trusting and cordial climate.

FINDINGS

Question 1: Who Are Difficult/Problem Patrons?

This item sought to gather information on the type of patrons that staff found to be difficult to serve and to identify specific things this clientele does to make working on the reference desk a tough and an unpleasant job.

As shown in Table 1, 90% of the reference desk staff who participated in the study indicated that difficult patrons were those patrons who wanted staff to give them the right/best response but would not give them enough time to search for the best source of information. During the interview, they explained that these patrons want librarians to give them the best response instantaneously, and thus become impatient when librarians go from one source to the other searching for the best information. Ninety percent also indicated that users who got angry over basic library rules and procedures are difficult patrons. Eighty percent of the library employees indicated that difficult patrons are those who do not trust the responses they received. During the oral interview, staff explained that these are patrons who doubt staff competence to provide information that is adequate and of high quality. These users want to direct the search strategies. Patrons who need information

TABLE 1. Difficult/Problem Patrons

Who Difficult/Problem Patrons Are	% of Reference Desk Staff Who Said So
Patrons who want you to give them the right/best response but would not give you time to search for the best source of information	90
Patrons who need information quickly to meet close deadlines	70
Patrons who do not trust the response you give to their questions	80
Patrons who do not know what they need and cannot explain it to you	40
Patrons who get angry over basic library rules and procedures	90
Patrons who want you to do their work for them	60
Patrons who lack basic library skills	70
Patrons who dispute library fines	10
Patrons who are rude	30
Patrons who only want items we do not own	20

quickly to meet close deadlines and those who lack basic library skills are considered to be problem patrons by 70% of the reference desk staff.

Question 2: How Do They Make You Feel?

This item sought information on how staff members feel when they encounter patrons who are not easy to provide service for and how the encounters affect them as they perform their job.

As shown in Table 2, 70% of the reference desk staff who participated in the study said that difficult or problem patrons make them feel inadequate, and incompetent. The same number of staff said they felt frustrated. Fifty percent of the staff acknowledged that they themselves felt angry and irritated. During the post survey oral interview it was apparent that a good proportion of the staff members felt (a) confused, (b) worried that they would not satisfy the difficult patrons, (c) were less willing to use all available resources to assist the difficult patrons, (d) felt challenged, (e) tried to find ways to quickly get rid of them, and (f) felt uplifted when they succeeded in assisting the problem patrons. However, only 10% indicated such feelings on the questionnaire.

Question 3: What Positive Outcomes Result from Encounters with Difficult Patrons?

This item sought to gather information on the positive aspects of encounters with difficult patrons.

TABLE 2. How Difficult/Problem Patrons Make Me Feel

How They Make Me Feel	% of Reference Desk Staff Who Said So
Inadequate/Incompetent/Need to know more	70
Frustrated	70
Confused	10
Angry/Irritated	50
Worried that I won't satisfy them	10
Less willing to use all available resources to assist them	10
Look for how to quickly get rid of them	10
Uplifting when I succeed in assisting them	10
Challenged	10

As shown in Table 3, 80% of the staff members were of the opinion that encounters with difficult patrons helped them identify areas where they needed to improve and 70% were challenged to learn more. Half of the staff affirmed that encounters with difficult and problem patrons made them try harder to assist them. Staff indicated they found that difficult patrons made them check more resources and think of more ways to assist the patrons. Fifty percent of the staff claimed that at the end of their interactions with difficult patrons it was good and rewarding to know that they knew which resources to use and what to say to satisfy such patrons. Encounters with such patrons enabled 50% of the staff to identify frequently asked questions. The participants made it clear that such encounters assisted them in identifying the reference tools and information, such as statistical tools and information, which students require but which are not easy to use or to locate. Therefore when such situations arise they brace themselves up to rise to the demand of the occasion. Forty percent stated that encounters with difficult patrons afforded them the opportunity to work on and practice their interpersonal skills. Further probing into this response revealed that (a) remaining calm, (b) allowing patrons to vent their frustration and anger, and (c) trying to be understanding were all helpful to library staff in confronting difficult situations. Fifty percent of the staff expressed that from dealing with difficult patrons they have the opportunity to teach this group of users the library skills they needed. The same number of staff also became aware of what to do to improve the services the library provides to the patrons.

TABLE 3. Positive Side of Encounters with Difficult Patrons

Positive Side of Encounters with Difficult Patrons	% of Reference Desk Staff Who Said So
Challenged me to learn more	70
Helped me identify areas where I need to improve	80
Make me try harder to assist them	50
Good and rewarding to know your stuff	50
Became aware of information frequently asked by patrons	50
Enable me to improve my interpersonal skills	40
Opportunity to teach patrons library skills	50
Be aware of what to do to improve our services	50

Question 4: What Can You Do to Prevent Users from Becoming Difficult Patrons?

This item sought to gather information on what individual reference desk staff members can do to minimize the incidence of difficult patrons and change such otherwise difficult people to pleasant and satisfied users.

Table 4 shows that 90% of the staff members were of the view that they could individually minimize the incidence of difficult patrons and change such otherwise difficult people to pleasant users by acquiring more of the knowledge and skills necessary for successful reference transactions, and by attending training sessions. Seventy percent suggested that they could individually prevent difficult patron situations by (1) not giving up easily on difficult questions and by letting patrons know that they genuinely desire to help them, (2) informing patrons that they would contact them later if they found more information, and (3) conducting the reference transaction in a professional manner. During the post survey oral session staff members explained that their being professional involved being calm, polite, respectful and cordial.

Question 5: What Can the Library Do to Help the Frontline Staff Reduce the Incidence of Difficult Patrons?

This item sought to gather information on what the library can do to minimize the incidence of difficult patrons and change otherwise difficult patrons to pleasant and satisfied patrons.

TABLE 4. What I Can Do to Prevent Users from Becoming Difficult Clientele

What I Can Do to Prevent Users from Becoming Difficult Clientele/Change Difficult Users to Pleasant Clientele	% of Reference Desk Staff Who Said So
Acquire more knowledge and skills	90
Attend training sessions	90
Persist/Let patrons see me sincerely desiring to help	70
Tell them I will follow up on the problem	70
Be professional	70
Refer them to professionals/Subject Specialists	50
Advise students to attend library training sessions	40
Offer alternatives	30
Advise them to report the problem	20
Bend the rule	10

As shown in Table 5, 80% of reference desk staff would like the library to provide training for them. During the post survey oral session staff members stated that the library should organize training sessions to better prepare them for the questions they have to deal with. Seventy percent of the participants wanted the library to provide basic and advanced information literacy training for patrons. The same proportion of staff members wanted the library authorities to listen to the staff suggestions. During the post survey oral conference, staff members stated that training sessions for patrons should be more publicized. They also wanted the library leaders to solicit and use input from staff because they are the ones who come into direct contact with the patrons and they know to a large extent what the realities of the reference desk are. Forty percent of the staff suggested that the library assign an adequate number of personnel to the reference desk. This, they said, would enable them to provide quality services to patrons with questions that require in-depth search.

RESULTS

Using the information from the literature review, staff response to items on the questionnaire, and the post survey oral interview/discussion sessions, the author concluded that to ensure consistent quality reference service at our new location, the primary focus has to be staff training on both professional and personal competency levels. Profes-

TABLE 5. What the Library Can Do to Reduce the Incidence of Difficult Patrons

What the Library Can Do to Reduce the Incidence of Difficult Patrons	% of Reference Desk Staff Who Said So
Provide training sessions for staff	80
Provide and publicize training sessions for patrons	70
Listen to suggestions from the staff	70
Have feasible policies and procedures	40
Provide adequate number of staff on the reference desk	40
Publicize rules, policies and procedures	30
Ensure technical problems are promptly resolved	30
Not much	30
Set clear expectations for what staff can do for patrons	20

sional competencies are comprised of knowledge and skills and the ability to use them effectively. Personal competencies consist of skills, attitudes, and values that promote frontline staff success on the reference desk. A training program that incorporates all these elements needed to be designed. The author relied on the knowledge of the frontline staff members for ideas and contents of the training program. Since 70% had indicated that they wanted their suggestions listened to, the author encouraged staff members to submit them anonymously. Here is a sample of their suggestions:

1. Databases on the Fast Track that contain information useful for the education content areas
2. Tests and measurement resources
3. Statistical resources
4. Children's book reviewing sources
5. Policies and procedures
6. How to demonstrate searching strategies
7. How to be an information intermediary
8. Interpersonal skills.

A staff training program focusing primarily on professional competencies was developed. Care was taken to make it possible for all the staff members to attend. A training session was scheduled for every other Tuesday from 1:30-2:45 p.m. The session was held when all but two of the staff members were on duty. Library staff members from other units worked at the reference desk to enable all Education and Behavioral Sciences personnel to attend the sessions. Professional librarians took turns to conduct and facilitate sessions on various topics, databases, and resources while paraprofessionals competent in routine reference desk transactions such as special charging of library items were assigned to lead such sessions. In addition to the regular training schedule, open discussions were held once a month on a Tuesday to allow staff members to share information, concerns, and discuss real or potential problems or situations.

To familiarize staff members with resources that our patrons will be using in other subject libraries such as the Social Sciences Library, Arts and Humanities Library, and Business Library, orientation and training sessions on resources in these libraries were scheduled. Additional assistance and resources were provided to reference desk staff on the revamped Education and Behavioral Sciences Library web page and the "How Do I . . ." links. Some of the topics covered under the "How Do

I . . ." include reference information on Curriculum Guides, Guides and Reviews on Children's Literature, Book Reviews, Test and Measurement, Statistics, Dissertations, Grants, Remote Access, Borrowing from Other Libraries, Non-Print Materials, and Penn State Information. A Reference Question Information Sheet was designed to keep track of the reference questions and to help identify topics for future training sessions.

CONCLUSION

The issue of problem or difficult patrons is a source of concern for library employees. Several factors may precipitate the problem. This article focused on addressing the issue from the perspective of taking steps to prepare the frontline staff and empowering staff members to provide quality reference services. It is hoped that when the frontline staff members possess the needed knowledge and skills necessary to handle reference questions well, they will provide quality reference services and that individuals on both sides of the reference desk will be happier.

Although the staff training program designed for the frontline staff of the Education and Behavioral Sciences Library is ongoing, it is yielding some good results. During the training sessions, Tuesday discussion meetings, and informal discussions, staff members express how topics and issues covered are enhancing the quality of reference services they are giving to patrons. The professional librarians are noticing appreciable improvement in the level of reference service the frontline staff is providing. Although the staff training now focuses on professional competencies, training on personal competencies will be offered in the future.

REFERENCES

1. Parus, Dale J. (1996). "The Reference Interview: Communication and the Patron," *The Katharine Sharp Review* ISSN 1083-5261, No. 2, Winter 1996. Retrieved April 25, 2000 from World Wide Web: <http://edfu.lis.uiuc.edu/review/winter1996/parus.html>. p. 1.

2. Rubin, Rhea Joyce (2000). *Defusing the Angry Patron: A How-to-Do It Manual for Librarians and Paraprofessionals, No 100.* New York: Neal-Schuman Publishers. p. 11.

3. Shuman, Bruce A. (1989). "Problem Patrons in Libraries–A Review Article." *Library & Archival Security,* 9: 2: p. 8.

4. Ibid, p. 8.

5. Rubin, Rhea Joyce (2000). *Defusing the Angry Patron: A How-to-Do It Manual for Librarians and Paraprofessionals, No 100*. New York: Neal-Schuman Publishers. p. 11.

6. Rubin, Rhea Joyce (1990). "Anger in the Library: Defusing Angry Patrons at the Reference Desk (and Elsewhere): in *The Reference Library User: Problems and Solutions* (ed: Bill Katz) New York, NY: The Haworth Press, Inc. p. 39.

7. Ensman, Richard G. (1997). *Defusing the Angry Customer.* Intertec Publishing Co. Retrieved March 22, 2000 from World Wide Web: <http://nrstg1s.djnr.com/cgi-bin/DJlnteractive>: p. 1.

8. Ibid, p. 1.

9. Rubin, Rhea Joyce (2000). *Defusing the Angry Patron: A How-to-Do It Manual for Librarians and Paraprofessionals, No 100.* New York: Neal-Schuman Publishers: 1.

10. Campbell, Jerry D. (2000). Clinging to Traditional Reference Services: An Open Invitation to Libref.com; *Reference & User Services Quarterly*, Chicago; 39 (3) Spring 2000: 224.

11. Bunge, Charles A. (1999). "Beliefs Attitudes and Values of the Reference Librarian" *The Reference Librarian* 66: 29.

12. Curry, Ann (1996). "Managing the Problem Patron," *Public Libraries* 35 (3): 181.

13. Benefiel et al. (1997). "Baseline Subject Competencies for the Academic Reference Desk," Reference Services Review 25 (1): 84 in Rockman, Ilene F., and Sarah B. Watstein (1999) "Reference Librarians/Educators Vision of the Future" *The Reference Librarian*, 66: 51.

14. Sherrer, Johannah (1996). "Thriving in Changing Times: Competencies for Today's Reference Librarian," *The Reference Librarian* 54: 13.

Core Competencies
of Front-Line Employees:
The German Contribution
to a New Service Culture

Wolfgang Ratzek

SUMMARY. The last decade of the 20th century and the beginning of the new millennium have seen unexpected changes. In Europe, especially in Germany, we are undergoing revolutionary changes in almost all domains of entrepreneurial, cultural and societal activities. These changes affect libraries too. Due to Electronic Data Processing, governmental regulations, and cultural changes, the workload for librarians has become more and more demanding. Traditional library education does not meet the needs of the 21st century. Customer service means more than doing a good job. This paper deals with some of these phenomena, focusing on libraries in Germany. *[Article copies available for a fee from The Haworth Document Delivery Service: 1-800-HAWORTH. E-mail address: <getinfo@haworthpressinc.com> Website: <http://www.HaworthPress.com> © 2002 by The Haworth Press, Inc. All rights reserved.]*

KEYWORDS. Personnel development, hard skills, soft skills, Germany, new steering model, political correctness, key qualifications

Wolfgang Ratzek is Professor of Business Administration for libraries, documentation centers and other institutions of information at the FH Stuttgart–HBI (University for Applied Sciences), Wolframstrasse 32-24, 70191 Stuttgart, Germany (E-mail: ratzek@hbi-stuttgart.de).

[Haworth co-indexing entry note]: "Core Competencies of Front-Line Employees: The German Contribution to a New Service Culture." Ratzek, Wolfgang. Co-published simultaneously in *The Reference Librarian* (The Haworth Information Press, an imprint of The Haworth Press, Inc.) No. 75/76, 2002, pp. 277-284; and: *Helping the Difficult Library Patron: New Approaches to Examining and Resolving a Long-Standing and Ongoing Problem* (ed: Kwasi Sarkodie-Mensah) The Haworth Information Press, an imprint of The Haworth Press, Inc., 2002, pp. 277-284. Single or multiple copies of this article are available for a fee from The Haworth Document Delivery Service [1-800-HAWORTH, 9:00 a.m. - 5:00 p.m. (EST). E-mail address: getinfo@haworthpressinc.com].

© 2002 by The Haworth Press, Inc. All rights reserved.
277

INTRODUCTION

As a result of the peaceful revolution of the people in Eastern Europe, and especially in the German Democratic Republic (GDR) during the late eighties of the last century, European countries have undergone heavy changes economically, societally, and technologically. In other words, Europe is no longer a homogenous entity of countries and cultures. The former Federal Republic of Germany represents an excellent example for these changes: unemployment, high taxes, racist tendencies, illegal actions by politicians and other top officials. On the other side can be cited: a blooming new economy, high potential or a high standard of infrastructure in the field of telecommunications. The main problem might be defined as the lack of a vision to replace the out of fashion vision of "Made in Germany." All these problems affect the cultural institutions of Germany: shortages in budgets, reorganization, integration of profit-oriented activities and a high quality of service do not always fit together.

As in other European countries, such as the Nordic countries or Great Britain, for example, libraries in Germany are undergoing major changes. These changes are taking place in both the public and the academic library sectors and are triggered by at least three factors which we find, more or less modified, in all countries: EDP, New Public Management, socio-psychological change of library users.

THE LOOMING OF EDP

Almost all libraries in highly industrialised countries, especially in Europe, integrated EDP for the improvement of their operation planning (key word: library automation) and library services. This entails a new organizational structure, i.e., the emergence of the virtual library or the OPAC. Without doubt, a new profile of skills for library personnel becomes necessary, which is quite different from the traditional skill pattern. To clarify the changes, let us look at the two waves of computerization which took place between the seventies and nineties of the last century:

1st Wave

During the seventies commercial companies discovered the library market. They stepped up their activities to sell products designed for computerising the library's acquisition, circulation and cataloguing systems. As a consequence of that, librarians turned their backroom work, for example, acquisition or cataloguing, into computer-directed routines, or better algorithm. This implied that the library's customers had to reorient themselves to the new way of getting bibliographic information, that is, through an online access public catalogue (OPAC). In addition, libraries started to implement databases for different purposes.

2nd Wave

The nineties are noted for the deployment of computer networks. There was a proliferation of campus, national and international networks, thus making it possible to access remote electronic resources. As a result of this development, information was no longer limited to in-house catalogues or bibliographic databases. Secondary information is the key word here. Within this framework another important factor has come into existence: electronic full-text versions of journals are now available. Via online systems, users have access to electronic documents from outside the library, i.e., from the user's private and/or work site.

THE NEW PUBLIC MANAGEMENT

In Germany the "Verwaltungsreform" of 1986 aims, among other things, to increase efficiency in public administration, to identify cost drivers, and to develop customer service. In the case of the German library sector, the reform of public management leads to a philosophy named "Neues Steuerungsmodell" (NSM)–the New Steering Model. Due to the new steering model, a new basis for legitimacy has become reality. Instead of the expenses in the older philosophy, cost accounting, range of services/products and customer service spread throughout the new framework. In other words, German libraries are changing from bureaucracies to service driven organizations. And here are some of the most important developments:

- Decentralization of managerial decision making, which means that library management is responsible for both material and personnel planning (global budgeting).
- Performance focus on steering from a distance, i.e., a library manager has to make a contract with the public administration. This

contract defines a range of products and services. Besides that, a performance measurement system must be implemented (key words: controlling, cost-benefit accounting system). Today, the former library user becomes a customer.

- Modernization of the organization, i.e., customer driven process structure, flat hierarchy and support from external consultants (if you can afford their fees).
- Human resource management, i.e., qualifications for a new range of duties, motivation through this widened range, and performance oriented payment (a strict uniform salary system for civil servants is the biggest hindrance to putting the new steering model into practice).

CHANGES IN THE PSYCHO- /SOCIO-DEMOGRAPHIC STRUCTURE OF LIBRARY USERS

The tremendous cultural change in the last two decades in the European countries has also changed the make-up of library customers. After the fall of the Berlin Wall in 1989, a stream of people from Poland, from the former Soviet Union, from the former Yugoslavia, from Africa, from Vietnam wanted to live in Germany. In addition to the new citizens, the German culture is strongly characterized by the Italians, Spanish, and the biggest ethnic group–the Turkish. When we speak of policy in public libraries' new target groups, their need for literature and access to information about their homeplaces becomes relevant. Another critical and logical result of the psycho- /socio-demographic structure of library users is hooliganism and drug dealing. A public library must be prepared to handle this kind of urban reality. In big public libraries in Germany, like the zlb (Zentral- und Landesbibliothek) in Berlin or the City Library of Cologne, librarians undergo special training sessions to help them cope with these real social situations. The socio-cultural side of librarian reality also means sticking to the rules of political correctness (PC). Political parties, the mass media, public authorities, and anti-establishment movements are eager to dictate the right use of words; otherwise a speaker or a writer is denounced as a racist, an anti-woman macho type or a friend of the economy. German librarians have to watch what they say, and even to anticipate what their conversational partner might understand. This becomes a very heavy burden in centers with various cultures such as Berlin, Cologne or Hamburg.

THE NEW LIBRARIAN

Having listed just a few phenomena which stand for the changes in the library sector, we can imagine that daily work requires a lot of skills from the library personnel which are different from the classical education and knowledge of a librarian of the good old tradition. We now want to look a little more closely at the skills the new librarian needs to meet the challenges deriving from the phenomena mentioned above, especially if we want to avoid situations that may be termed as problem patron encounters.

Against this background we have to look more closely at the competencies required to meet the challenges. The most important areas of competency are:

Methodological Competencies

It is trivial, but we have to mention that librarians need both profound knowledge and capabilities for the performance of library specific work. In that way, librarians are able to assess the (potential) needs of their customers, e.g., acquiring current information, in whatever media format they are stored; indexing according to content by employing differentiated library rules; making the information available to customers, including information on collecting; providing access to information that is not available on site but throughout the world, no matter whether physical or electronic.

Academic Competencies

As a part of communication and consultative skills, a specialized knowledge is required to

- select the most useful information from a worldwide supply for a customer from a research and development (R&D) Institute, and to be accepted as a competent, reliable, and trusted partner. Anything short of that diminishes how users look at librarians or information specialists, and may trigger the way for many dissatisfied scenarios.

Social Competencies

- Post-modern librarians are customer oriented. For better communication with customers and colleagues a successful librarian needs a basic knowledge of psychology and pedagogy to help them with conflict management. When communicating with a customer we are representing our library in every way imaginable. This means that we need to know the structure of our library and make it comprehensible to our customers. In addition we owe it to our users to assist them in finding relevant information via OPAC, CD-ROM and/or the Internet in a friendly and competent manner. We also need to master the skills of working as a team so that we can provide excellent and consistent service that convinces our clientele of a uniform organizational, structural and decision making pattern in our libraries.

Cultural Competencies

Librarians are not only a part of a culture, they take care of cultural matters and they even create culture by organizing cultural events for different target groups, for example, children, students, blind people, ethnic groups. In cities or rural environments there is a need for both local information and public places where people can meet and/or get the latest news or gossip. A library should be part of at least the local network for the distribution of local news. As mentioned above, we have to keep in mind that especially in mixed cultures, politically correct communication methods and behavior are of importance for a librarian with customer contact. A lot of inhabitants in Germany as well as in the USA are originally from other countries. In other words, in Germany the multicultural aspect becomes more and more important. Learning from America what political correctness implies, we Germans have made a cult out of it.

Business Administrative Competencies

Since the New Steering Model influences the daily task of a German librarian, special aspects of business administration belong to the tools a librarian has to be aquaintanced with. Some examples are cost-benefit analysis, personnel development, and marketing. In other words, libraries are public institutions and widely financed by taxes. Shortages in budgets force libraries to develop cost cutting programs. Besides the state or township, taxpayers also want to know whether their money is spent in a useful manner. Due to this fact, libraries are forced to justify their need for money. The best way, of course, is to argue like business economists do. This leads us to another domain of business administration: general management and its fulfillment, which includes human and material resources as well as budget planning. Competency in business administration enables librarians to negotiate good conditions in cost-reducing delivery conditions, licensing fees and service performance for information retrieval; to calculate the relationship between costs and services; and control and optimise the services offered by their library, and the internal work processes dealing with service measurement and controlling.

Value-Adding Competency

Due to the continuing flood of data, the library's role is changing rapidly–from the classical circulation plant toward a service driven information agency. Librarians become information experts, who navigate customers through the analog and digital world of media. One important basic task is to instruct customers in how to use electronic sources of data, i.e., to explain how the Internet is functioning, and to assist a customer in developing difficult search strategies. But these services are far from complete. More and more public libraries are preparing for new target groups. Due to cuts in budgets, libraries are forced to find other sources of income. In that case, small and medium-sized enterprises (SME) are a very interesting focus group. The public librarian becomes a partner in helping to create value-added service. A leading role might be played by the German Stadtbibliothek Köln–the City Library of Cologne, which has become part of the local spurring of economy.

Technological Competence

In every domain of the library spectrum librarians are confronted with a still ongoing IT-dynamic which leads to the digital or virtual library. Computers, networks, databases and other electronic media belong to the tools a librarian uses to do a good job. We have to consider that the deployment of EDP opens two options in all kinds of libraries: first, the internal work processes might be accelerated, improved and/or streamlined; second, another information carrier and storage medium, besides print media, is available and must be integrated into the historical library systems. A contemporary librarian must be able to span the gap between the "real world" and the "virtual reality" of cyberspace. Without a basic IT-knowledge and practical experience a library will not be able to offer a high quality of service.

CONCLUSION

The new librarians are multi-skilled persons with competencies in EDP, psychology, cultural communication, and business administration. They are competent in evaluating, structuring and presenting information from different analog and digital sources for clients from different branches or cultural origins. Librarians offer their services for life long learning, co-determining the service quality, the image and the atmosphere in their library. As shown above, we should not concentrate only on EDP or classical library knowledge, but also on socio-cultural competence as well as on business administration. In this respect a library takes on more and more of the features of an enterprise. In spite of EDP, the daily workload of a librarian becomes more and more demanding, especially the psychological pressure resulting from technological problems such as computer crashes and viruses, from shortages in budget, from a continuous improvement of quality and–last but not least–demanding customers with different cultural and technological backgrounds. The person who is responsible for personnel development and training must look at this phenomenon more closely. In consideration of the above mentioned situation, the following ideas may be excellent workshop topics to prepare librarians to deal with problem patron situations and how to resolve them: conflict management–how to turn combatants into winners; political correctness–what is meant by non-discriminatory communications; counselling strategies–what we can learn from management consultants; and quality service–what library staff needs for a better work performance.

Partnership with Community Resources– Campus Police: Revisiting Policies to Reflect the 21st Century

Joyce C. Wright

SUMMARY. It is the policy of the University of Illinois at Urbana-Champaign to maintain a quiet and otherwise appropriate environment to assure an atmosphere conducive to study in all units of the University Library System. It is incumbent upon library users to conduct themselves in accordance with the rules of the University Library. It is expected that those who use the University Library System will do so responsibly and appropriately without harassing other users or library staff and without damaging the Library's facilities or its collections.

At Illinois, partnerships have been organized with the campus police to make the library a safe place for all users. With the assistance of our library security staff we have an excellent working relationship with the University Police Department. These partnerships promote initiative for learning and build a desire to pursue a deeper sense of being.

This paper will examine the partnerships that are available in the Champaign-Urbana academic community. *[Article copies available for a fee from The Haworth Document Delivery Service: 1-800-HAWORTH. E-mail address: <getinfo@haworthpressinc.com> Website: <http://www.HaworthPress.com> © 2002 by The Haworth Press, Inc. All rights reserved.]*

Joyce C. Wright is Head, Undergraduate Library, and Associate Professor of Library Administration, University of Illinois at Urbana-Champaign, 1402 W. Gregory MC-522, Urbana, IL 61801.

[Haworth co-indexing entry note]: "Partnership with Community Resources–Campus Police: Revisiting Policies to Reflect the 21st Century." Wright, Joyce C. Co-published simultaneously in *The Reference Librarian* (The Haworth Information Press, an imprint of The Haworth Press, Inc.) No. 75/76, 2002, pp. 285-290; and: *Helping the Difficult Library Patron: New Approaches to Examining and Resolving a Long-Standing and Ongoing Problem* (ed: Kwasi Sarkodie-Mensah) The Haworth Information Press, an imprint of The Haworth Press, Inc., 2002, pp. 285-290. Single or multiple copies of this article are available for a fee from The Haworth Document Delivery Service [1-800-HAWORTH, 9:00 a.m. - 5:00 p.m. (EST). E-mail address: getinfo@haworthpressinc.com].

© 2002 by The Haworth Press, Inc. All rights reserved.   *285*

KEYWORDS. Library security, campus collaboration, collaboration with police

The person who we called the police on this past weekend has been issued a no trespass letter. His name is . . . and if you see him in the library, please call our security or the campus police immediately.

–Undergraduate Library Staff Member
University of Illinois @ Urbana-Champaign

The Undergraduate Library is the most popular of all the departmental libraries in the system. Serving an undergraduate population of over twenty-six thousand, it is open 107 hours a week and during finals the library is open twenty-four hours. In 1992, the Library Administration agreed to hire security for the library. This was a welcome for our staff and users. As a public institution the library is open to all Illinois residents.

According to Shuma "library security has always been a problem, although in the past it was somewhat less problematic than it is now. In the Middle Ages, security, inventory, and bibliographic control weren't nearly as difficult as they are today."[1]

As a public institution the library is open to the entire Urbana-Champaign community. Having a facility this large open to the public is problematic at times. There are currently two partnerships in place to assist staff and library users: (1) Library Security Guards, and (2) University Police.

The Library Security Guards patrol the building from five o'clock p.m. until closing time weekdays and weekend hours. If a situation occurs where staff cannot handle the problem, library security is called upon. Last semester a student "reported that a patron hung out by the women's bathroom on the lower level east side for hours; many of the female students feel uncomfortable when they go to use the bathroom." The patron continued this behavior even after a library staff member spoke to him. Our policy indicates that whenever a situation makes someone feel uncomfortable–whether involving theft, unruly patrons, or anything else–the security guards are paged immediately.

Our first approach was to establish a basic library policy governing public use. These policies were drafted by the Associate University Librarian for Budgeting and Planning and passed by the Library Administrative Council.

The following rules governing use of the University Library have been established to provide a safe environment for library users and staff; to prevent activities which could endanger the library, its equipment or collections; and to maintain an atmosphere which permits the intended uses of the University Library. These rules may be modified from time to time.

POLICIES

Patron Conduct in the Library System:
Basic Library Policy Governing Public Use

The University of Illinois at Urbana-Champaign Library's mission is to encourage scholarly research by maintaining an environment conducive to study in all units of the University Library system. Library users are expected to act responsibly, appropriately, and courteously to preserve the library facilities, environment, and collections.

The Library Administrative Council established the following policies in accordance with the Library's mission. Library administration reserves the right to authorize temporary suspension of any of these policies to accommodate University of Illinois sponsored, or Library sponsored events and receptions.

Persons who violate any of these policies may lose their privileges to use the University Library, be subject to University-imposed discipline, and/or be subject to criminal prosecution or other legal action, as appropriate.

Consumption of Food and Beverages

Eating and drinking, and using tobacco pose threats to the mission of the Library by creating litter as well as damage to equipment and materials, and are, therefore, not allowed in the Library, with the exception of the consumption of non-alcoholic beverages in spill-proof, covered, plastic or metal containers. Some units may not allow even spill-proof containers, because of the uniqueness of materials in their collections, e.g., Rare Books and Special Collections, and University Archives.

Disruptive Behavior

Disruptive behavior is detrimental to the Library's mission and to staff and patron safety. Disruptive behavior includes, but is not limited to, the following:

- Abusing, threatening, or intimidating Library staff or patrons through language or actions.
- Fighting or other behavior that creates excessive noise or commotion.
- Bringing weapons, simulated or real, into any Library facility.
- Playing musical instruments or audible electronic devices.
- Using bicycles, skateboards, or skates.
- Refusing to leave a Library unit at closing time.
- Entering areas of the Library marked "Staff Only."
- Engaging in sexual harassment and/or overt sexual behavior.
- Displaying overt signs of substance abuse, including drunkenness.
- Petitioning, conducting unauthorized surveys, or direct distribution of any non-library materials.
- Soliciting goods, services, or donations.
- Bringing bedding into any Library facility.

Staff will take-appropriate action to remedy disruptive behavior.

Damage to Library Property

The University Library prohibits behavior that will damage University Library equipment, collections, or facilities. Protection of University Library materials is defined by Illinois criminal law (720 ILCS 5/16B). The types of behavior which are not permitted include, but are not limited to, the following:

- Defacing University Library buildings, equipment, or collections.
- Deliberate misuse of University Library equipment or collections.

Criminal Behavior

The University Library will notify law enforcement authorities concerning any criminal behavior in the University Library. Among the areas in which the University Library will be particularly vigilant and pursue legal remedies are:

- Theft of University Library equipment or collections.
- Vandalism.
- Deliberate misuse or damage to University Library equipment or collections.
- Exhibitionism.
- Assault, including verbal threats.

Unattended Children

Children under the age of 11 may not be left unattended for any period of time. The University Library is not responsible for the safety of children left unattended in any part of the University Library.

Library staff will take appropriate action upon discovering unattended children. This action may include contacting parents, Library Security, and/or juvenile authorities.

Patron Use of Library Staff Telephones

The University provides pay telephones and Campus telephones for the use of patrons. Patrons may not use staff telephones.

Paging Library Patrons

Staff will page Library patrons only in case of emergency.

Animals

Animals (with the exception of assistance animals) are not permitted in any University Library facilities.

Personal Mobile Phones and Pages

The Library is a research area where users expect to work undisturbed, therefore the use of mobile phones and pagers must be limited to designated public telephone areas. Please set mobile phones and pages to nonaudible signals while in the Library.

Personal Property

Theft is an unfortunate reality in the Library. Please take every precaution to ensure the security of your personal belongings, especially that of purses, wallets, backpacks, books, portable computers, and other electronic devices. In addition, sleeping in the Library increases the potential for theft of personal belongings. For this reason, library staff will wake sleeping persons.

The University Library has no facilities to store personal property, and will not under any circumstances take responsibility for theft, damage, or loss of property.[2] Approved by Library Administrative Council on April 30, 2001.

Campus Police

Campus Police officers are sworn police officers under state statutory authority and are trained to cope with emergencies and other problems on campus and in the immediate area of the campus. Their primary responsibilities are to protect the people and property under their jurisdiction, to maintain peace and order, and to protect constitutional rights. Campus Police officers investigate crimes and enforce state criminal statutes, the Illinois Vehicle Code, and University rules and regulations. All officers operate under the community policing philosophy within defined "focus areas."[3]

The officer assigned to the University Library has been very helpful over the years by attending staff meetings, putting on workshops and working in areas where staff needs assistance in the following:

- Patrons and students disgruntled or enraged with library policies or with a staff member's attitude or behavior.
- Individuals with irrational behaviors, mental problems, domestic disturbances, sometimes augmented and exacerbated by drug or alcohol abuse.
- Former employees seething with resentment and looking for a paycheck for being demoted, passed over for promotion, fired, or downsized.

So far the partnership approach at Illinois has been very successful and the library staff has responded positively.

REFERENCES

1. Shuman, Bruce A. Library Security and Safety Handbook: Prevention, Policies, and Procedures. Chicago: American Library Association, 1999.

2. Patron Conduct in the Library System, Basic Library Policy Governing Public Use, Urbana, IL, 2001.

3. Academic Staff Handbook, University of Illinois at Urbana-Champaign, 2000-2002.

Index

© 2002 by The Haworth Press, Inc. All rights reserved.